The Hot Guyde

How to Become an Attractive Man

By Howie Reith

Contents

Acknowledgments

I would like to thank Erin L. Sullivan and Jordan Allen for your help and feedback as I developed this book. It would not be the same without either of you. Thank you to Jane Lincoln Taylor for editing this work for publication, and figuring out how to say the words in my head better than I knew how to say them. Thank you to Janet Dado for contributing the cover art, and to Elizabeth Clark Libert for taking the author photo. Thank you to the many scientists and authors listed in my references for your contributions to my own personal development and this work. Thank you to Quora, to my followers and supporters who use the site, and to everyone else who's sought advice from me, for inspiring me to write. I undertook this project because you showed me it was worth it. I hope it helps you and many others.

Introduction

For two years I'd had a crush on her. She was beautiful, smart, a talented dancer, and living down the street from me to boot. All of my friends—hell, most of the school—knew about my feelings. They'd been trying to get me to ask her out, and I'd decided the moment had come. It was the night of our eighth-grade end-of-the-year social, and I resolved to ask her to dance. After two hours of talking myself into it, I walked up to her and…froze. I couldn't do it. The anxiety was too extreme. My buddy, who'd been watching, wasn't going to let me get away with that. He snuck up, tapped her on the shoulder, and ran away, spurring her to turn and face me. I was surprised, but blurted out, "You want to dance?" Her reply was instant. "Noooooooooooooooooooooo!"

It was my first rejection—the first of hundreds. I sulked for the next couple of days, but on the third day, as I sat in art class, I made myself a promise. "This isn't how my story's going to end." I know, melodramatic, huh? "From this day on, I will do everything I can to become the most attractive man I can be until I'm thirty years old." Why thirty? I don't know. It seemed far off at the time, and I figured I'd get married by then. (Funny to think about, now that I'm twenty-nine….)

Fortunately for me, I followed through. Every year since, I've done my best to learn about dating, relationships, and becoming more attractive. I asked my female friends what they liked in guys, I tried out new fashions and hobbies, and I started working out. Later on, I began studying psychology, self-help, and anything else remotely relevant I could get my hands on. Most of my early efforts were misguided, but every year, without fail, I had more success than the year before. I went from the "creepy" guy in high school to a guy who intrigued pretty much every woman he met. In recent years,

I've never lacked sexual companions, and today, I'm in a relationship that makes me happier than I've ever been.

Around the age of twenty-three, I made a discovery. Trying to "be attractive" is actually a pretty damn unattractive thing to do. Attraction is something other people feel toward you, not something you do, so when you're trying to "be attractive," you're looking to warp other people's perceptions. It's manipulative, and when women realize you're doing it, they find it creepy. I learned that you can't control how anyone sees you, or whether anyone likes you, and you shouldn't try. All you can control is how you see yourself — and whether or not you ask out the women you like. Attractiveness isn't something you can work to have; it's something you develop as a side effect of living an interesting life. Once I understood that, the way forward became clear. I needed to learn to be direct, authentic, and comfortable with dating, and doing that was just a matter of removing the obstacles on that path. My biggest barriers were a lack of confidence in myself and a lack of social skills. If I could address those problems, I figured I'd be golden, and I was right. Of course, those weren't exactly small problems to solve.

You've picked up this book looking for dating advice, and if you're anything like I was, you've pored over endless volumes on this subject and found most of them to be bullshit. Perhaps you've delved into the seduction community, or the work of "alpha male" evangelists, or the books on achieving dating success through various spiritual movements. Maybe you've just had friends offering you platitudes such as "Be yourself." You're frustrated, and you're probably wondering if *The Hot Guyde* will be more of the same.

I never expected to give dating advice. It's something I more or less stumbled into when I started answering questions about dating on the Q&A website *Quora*. I began answering those questions out of boredom, but after several months, hundreds of people were telling me how my advice had changed their lives. My writing got published in the *Huffington Post, Time, Lifehacker, Thought Catalog,* and elsewhere. People kept asking me where to learn everything I had to say, and all I could do was give them a long reading list, each item of which was only partially applicable to their needs. I was encouraged to write a book that focused on the most important lessons, so I have. I've designed this book to be the resource I wish I had had when I was younger, and I've tried to keep it free of all the shit that annoys me most about the dating-advice industry and the self-help genre. This book is structured around problems, solutions, explanations, and exercises that put those solutions into practice. Everything I recommend is based on scientific research, mostly in the fields of cognitive therapy, social psychology, and couples therapy. You will find no misguided appeals to the "Law of Attraction," pop evolutionary psychology, neurolinguistic programming, or any such pseudoscience. I also offer references for everything I suggest, so if you care to look into why I recommend what I do, you can read any of my sources for yourself.

Who Is This Book For?

I wrote this book for heterosexual guys who'd like to have more success in dating, though come to think of it, most of the insights I'm sharing can help anyone in any sort of relationship. Do you freak out about how women judge you? Are you depressed because you think you'll be alone forever, and that depression keeps you from meeting women? Do you have bitter, misogynistic views? Are you stinky? This book will help with all of that and more. I also hope that when you finish this book, dating success will be the least of the benefits you enjoy. It's not a guide to getting laid; it's a guide to becoming an attractive man, and that entails a lot of personal changes that are incredibly beneficial in their own right. Yes, women will love you, but more important than that, you'll love yourself.

The Hot Guyde Approach

There are no pickup lines or routines in *The Hot Guyde*. Since the root of most men's dating struggles lies in our own self-limiting ways of thinking, the most important component of this book is a collection of clinically effective techniques to address self-defeating thoughts. You will learn how to deal with shame, low self-esteem, fear, laziness, and bad habits.

The next big issue most men face is a lack of social skills. We will discuss at length the mechanisms underlying social interactions as understood by psychologists. *The Hot Guyde* will teach you to be socially aware and adept. You will be capable of mustering confidence, sensitivity, humor, and sexuality as needed.

With these first two sections alone, you will enjoy more dating success than anyone you know, but we're not stopping there. While looks are nowhere near so important as your self-esteem and personality, we'll also talk about how to improve your physical appearance through hygiene, grooming, and fashion, and discuss the most clinically effective approaches to diet and exercise.

The fourth section will talk about actual dating. You'll learn how to meet women, flirt, plan dates, kiss, cuddle, and be good in bed. We'll talk about common problems in long-term relationships, both monogamous and casually sexual. Every chapter will have exercises to help ingrain the lessons into your personality. Some of these exercises will be one-time things, some will be ongoing, some will need to be done in specific circumstances, and some will require a partner. Only you can know what exercises will benefit you most, and you will need to design your own personal schedule and "workouts" to practice and improve. The last chapter will give you an example of how to do this, and you're welcome to visit *thehotguyde.com* for additional help and support.

How to Read This Book

This book isn't a collection of fluffy anecdotes to make you feel inspired while you're taking a dump; it's a cross between a handbook and a textbook, and it's extensive. You're going to have to study, practice, and take notes. Don't try to make all your changes at once, or you'll be overwhelmed.

Here's how I suggest you go about the program. Read through this book once. At the end of each chapter, there are exercises labeled "Immediate." Do these exercises as soon as you finish a chapter. Ignore the rest. After you've finished the book, when you have a solid idea of what your biggest issues are, look back through the exercises and focus on ones from the chapters you're most concerned with. "One Time" exercises are meant to be performed once. "Ongoing" exercises require extended practice. "Responsive" exercises should be performed in the specified circumstances. "Partner" exercises are done with a partner. Incorporate the exercises you find most valuable into your daily routine, but take your time doing so. Remember, you're human. You're not going to change overnight, and there are only so many changes you can make at once. Your transformation will take months and could take a couple of years. However long it takes you, *The Hot Guyde* will help you all along the way, and if you're struggling, you can always ask for help at *thehotguyde.com*.

While you're reading, you might sometimes wonder why I'm asking you to learn a particular skill. For example, in chapter 2, we're going to talk a lot about "talking back to your inner critic." You might be confused about how this technique applies to dating, but then, three weeks later, when you're making your first approach and your brain starts to flood with thoughts such as "She won't want to talk to me, she won't find me attractive," that's when you'll realize, "Oh shit, this is what he was talking about," and you'll know how to deal with it. Likewise, you might not know how "habit-reversal therapy" applies to dating, but when you start taking a look at your posture and you realize, "Whenever I walk, I hunch my shoulders," that's when the tool will make sense. Every word in this book has a purpose, so if something doesn't make sense, just keep reading; its value will become clear later on.

The Hot Guyde is a labor of love. I remember the pain and loneliness I went through, and how powerless I felt to change things. I remember my frustration when all the advice I could find was manipulative and misogynistic. I wanted to write a book that would help everyone who struggles as I did. Despite what you may have been told, you don't have to be a "bad boy" or practice dozens of routines to date women. You just need to learn how to be the most authentic, confident version of yourself. There are women out there who will want you, eagerly. I hope this book helps you find them.

Disclaimer

The Hot Guyde is not intended as a substitute for the medical advice of physicians or the psychological care of a psychotherapist. Readers should regularly consult professionals in matters relating to their mental and physical health and particularly with respect to any symptoms that may require diagnosis or medical attention. The physical exercise recommended in this book, like all sports, poses some inherent risk. The author and publisher advise readers to take full responsibility for their safety and to know their limits. Before practicing the skills described in this book, be sure that your equipment is well maintained, and do not take risks beyond your level of experience, aptitude, training, and comfort. The reader assumes full responsibility for his or her actions and use of the material in this book. Adherence to all laws and regulations, whether federal, state, local, or in other jurisdictions, is the sole responsibility of the reader. The author and publisher assume no responsibility or liability whatsoever on behalf of any purchaser or reader of this book.

Part I: Psychology

Chapter 1 – The Problem

The moment has come. After two long years of preparation, Phil is ready to tell Becky that he likes her. Deep into the night he sits hunched over his smartphone, crafting every syllable of his 200-word text message. Yes, they're from different social circles, and he'd made that weird comment that one time, and he knows that someone as beautiful as she is probably has other options, but he hopes that somehow she will find it in her heart to go out with him. Phil clicks "send." The servers strain to process the behemoth of a message. Hours go by. Then days. Becky never replies.

Romance is a funny thing. It brings out the best and the worst in us. Every tiny insecurity we have feels amplified when we try to show interest in someone we find attractive. Some of us fall in "love" with a longtime friend, but we think if we show it, we'll lose her forever, so we hide our feelings and hope that somehow the stars will align and romance will appear. Some of us are uncomfortable with sex. We think it's immoral, fear we aren't any good at it, or view our sexual desire as objectifying and wrong. Some of us are afraid of social judgment. We think that if women reject us, it means we're worthless—we're somehow lesser men. Some of us are even afraid of success. Success means change, and change can be scary. Any and all of these can sap our dating resolve, and lead to the sort of needy behavior we just saw in Phil.

Whatever insecurities are at the core of your dating struggles, you're not alone. We don't like to talk about it, but most other men suffer the same fears and setbacks. Most of us are our own worst enemies. We can't find love and sex not because no one thinks we're attractive, but because we assume that they don't, and we're terrified of confirming our fears. Unless we know beyond the shadow of a doubt that someone likes us, we don't even try. What are we so afraid of?

Shame

I had a conversation once with a woman who noted how bizarre it was that men are so scared of women. Why would a six-foot-tall, 180-pound guy shudder at the thought of talking to a five-foot-nothing, 110-pound woman? He's not afraid of her; he's afraid of the shame she potentially represents. What if she rejects him? What would that mean? For most of us, it's not the rejection that scares us; it's the implications. Rejection floods our minds with painful, shameful thoughts: "I'm worthless." "I'm a bad man." "I'll be alone forever." "No one loves me."

The fear of shame discourages us from being vulnerable, and it's that discomfort with vulnerability that drives us to hide our feelings and act in awkward, unattractive ways. Not only does it discourage us from asking women out and connecting with them, it influences our body language. Everything about how you move and the way you talk echoes your belief in your own worthlessness, and when people see you acting that way, they believe you. Just like you want to be with a woman who excites you, a woman wants to be with a man who excites her, and it's hard to feel excited by a guy who's nonverbally telling her she'd be better off with someone else. In order for most people to like you, you have to like yourself.

No one chooses to adopt these negative beliefs. No one asks for social anxiety. These patterns are thrust on us in childhood by parents, teachers, and peers who don't know better. You didn't cause your struggles, but you do choose whether to continue them or to vanquish them. You are the only person with control over your mind, and you're the only one who can change it. The voices in your head telling you that you suck, that your emotional needs are flaws, and that women will never love you have only as much power as you give them. You, and only you, perpetuate your shame.

The "Nice Guy"

Jeremy works a desk job at a local financial firm. Every day, his co-workers and superiors unload a deluge of work into his inbox. His work is adequate—good, even—but when he makes mistakes, he apologizes as if he's just committed murder. Jeremy hasn't had a raise in five years. He's the first to offer help, but never asks for help himself, nor does he ever complain. As a child, Jeremy was a good boy. His parents and teachers said he never gave them a moment's trouble. He went to school and got good grades, and when he made a mistake, he made sure to punish himself for weeks longer than his parents and teachers did. Jeremy is a "nice guy."

Millions of men all over the world live lives similar to Jeremy's. They grew up with parents and other authority figures who taught them, through words and actions, that people-pleasing and self-shaming would put them on the path of least resistance through life. When these "nice guys" followed the rules and pleased their parents, they got toys and affection. When they made mistakes, parental love was withdrawn and they were punished. The "nice guys" learned a clear lesson: "If I can be what other people want me to be, I will get what I need to be happy." They learned never to impose themselves on other people, and they bring these lessons into their adult lives. Whatever situation they find themselves in, they will change themselves to be as inoffensive and pleasing as possible.[1]

The deeds of the "nice guy" are primarily motivated not by love or personal fulfillment but by fear of abandonment. Every moment of his life is filled with a quiet terror that people will discover the rotten human being he "knows" himself to be. He feels that people love him for his intelligence, his humor, his talents — the sorts of things that earned him approval and affection when he was growing up. People love him because he has a hot wife or a cute baby. They love him for his work or his body. They don't love *him*. If they knew the real "him," they would abandon him.

No matter how hard the "nice guy" tries to please people, he inevitably fails. The bullies still bully him, his parents are still disappointed, and his boss never gives him the promotion. Despite the evidence, since it's the only life strategy he ever learned, the "nice guy" continues to assume that as long as he keeps being "good," he'll be rewarded eventually. This leads to one of the most toxic habits of the "nice guy": the covert contract. Though he'll never say it explicitly, every "nice" thing the "nice guy" ever does is secretly designed to win approval and avoid abandonment, and nowhere is this more manifest than in how he interacts with women. "Nice guys" have been taught to see sex and love as the highest forms of approval they can achieve. Every time the "nice guy" watched a movie, read a comic book, or listened to a story and saw the hero's struggles rewarded with love, he learned that the love of women was the ultimate reward for being a "good" man. He thus figures that being "good" to women is the best way to earn the love and affection he desires. He turns himself into a protector, comforter, problem-solver, and confidante for all of the women in his life, hoping that one day he'll cross the "love" threshold and enjoy his sweet reward.

If this section is resonating with you, you've probably learned the hazards of the "nice guy" paradigm at first hand, and you've picked up this book because you know, deep down, that your paradigm is misguided. Being "good" might have been all that was necessary for rewards when you were a child, but in the world of adults, that people-pleasing, self-shaming behavior isn't a strength; it's a liability. Women aren't stupid. They recognize the behavior of the "nice guy" for the manipulation it is, even if the "nice guy" doesn't. They know that everything he does reflects a secret agenda to fulfill his unspoken needs, one of which involves getting into a woman's pants. Since he's not being direct, women can only assume he has questionable intentions, which encourages them to stay away from this sort of guy whenever they find him.

Even when women aren't creeped out by the "nice guy," they will never be attracted to him. Just because your family and teachers praised you for being "good" doesn't mean women find it sexy, no matter what Hollywood says. Sexual attraction isn't "earned"; it's felt. Nothing about helping your crush move boxes, listening to her problems, or surprising her with gifts is sexy. She may appreciate the gestures, but she won't feel turned on, so she'll never "feel that way" toward the "nice guy." Since "nice guys" are obsessed with pleasing women, but terrified of disapproval, they never do the only thing that might actually turn the women they're attracted to on: expressing direct sexual interest and risking rejection.

As the needs of the "nice guy" remain unfulfilled, and as he sees women giving their approval to "less good" men, he grows resentful. Most "nice guys" develop a quiet rage toward women. They project a façade of kindness thickly plastered over a core of victim bile. When they've had enough, they erupt in "victim vomit" tantrums that terrify those unfortunate enough to see them. If nothing changes, many "nice guys" eventually turn to a path that's not nice at all.

Where Do You Get Your Self-Worth?

The first and most vital step in overcoming a "nice guy" mentality, or any of the self-shaming beliefs we touched on, is changing how you define your self-worth. The defining feature of most people who suffer social anxiety is that they base their self-worth on the opinions of others. When they make other people happy, they're "good men." When they upset people, they're "bad men." By giving so much importance to other people's opinions, they've enslaved themselves to their whims.

The solution is simple, but not easy. Instead of getting your self-worth from other people, what if you could get it from yourself? What if whether you were a "good man" or a "bad man" depended on your own judgments? If you're willing to entertain that thought, you'll realize that the benefits are impressive. It's more difficult to manipulate a man who isn't obsessed with pleasing people. When you're not trying to make people like you, you'll be less anxious and more confident, and you won't be projecting that needy, manipulative vibe that characterizes the "nice guy." You can still be nice to people, but when you are, you'll be doing it because you want to, on your own terms, not because you're terrified of disapproval. As odd as it might sound, when you're not obsessed with being "nice," being genuinely nice is easier, and people will like you a lot more.

Just as we don't want our feelings of self-worth to hinge on the whims of others, we also don't want them to depend on random events. For example, if you define your worth by how much money you have, the moment you suffer a medical emergency, or the stock market takes a tumble, you'll fall into depression. Ideally, you want your self-worth to be based on factors completely within your control. With these points in mind, here's what I recommend you adopt for a core belief about your worth:

"I have worth when I am behaving according to my goals and values."

You choose your goals, you choose your values, and you control your behavior. You're in control of everything. Neither fate nor other people have any say. As long as you're taking actions to accomplish your goals, you're doing things right and you reap all the benefits. Your worth doesn't depend on closing the deal; it depends on making the pitch. The woman doesn't have to sleep with you; you just have to ask her out. The more positive actions you take, the better you'll feel about yourself. People will make their judgments, and the stars will project what tragedies they will. You will face them as they come, you will always be there for yourself, and you will always have worth.

This is the essence of high self-esteem. It promotes what psychologists call an internal locus of control—a sense that you have power over what happens to you—and it's a mentality associated with lower rates of depression,[2] greater success in school,[3] job satisfaction,[4] superior problem-solving skills, and a better ability to deal with stress.[5] By every measure, when you're thinking this way, you're better off, and that applies to dating as well. When you're not trying to control people because you've stopped worrying about how they're controlling you, you free yourself to make genuine connections, and that's the stuff that makes friendship and love possible. This is vulnerability, and this is courage, and as I hope you're going to discover, it's the most attractive thing in the world.

Other Manifestations of Shame

I expect most men who pick up this book to be dealing with the "nice guy" mentality to some degree, but "nice guys" aren't the only ones who can benefit from a change in perspective. Sometimes we deal with our shame not by obsessively pleasing others, but by numbing all of our emotions. It helps us hurt less, but we also limit our capacity for good feelings such as passion and love. Our friends and lovers start to find us distant and emotionally unavailable.

Sometimes "nice guys" turn away from their "please everyone" paradigm toward an "everyone sucks" paradigm, adopting a "kill or be killed, exploit or be exploited" approach. They think this perspective is more "alpha" and that it will attract more women, only to find themselves enjoying little more success than they did before, and what "success" they do have invariably comes in the form of toxic relationships.

Whatever mask you're wearing, it's preventing your romantic success. Our next several chapters will teach you how to shift your perspective from "I'm worthless" to "I am enough" and "I have worth." Once you're thinking that way, you'll feel comfortable stripping away your mask and living as your authentic self. You won't see rejection as a judgment of your worthiness as a man; you'll see it as a way to screen out what you don't want. You'll learn to make yourself the priority while still being sensitive to the needs of others. You won't hide your fears behind arrogance or a macho persona; instead, you'll show genuine confidence through comfort with vulnerability, and that, in turn, will be a new beginning for your romantic life.

Chapter Summary

• "Nice guys" harbor a secret belief in their own lack of self-worth, and do "nice" things in hopes of manipulating others into meeting their emotional needs.

• Shifting your paradigm from "I have to please everyone" to "I will live according to my own values and goals" frees you from shame and anxiety.

Exercises

Exercise 1.1 – Immediate – Start Your Journal

Open a new document on your word processor or a fresh

notebook to serve as your progress journal. For your first entry, describe what changes you'd like to see in your dating life. Do you want to become more confident in approaching women? Fight less in your current relationship? Have better sex? List and describe your dating and relationship goals.

Exercise 1.2 – Immediate – Explore Your Problems

On a fresh page of your journal, answer the following questions:

• What are three ways I sabotage myself in dating? Why do I do so?

• What are three ways in which I hide my flaws from other people? Why do I do so?

• What are three ways in which I seek external approval? Why do I do so?

• Do I engage in covert contracts? If yes, give two examples.

Chapter 2 – Overcoming Self-Defeating Thoughts

Jesse has been sitting at his favorite bar, nursing his beer, for more than half an hour. Across the room sits a tall brunette in a sparkling dress, sipping her cosmopolitan. She hasn't moved since he arrived, and he would swear she's been staring at him, even smiling. Jesse doesn't usually have problems talking to people, but as he thinks about walking up to her, his stomach feels like lead. His hand trembles as he holds his glass, his mouth goes dry, and he feels ready to vomit. "I guess I've had too much," he mutters to himself. "Better call it a night."

Sometimes our emotions are crippling. Anxiety, fear, depression, and shame sap our willpower and keep us from reaching for the things we want. For "nice guys" especially, being sexually direct, or doing anything that could lead to disapproval, can feel so painful that we might not even think those actions are possible. If we're going to get anywhere in our romantic lives, we need to learn to deal with the emotions that keep us from taking risks.

As you read these words, thoughts are going through your head. You recognize the language and your brain organizes it into sentences. This is your conscious, directed thought, and it's what you're most aware of. There is another layer of thoughts, however—a subtler layer—that lingers in the background of your mind. You've probably never noticed these thoughts before, and if you have, you've noticed them only in terms of their most obvious consequences: emotions.

According to the theory behind cognitive behavioral therapy (CBT), which is one of the most clinically effective approaches to addressing depression and anxiety,[6] our moods and emotions are driven by these thoughts. It is not our experiences themselves that cause our emotions, but how our background thoughts interpret those experiences.[7] Jesse didn't become anxious because an attractive woman was looking at him; he was anxious because his background thoughts interpreted her attention as a threat, activating his "fight or flight" response. If we can become aware of our background thoughts, and change how they interpret our experiences, we can manage our self-limiting emotions.

Automatic thoughts aren't bad. They're totally normal, and most of them are good. What we're concerned with are any automatic thoughts that interfere with our goals. It's useful to feel anxious when you're standing at a cliff's edge. The automatic thought "I'm going to fall if I get too close" generates fear and encourages you to step back. That emotion is less useful when you're asking out your crush. The automatic thought "She'll think I'm stupid and I'll be humiliated" could ignite anxiety, setting in motion a barrage of physiological responses that make your thought a self-fulfilling prophecy. These self-limiting, distorted thoughts are the ones we want to change.

Cognitive Behavioral Therapy

The first thing to understand about any sort of psychotherapy is that your therapist isn't there to give you answers, but rather to help you find your own. You're a unique individual with your own personal cocktail of psychological strengths and weaknesses. Only you can figure out what automatic thoughts are limiting you, and only you can fix them. The tools in this chapter will help you do that, but you, not this book, will be the one solving your problems.

Start by imagining a scenario that's emotionally distressing for you that you wish weren't so. Let's say you're trying to ask your crush on a date. Notice the emotions you feel in this moment, and as you feel them, ask yourself: what's going through my head right now? We're not looking for thoughts such as "What am I going to say to her?" or rationalizations such as "I'm anxious because I'm insecure." The thought we want is the one directly provoking the emotion. "I will look stupid." "She will be annoyed with me." Another approach is to ask yourself, "What thought, if it went away, would make the emotion go away too?" If you can identify that thought, that's the one you're looking for.

When you've figured out what thought in your head is provoking your troublesome emotion, write it down in your journal. Usually such thoughts don't accurately reflect reality. They rest on assumptions that seem true, but after a little scrutiny, really aren't. Determining what's distorted isn't always easy, and this is where a therapist can be a big help. If you're not working with a therapist, you'll need to try to judge your thoughts for yourself. Fortunately, we have a few tools to help us do that. In *Feeling Good: The New Mood Therapy*, David Burns suggests ten of the most common types of distortions that people tend to make.[8] If your thoughts fall into any of these categories, they're probably distorted.

1. All-or-Nothing Thinking
You evaluate your personal qualities in extremes. All setbacks are disasters. Anything short of perfect is failure.

2. Overgeneralization
You feel that the thing that happened once will always happen. "This rejection means no one will ever like me."

3. Mental Filter
You focus on negative details and ignore the positive.

4. Disqualifying the Positive
You systematically interpret positive and neutral experiences as either negative or invalid. When that woman complimented you, it wasn't because she liked you; she was "just being nice."

5. Jumping to Conclusions

You make assumptions quickly by "**mind reading**" and "**fortune telling**." Mind reading is when you assume that people don't like you. Fortune telling is when you assume that bad things will happen.

6. Magnification and Minimization

You distort reality in one direction or another. Magnification is when you exaggerate the importance of errors, fears, and imperfections. "If she rejects me, my life will be over." Minimization is when you ignore or downplay your strengths. "She's with me only because everyone else sucks."

7. Emotional Reasoning

You use your emotions as evidence of your self-deprecating beliefs. "I feel overwhelmed, so I must be incompetent."

8. "Should" Statements

You frequently make "should" or "must" statements, causing you to feel pressure and resentment.

9. Labeling

You label yourself with a negative self-image. Instead of "I missed," you think "I'm a loser."

10. Personalization

You take responsibility for things you shouldn't, such as when you apologize for bad weather.

Reprogramming Your Distorted Thoughts

Think of your automatic thoughts as a computer program, and the way you have been writing the "code" of this program is by thinking the same thing over and over again. When you enter a situation, your brain activates your "programming," leading you to think that series of automatic thoughts and triggering the relevant emotions. If you practice a different series of thoughts in the same circumstances you will rewrite your programming, so the next time you're in that situation, you'll default to that new program and avoid your old, limiting emotions. In other words, if your old thought

"I'm ugly, she'll hate me" triggered approach anxiety for you, replacing it with "She might like me" will encourage you to approach and talk to her.

In cognitive behavioral therapy, the way we do this is by talking back to our distorted automatic thoughts with our desired rational responses. The more we argue with our distorted thinking, the quieter it gets and the more prominent our rational thoughts become. Eventually, the rational response will be as automatic as the original thought, replacing or accompanying it every time and evoking a more reasonable emotion.

Finding Rational Responses

To figure out what "rational responses" will work best for us, we're going to use a tried-and-true cognitive behavioral therapy technique called the **Column Method.** In your journal, arrange six columns labeled Date, Event, Emotion, Automatic Thought, Cognitive Distortion, and Response. An Excel template can be downloaded at *thehotguyde.com/resources*.

Date	Event	Emotion	Automatic Thought	Cognitive Distortion	Response
24-Jun	Sent an email to the wrong person	Fear	My boss will think I'm incompetent.	All-or-nothing thinking, Magnification, Mind reading	It was an honest mistake and I took care of it. It didn't cause any harm. My boss makes mistakes too.
24-Jun	Didn't prepare a date idea before meeting Kathy; she had a bad time	Shame	I'm an idiot.	Labeling	It probably would have been better if I'd thought of something fun to do, but my not doing that doesn't make me a bad person. I made a mistake and I recognize it; I'm not stupid. Next time I will plan ahead so this doesn't happen.

25-Jun	Someone complimented me on my shirt today	Discomfort	She's lying.	Disqualifying the positive, Mind reading	She had no reason to compliment me except that she genuinely liked my shirt. It doesn't make sense to assume she was trying to manipulate me.

In each column, record the date, event, emotion, and the automatic thought or thoughts going through your head. In the fifth column, determine whether each thought falls into any of Burns's ten categories of distorted thoughts, and write it down. In the sixth column, with the knowledge of what distortion is involved, write a brief response to the automatic thought. Think of the thought as if it's another person — a really stupid, annoying person. Tell it why it's wrong and what the right answer is. For example, let's say we had the thought "I'll just annoy her." This would be a case of "fortune telling" and "mind reading." We're assuming we'll annoy her; we don't know it. In response to the thought, we tell ourselves the truth: "I don't know if she'll be annoyed. I should find out. If she rejects me, I'll leave, and I'll be free to meet someone else."

Talking Back to Your Inner Critic

For many of us, our toxic automatic thinking takes on a specific form: the inner critic. He's the voice in your head that berates you. Whenever you try something, he's the first to tell you you'll fail. Nothing you do can satisfy him. He reminds you of the expectations you're not meeting, and he provokes your shame.

The key to overcoming your inner critic is to make the "rational" voice in your head louder and more influential than the critic's. One helpful tool I found to do this was to give the critic a name. I like "Dumbass Brainwash Voice." I also like to preface my responses to automatic thoughts with "Shut the fuck up." For example, my particular brand of approach anxiety was rooted in a fear that any woman would be "creeped out" by me, and if I talked to her, I was "bad." I would be harming people by being social, and the world would be better off without me. When my inner critic reminded me of this, I learned to reply, "Shut the fuck up, Dumbass Brainwash Voice. Plenty of people have liked chatting with me, and who's to say I'm not the guy she wants to meet tonight? She's out to have fun. I'll go up and say 'Hi,' and if she doesn't want me to stick around, I'll leave. No harm done."

Another helpful way to address your inner critic is to imagine a bully attacking your best friend. He tells your friend he sucks, that he's not good enough, that he's too short, or ugly, or stupid. Imagine that you're bigger, stronger, and smarter than that bully. How would you defend your friend? You'd say "Fuck off." "You're a lying asshole." "Get the hell away from him." What would you tell your friend? "He's an idiot; don't listen to him." "He's trying to manipulate you. He's the one with the problem, not you." Treat yourself like your friend, and your critic like the bully. Be ruthless with him and infinitely compassionate with yourself. Do both consistently and eventually he'll quiet down.

Identifying Core Beliefs

The first time you try talking back to your distorted thoughts, you'll be surprised by empowering it can be, and you might even see immediate improvements in your feelings. Asserting yourself against your own toxic thoughts might be the most liberating thing you've ever done. There are, however, hazards. Sooner or later, something will happen that will give your inner critic a boost. You might fail a test, get rejected, or creep someone out. In these moments, your inner critic will be saying "I told you so; you should have listened to me," and you'll be in danger of relapse. To prevent this, we need to go beyond talking back to our automatic thoughts. We need to go to their root, to the core beliefs that create them. If you can replace your toxic core beliefs with self-actualizing ones, you'll maximize your chances that your toxic thinking will disappear for good.[9]

To figure out what our core, toxic beliefs are, we'll be using another tried-and-true CBT method: the **Downward Arrow Technique**. When you've identified one of your toxic automatic thoughts, the downward arrow technique digs into that thought with a second question: "Suppose that were true. What would that mean?"

Here's an example. Imagine you had the thought "If I ask her out, she'll be annoyed with me." What would that mean? "It would mean I had upset the woman I love." Suppose that were true too. What would that mean? "It would mean I'm abusive and a bad person." Whatever implications you believe about your thoughts, whether you think they're rational or not, write them down. Keep asking yourself "What would that mean?" until you can't go any deeper. These are the beliefs that control your emotions, and the last one you can dig into will be your personal, core belief, from which all of your distorted thinking derives.

Take your list of thoughts and what those thoughts mean, and arrange them in three columns labeled Thought, Cognitive Distortion, and Response. As we did with the column method, identify what cognitive distortion is at play with each thought on your list, and write a rational response to that thought.

Automatic Thought	Cognitive Distortion	Response
She will be annoyed with me.	Fortune telling	I don't know that she will be annoyed with me. Perhaps she wants me to ask her out. If she rejects me, I can back off and go for someone more right for me.
I will have upset the woman I love.	Fortune telling	I don't know that she'll be upset. If sharing my feelings upsets her, that is her problem, not mine. I might not want to be friends, much less in love, with someone hostile toward me because I was honest about my romantic feelings.
I will be an abuser and a bad person.	Magnification, Labeling	Telling a woman I want to go out with her is not abuse. She will be just fine. I am not a bad person for having romantic feelings, nor am I bad for being honest about them.

Whenever you find yourself thinking your distorted thoughts in the future, remember your response to your core belief and add it into your response. "She will be annoyed with me." "Shut the fuck up, Dumbass Brainwash Voice. I don't know that. Having romantic feelings doesn't make me a bad person. She and I will both be better off if I find out how she feels." Every time you argue with your core belief, you will shift your paradigm a little closer to the self-actualizing "I am worthy when I'm living by my own values" belief we discussed in chapter 1. Eventually, that belief will define who you are and how you think, just as this toxic belief is doing now.

Ironic Rebound

There's a common mistake folks make when experimenting with distorted thinking, and it's worth talking about before we close this chapter. Some people realize that their thoughts are toxic, but instead of doing the "thought replacement" approach we're using here, they try to ignore or suppress their thoughts. "Just stop thinking about it!"

The problem with thought suppression is that it creates a paradox. In order to stop yourself from thinking a thought, part of your brain—what psychologist D. M. Wegner calls the "monitor"—has to think about that thought to make sure other parts of your brain aren't thinking about it. Brain scans show that when people attempt to suppress a thought, it remains active just outside their conscious minds.[10] Sooner or later, the thought boomerangs backs in, stronger than ever[11]—what Wegner calls "ironic rebound."[12] To make things worse, the more often we think a thought, the more likely we are to believe it's true.[13] In one study, when people tried to push away thoughts such as "I'm such a loser" and "People think I'm stupid," their self-esteem plummeted, even when they were emotionally healthy, and even when their efforts at consciously suppressing the thoughts were successful.[14] By suppressing our toxic thoughts, we make ourselves even more vulnerable to them.

When you have toxic thoughts, make sure you're not trying to stop yourself from thinking them. Let your inner critic say his piece, and instead of suppressing him, tell him to go fuck himself. Giving yourself permission to think the thoughts saps their potency,[15] and responding to them gives you the upper hand. Don't fight your thoughts; replace them.

Chapter Summary

• Our emotions, behaviors, and physiological responses are governed by how our automatic thoughts interpret our experiences.

• Some of our automatic thoughts are distorted, causing us to experience unpleasant emotions.

• By replacing our automatic thoughts with more-rational ones, we can change the way we habitually feel, behave, and react.

• We replace our automatic thoughts by talking back to them in our minds.

• The column method is a way to structure your responses to your distorted automatic thoughts.

• Your automatic thoughts come from your core beliefs. We can use the downward arrow technique to identify them.

• Don't try to suppress toxic thoughts.

Exercises

Exercise 2.1 – Immediate – Identify Automatic Thoughts

Read the following vignettes and imagine yourself in the position of the character described. What automatic thoughts might be provoking the feelings each character is experiencing? For example, if the vignette says "I got a B on the exam, and I felt utterly depressed," the automatic thought might be "If I don't perform perfectly, my life will be over," which is all-or-nothing thinking and magnification. There are no right answers; just try to imagine possibilities. Identify the cognitive distortion at play with each automatic thought you come up with.

1. I was about to turn in my project, and I felt nervous.
2. As I began writing my resume, I felt apathetic and wanted to put it off.
3. As I started to do my chores, I began to feel resentful.
4. As I presented my proposal to the meeting, I started to

sweat and I stammered.

5. I'd been in bed for twelve hours, but still couldn't find the will to get up.

6. I want to ask Rebecca out, but every time I try, I find excuses to delay.

7. My sister was sad (for a reason unrelated to me), and I felt guilty.

Exercise 2.2 – Immediate – Practice the Column Method

Have a look at the following automatic thoughts. Identify the type or types of distortion at play and write out a rational "replacement thought" to counter these distorted thoughts.

1. "If I lose this job, I'll live in poverty."

2. "If this clique doesn't accept me, I'll never make any friends."

3. "If I fail in this approach, I'm unattractive and no woman will ever want me."

4. "It doesn't matter if other women like me. If she doesn't accept me, I suck."

5. "I must get a bigger apartment or people will think I'm poor."

6. "I tried telling her I liked her and I was humiliated. It will always be that way."

7. "I'm a fuckup. Always have been, always will be."

Exercise 2.3 – Immediate – Practice the Downward Arrow Technique

Choose any two of the automatic thoughts from Exercise 2.2. Imagine that you are the person thinking each of those automatic thoughts. Use the downward arrow technique, asking yourself, "Suppose that were true; what would that mean?" to identify a core belief that might be at the root of each of those automatic thoughts. Write rational responses for each level of thoughts you discover.

Exercise 2.4 – Immediate – Analyze Your Past Experiences

Take a look at your answers to Exercise 1.2. What sorts of

emotions are involved in your people-pleasing behavior and the way you hide your flaws? Can you identify any automatic thoughts associated with these emotions? Write about your findings in your journal, identify any cognitive distortions at play, and brainstorm some rational responses you can use to replace those toxic beliefs.

Exercise 2.5 – Responsive – Document Your Automatic Thoughts

For the next two weeks, carry a small notebook or portable electronic device. Whenever you feel a distressing emotion that interferes with your life, document the date, activity, emotion, and what was going through your mind in that moment, as described in the section of this chapter about the column method. When you get home, identify any cognitive distortions at play and write a rational response to your automatic thoughts. Feel free to use the column method template available at *thehotguyde.com/resources*.

Exercise 2.6 – One Time – Perform the Downward Arrow Technique for Your Automatic Thoughts

After two weeks of documenting your automatic thoughts, choose three that have come up several times. Perform the downward arrow technique with these automatic thoughts and identify what core beliefs you carry with you that are at the root of your limiting emotions. Write out rational responses to replace them.

Exercise 2.7 – Responsive – Talk Back to Your Inner Critic

In the weeks you're practicing Exercise 2.5, and for no fewer than two weeks following the completion of that exercise, practice talking back to your inner critic with the rational responses you came up with in Exercises 2.4, 2.5, and 2.6. Tell your critic to "shut the fuck up," and assert yourself with the more-rational, self-actualizing belief. Keep track of your progress in your journal.

Chapter 3 – Dealing with Fear

It was November 13, 2010, a cold evening in South Burlington, Vermont, and the last day of my business trip. I'd made myself a promise. While I was there, I was to do the scariest thing on the face of the earth: talk to a stranger. I'd procrastinated all week, and when I walked into the hotel bar and ordered a cider, there were only two other people there: a big, burly man and his wife. Mustering the biggest surge of willpower in my life, I turned to him and said, "Excuse me, I'm trying to overcome my social anxiety. May I introduce myself to you?" Graciously, he said "Sure," and what followed was probably the most awkward conversation this man had ever had. He tried to connect with me on sports, travel, where I was from, and anything else he could think of as his wife sat by, visibly uncomfortable. It wasn't the best conversation of my life, but as I exited that bar, I jumped for joy, overwhelmed with euphoria. I'd done something I thought was impossible. Nothing would ever be quite as scary again.

We have to face a lot of scary stuff while we're dating—everything from rejection to opening up about our deepest insecurities. It takes courage, so we need to learn how to be courageous. Talking back to our anxious thoughts, as we talked about in chapter 2, can help a lot,[16] but when it comes to fear in particular, we have a tool that's even more effective: **Exposure Therapy**. Exposure therapy is exactly what it sounds like. The best way to overcome fear is to face it,[17] especially when that fear is social phobia.[18] No matter how much you practice, there will always be things that scare you, but with this approach, you can get your fear down to a manageable level.

Flooding vs. Graded

There are two types of exposure therapy — flooding and graded. Flooding is when you face your greatest fear directly and immediately, as when I talked to the guy in that hotel bar. Graded exposure involves starting small and increasing the level of difficulty over time, such as when a guy who's afraid of heights climbs a little higher every day. Both techniques are effective. I will focus on graded exposure, as it's the method most commonly used by therapists.[19] If you want to accelerate things, all you need to do is expose yourself to scarier situations earlier. Just be careful not to "alpha" your way through this. Trying to deadlift 300 pounds on your first trip to the gym won't make you stronger; it will discourage you. Flooding can do the same.

Exposure Hierarchy

Your first step is to decide what fear you want to overcome. Are you afraid of talking to women? Going to parties? Sharing your feelings? Describe your fear in your journal and list ten to fifteen associated activities that you'd find scary to do. For example, if "talking to women" is what scares you, some activities might be "Saying hi to a woman" or "Holding eye contact with a woman." Rate these activities on a scale from 1 to 10. A "1" should be something you can do with no problem. A "10" would put you in the fetal position, pissing your pants. A "5" is in between: something you can do, but it might take some willpower or encouragement. Make sure to include several activities rated 7 or higher. The scariest activities are the most important.

Activity That Provokes Approach Anxiety	Fear Level
Asking out my crush	10
Approaching a woman on the street	9
Approaching a group of women in a bar	8
Approaching a stranger in a bar	7
Asking a woman I am acquainted with on a date	6
Asking a woman on a dating website on a date	5
Talking with a woman in person one on one	4
Hanging out with a woman in a group of friends	3
Instant messaging a female friend	2
Looking at a picture of a woman	1

Every item on your list should be action oriented, by which I mean something you are going to do, not something you're going to stop doing. For example, don't write "Stop looking at porn." Keep things as specific as possible. "Talk to a woman in a club" might be easier for you than "Talk to a woman at the beach," and that important distinction would be hidden if you just wrote "Talk to a woman." If you're exposing yourself to anything more dangerous than talking, keep safety in mind. Nothing you do should hurt you or anyone else.

Your Exposure Schedule

When you go out to conduct an exposure, you can think of it as a "courage workout." As with any good workout plan, you'll get better results if you give it some structure and document your progress. When I was overcoming my approach anxiety, I found that two exposures per week (in the form of salsa lessons and bar socializing) worked well. When I was overcoming my fear of heights, several flooded exposures on a trip to Six Flags were enough. The more often you undertake this courage workout, the faster your progress will be. I wouldn't recommend anything slower than one exposure per week.

Every time you conduct an exposure, record when you get home how things went. I recommend keeping track of the date, activity, predicted fear level, actual fear level, and how satisfied you felt after doing it. You can grab an Excel template at *thehotguyde.com/resources*.

Thursday Night Salsa Lessons Fear Chart				
Date	Action	Predicted Fear	Actual Fear	Satisfaction
4-Oct	Go to first salsa class	4	4	6
11-Oct	Talk to a male stranger at salsa class	5	4	5
18-Oct	Talk to two strangers at salsa class	5	5	5
25-Oct	Talk to a woman at salsa class before dancing	7	5	7
1-Nov	Talk to five people; two must be women	7	5	8
8-Nov	Ask a woman to dance at the salsa club after class	8	6	10
15-Nov	Ask at least two women to dance at the salsa club	8	5	10
22-Nov	Ask for one woman's phone number	9	6	10

When Should I Move to the Next Exposure?

In *Face Your Fears*, David F. Tolin suggests that you have "mastered" your fear when your fear level drops to 50 percent of what it was when you started. At that point, you should move on to the next activity.[20] For example, if your fear level for "Approaching a stranger at a bar" was a 7, when your "actual fear" level gets down to 3 or 4, it's time to move to the next level.

Stay in the Exposure!

When you face your fear, your body will flood your bloodstream with adrenaline, activating your "fight or flight" response. You will feel a compelling urge to get away. Don't fight this feeling; accept it. Go ahead and say in your head, "I'm afraid right now; I don't have to run away." Feeling an emotion doesn't compel you to act on it. Your limbic system doesn't know the difference between a real threat and a perceived one, but you do. All you have to do is stay.

After several minutes, your fear will subside for purely biological reasons. Your body can't produce adrenaline forever, and eventually your cells reabsorb what's already flowing and your amygdala surrenders control back to your frontal cortex. This is why we stay. Your goal is to teach your body that it doesn't have to activate your fear response in these circumstances. As long as you can stay in the exposure without leaving, your brain will reprogram itself accordingly, and it will get easier. If you run from the exposures before your brain can calm down, the primitive parts will never learn their lesson, and your fear will be just as potent every time.

Safety Behaviors

Andy is scared of approaching women, but being a "clever" dude, he has a solution. He gets drunk. Unfortunately for Andy, drinking doesn't help him much beyond his first approach, and on the rare occasion when the woman sticks with him for more than two minutes, things tend to fall apart. His drunken conversation isn't as interesting as he thinks it is, and that "fearlessness potion" isn't the best helper when he tries to perform in bed. A lot of guys follow Andy's example, and all of them would be better off not relying on the booze.

Fear is uncomfortable, and often people resort to various crutches to make facing their fears a little easier. These crutches are called "safety behaviors." Though they make an exposure easier in the short term, they'll handicap your long-term progress. Here are some common examples:

• Doing exposures only when your friends are around

• Carrying a lucky object with you that is the source of your success

• Keeping a tool nearby to help you, such as someone facing his fear of the dark clutching a flashlight

• Drinking alcohol

• Performing a ritual before the activity

• Distracting yourself to keep your mind off the activity

By using these safety behaviors, you're teaching your brain that the situation you perceive as scary is safe only when the safety behavior is involved. The moment the safety behavior isn't available, your anxiety comes back in full force. If you want to make real progress, you need to teach your brain that the scary activity is always safe, not only in certain circumstances.

Take a few minutes to brainstorm any safety behaviors you might be using and see if you can divorce them from the activities you've attached them to. For example, "Go to a bar with friends" might be easier than "Go to a bar by myself." "Ask a woman out" may have a tougher rating than "Ask a woman out while drunk." With the safety behavior removed, give the activity whatever fear rating it deserves, add it to the appropriate spot on your exposure hierarchy, and start working toward it.

Generalized Courage

Being a skydiver might not teach you social skills, but it will teach you to deal with fear. The more often you subject yourself to scary situations, the easier unexpected ones will be.

Make a list of twenty activities that scare you and give

them a fear rating from 1 to 10. They don't have to have anything to do with dating, and it's probably better if they don't.

Action	Fear Level
Emailing my boss asking for time off	2
Skydiving	9
Cliff diving	10
Approaching a woman at a bar	5
Asking a woman out after chatting	4
Sending my writing out for people to read	5
Going down Geronimo at Water Country	6
Going alone to a foreign country	7
Telling a bully I don't appreciate how he's treating me	5
Public speaking	4
Cold calling	8
Riding a roller coaster	5
Auditioning for a show	6

With this list in hand, I suggest adopting a new policy on fear: If something scares you, that alone is reason enough to do it. Get in the habit of facing your fears at every opportunity. If you want to give this new policy some structure, try the following:

1. Every week, face one fear ranked 5 or lower.

2. Every month, face one fear ranked 6 or higher.

3. When you encounter a fear ranked 4 or lower, always do it.

4. Revise the list every month with new fear ratings and new challenges.

Imagined Exposures

Sometimes there are activities we can't do in person. Maybe it's a one-time event, such as a presentation at work. Maybe it's too legitimately dangerous to do several times. In these cases, unless we have access to a virtual-reality program, the best we can do is imagine the exposure.

Sit in a comfortable chair. For the next twenty minutes, imagine doing the thing that scares you. Envision every detail: smells, sensations, temperature, sounds, people, tastes, and anything else you can think of. If you like, write out a narrative of the activity, record yourself reading it, and then listen to the narrative as you imagine your exposure.

Imagining the exposure helps you approximate the real experience. Since it isn't real, your imagination serves as a permanent "safety behavior" you can never abolish, so it's not so good as the real thing, but it can help. When I do imagined exposures, I like to imagine things going as badly as they could possibly go. When I face the real thing, if it turns out not to be so bad, it's a lot easier to deal with.

Chapter Summary

• Exposure therapy involves overcoming fear by facing it. Flooding exposes you to your worst fears immediately. Graded exposures increase in intensity over time.

• Identify activities that scare you and rate them from 1 to 10. Expose yourself to these fears, moving up the list when your fear rating drops to half of where it started.

• Stay in exposures for at least twenty minutes.

• Watch out for safety behaviors—crutches you use to make the exposures easier.

• If something scares you, that is reason enough to do it. Get in the habit of behaving this way.

• When facing a fear in person is not possible, imagine it.

Exercises

Exercise 3.1 – Immediate – Explore Your Fears

What sort of fears hold you back from dating success? Are any of your undesired behaviors you described in Exercise 1.2 connected to fears? What sorts of activities could you design as part of an exposure plan to systematically desensitize you to those fears? Discuss these issues in your journal.

Exercise 3.2 – Immediate – Make Your Exposure Plan

Identify a fear you would like to overcome and make a list of associated activities with fear ratings from 1 to 10. For suggestions related to dating and social anxiety, see below:

• Go to a bar or other social venue and stay for at least thirty minutes.

• Go to a bar and sit next to a woman.

• Go to a public place and dance where people can see you.

• Walk down the street and hold eye contact with every stranger you pass.

• Walk up to a group of people at a bar and say, "Hi, I'm trying to overcome my social anxiety; can I hang out and chat with you guys?"

• Send a message to an attractive woman on an online dating site.

• Compliment a woman on how well she dresses.

• Compliment a guy on how well he dresses.

• Ask a stranger for directions, or for the time.

Exercise 3.3 – Immediate – Make Your Generalized Exposure List

As suggested in this chapter, make a list of activities unrelated to dating that scare you. Rate them for fear levels ranging from 1 to 10.

Exercise 3.4 – Ongoing – Practice Exposure Therapy

Execute your exposure plan. Do your exposures no less frequently than once per week. Document your progress in your journal. Feel free to use the template at *thehotguyde.com/resources*. After one week of exposures, review your progress for any safety behaviors or other problems.

Exercise 3.5 – Ongoing – Practice Rejection Exposure Therapy

For two weeks, put yourself in a position to be rejected at least once per day. This can be a romantic rejection, but it does not have to be. Examples include:

• Asking someone on a date

• Inviting someone to hang out

• Inviting someone to get coffee or a drink

• Asking someone for money

• Offering someone money

• Asking for a small favor

• Asking for a ridiculous favor

• Inviting someone to dance at a club or party

• Bringing bubbles to a park and offering them to someone to play with

Exercise 3.6 – Ongoing – Explore Generalized Exposures

Execute your generalized exposure plan and specify what your first month of activities will be. Plan four scary activities with ratings of 5 or lower and one scary activity with a rating of 6 or higher. From this day forward, any time you encounter a fear with a rating of 4 or lower, do it immediately.

Chapter 4 – Willpower

Ted is a couch potato. Every day he has the same routine: come home from work, binge-watch TV, go to bed. At twenty-eight, he has finally realized that this isn't the behavior of a healthy guy. He's depressed and lonely.

Ted decides to change. He starts to hit the gym. He devours dozens of books, podcasts, and articles on self-help. He hangs motivational posters in his bedroom and shares inspiring memes on social media. Ted wants to make his life better, and he seems to be taking all the right steps.

As the weeks wear on, the piss and vinegar that characterized Ted's early drive starts to fade. He falls back into his old routine. Hitting the gym gets harder and harder, and he starts to rationalize why he can't go. He's too tired. He deserves a break. There will be time tomorrow. Despite his early promise, Ted reverts to his old habits.

Nearly every person you will ever meet who purchases a self-help book or goes to a self-improvement "boot camp" can tell you Ted's story. Inspiration doesn't last and real life gets in the way. As you work through *The Hot Guyde*, you will be tempted to give up on your self-improvement goals and accept the status quo. You will get lazy and frustrated, and you will break. I'm saying this not to discourage you, but to help you beat the odds. Acknowledging that you're human, and that you'll be tempted the same way your peers are, doesn't mean you're going to succumb; it means you have to prepare for when it happens.

A Willpower Primer

Right behind your forehead is a part of your brain

called the prefrontal cortex, the headquarters of your willpower. When the impulsive centers of the brain, like the reward system, are screaming to have their ways, the prefrontal cortex intervenes to choose what desires are most important. When your brain is running low on blood sugar, it starts to shut down what evolution has determined to be "non-essential areas," one of which happens to be the prefrontal cortex[21] (even though it doesn't actually take that much energy to run[22]). As such, your willpower is dependent on your nutrition. You will be more likely to give in to temptation when you're hungry, and the better you eat, the stronger your discipline will be.

There are three types of willpower: "I will," "I won't," and "I want," each of which is associated with a separate region of the prefrontal cortex.[23] "I will" power concerns doing things you're reluctant to do. "I won't" power concerns restraining your impulses. "I want" power involves remembering your long-term goals in the face of immediate gratification.

Just as our bodies have a "fight or flight" response to deal with threats, we have another response to deal with difficult choices: the "pause and plan" response,[24] the strength of which is associated with a physiological quality called heart rate variability (HRV), which is the amount of change between the intervals of your heartbeats. The higher your HRV, the stronger your willpower.[25] Factors such as air pollution,[26] depression,[27] and illness[28] have all been found to harm HRV, while proper sleep, nutrition, and exercise improve it. If you're finding yourself frequently lacking willpower, taking better care of your health will help.

Willpower is like a muscle. The more we use it, the stronger it gets, but no matter how strong we become, it will always have a limit.[29] In a study where alcoholics were asked to resist drinking, they became physically and psychologically weaker.[30] When smokers resisted cigarettes, they gave in to eating ice cream.[31] Every time you use your willpower, you tire yourself out, so no matter how strong you get, you will always have a breaking point.

Things That Don't Work

Shame

Often when we fall short of our goals, we beat ourselves up. We figure that by punishing ourselves, we can stay motivated to stick to our goals and avoid self-punishment in the future. The reality is the opposite. When we're feeling down, our brains make feeling better a top priority, and most of the time, that means turning to short-term pleasures. In several studies, when feeling crappy, addicts felt their urges more strongly,[32] diners perceived cake as more delicious,[33] and dieters ate more.[34] Janet Polivy and C. Peter Herman call this the "What the hell" effect.[35] We're already pieces of shit, so why not indulge? By shaming ourselves, we cause the very failures we're trying to avoid.

The key to overcoming the "What the hell" effect is to focus on the opposite of shame. In a 2007 study, when dieters who gave in to their urges were comforted, they retained more willpower and adhered to their diets better than those who were shamed.[36] In another study, students who procrastinated and then shamed themselves procrastinated more on future assignments than students who forgave themselves.[37] Having compassion for ourselves encourages us take responsibility for our actions,[38] boosting our willpower. Shame saps it.[39] The next time you find yourself facing failure, instead of beating yourself up, treat yourself with compassion.

Resolutions

Every New Year's Eve, millions of people decide to change their lives. Eight percent succeed.[40] For those of us hoping to change our lives in the new year, the odds aren't good.

Promising ourselves to change fills us with hope and good feelings. We make big plans and demand big improvements, and the bigger the demands, the better the feelings. It's what a lot of folks feel when they start a new self-help program or a new diet.

All of these things are wolves in sheep's clothing. Instead of spurring change, they function as just another kind of instant gratification. The euphoria we feel only sets the stage for our downfall. The first time we encounter resistance, frustration sets in, we feel bad, and our willpower fails. Polivy and Herman have dubbed this tendency the "false hope syndrome."[41]

When you're setting out toward a goal, pay attention to how your plans make you feel. You should be optimistic, but there's a difference between optimism and a fantasy-induced "hope high." Remind yourself of the real challenges that are ahead of you. Stay focused on the next step of your plan, not on how great life will be when it's done. Every step is worth taking, and its own reward. Good feelings and fantasy will not change your life. Sticking to your plan will.

Making It Moral

Most of us like to be decent people, but we aren't trying to be angels. When we do good things, we feel we've earned some leeway and have permission to be a little bit bad.[42] In a study conducted in 2001, when researchers asked students how they felt about a sexist statement, those who disagreed most strongly with the statement were the most likely to behave in a sexist way in a subsequent experiment.[43] People who wrote stories about being altruistic donated 60 percent less money than people who didn't, and when managers thought about occasions when they acted ethically, they were less likely to reduce factory pollution.[44] These people weren't all hypocrites; they were falling victim to a human tendency called moral licensing.

People often label their goals as morally good, and the failure to achieve those goals as morally evil. When you stick to your diet, you're being good. When you indulge, you're being bad. The problem with this approach is that the more we stick to our goals, the more inclined we are to license ourselves to turn away, killing the progress we just made.[45]

Instead of making your goals a moral issue, think of them in terms of "I want" and "I don't want." You're not avoiding that cake because it's naughty, but because you want to lose weight. You're not facing your exposure because you're "good"; you do it because you want to be braver. If you're facing a moment of weakness, remind yourself of why you have your goals and why you have resisted giving in to temptation in the past. This will strengthen your will more than praise or shame.

Believing in Super You

In 2009, R. J. Tanner and K. A. Carlson conducted a survey of recent purchasers of exercise equipment, asking them how much they planned to exercise in the next month. They asked another group of participants how much they would exercise in an ideal world. Their responses were identical. The people who had just bought exercise equipment were imagining exercising in an ideal world by default. When surveyed later on, those who failed to live up to their expectations became even more optimistic about the future.[46] "These weeks were hard. I'll make up for it next week, when it's easier." We rationalize our laziness by expecting things to get better. If you can catch yourself thinking this way and remind yourself that the future will be just as hard as the present, you'll be more likely to follow through on your goals.

Another factor at play is that most of us would rather have someone else do hard work than do it ourselves. As odd as it may sound, we have this same attitude toward our future selves. When students in a study were deciding when to do unpleasant tasks, their treatment of their future selves resembled their treatment of strangers.[47] Brain-imaging studies showed that when imagining their future selves, many participants had no activity in the regions associated with self-reflection. They literally thought of their future selves as other people. The less these participants related to their future selves, the more likely they were to embrace instant gratification.[48]

It's important to remember that in the future, you're still going to be you. All of the good things you're doing today will benefit you, and all the bad things will harm you. If that's something you struggle to accept, here are a few techniques that have been shown to help:

• Imagine your future self and write him a letter. Visualizing the future in this way was found to have strong effects on present willpower.[49]

• Instead of changing your behavior, make it consistent. "I will smoke the same number of cigarettes tomorrow as I smoke today." This keeps your vision of the future realistic.[50]

• Plan your indulgences ahead of time. "I will play Starcraft for thirty minutes after my homework is done." When your indulgence is part of your plan, you'll preserve your willpower.

Things That Work

Meditation

As I mentioned above, willpower is like a muscle. The more you exercise it, the stronger it gets. Wouldn't it be nice if there were a willpower workout that got reliable results?

It turns out that there is. Clinical evidence has found a technique that might be the best "willpower workout" around. People who practice it possess superior focus, stress management, impulse control, self-awareness,[51] and heart-rate variability.[52] This "workout" is meditation.

Our minds are constantly shifting to all of the distractions we deal with every day. You think about work, and then the apps on your phone, and then food, and then the itch on your ass. When you meditate, you practice turning your mind away from these distractions and toward a central focus, usually your breath. Every time your recenter your mind, you exercise your willpower.

To practice meditating, do the following:

- Sit. Do not move.

- Close your eyes.

- Slowly think the words "inhale" and "exhale." Breathe accordingly with each thought.

- When your mind wanders, return to the words "inhale" and "exhale." Continue to breathe.

When you're starting out, limit yourself to five minutes of meditation. Set a timer so you don't have to keep track of the time. After several days of practice, instead of returning your mind to the words "inhale" and "exhale," see if you can turn it just to the sensation of breathing. If you find that you are "bad" at meditation, and your mind wanders frequently, that's okay. All that means is that you stand to benefit the most. Practice regularly, and at your own pace.

Other Willpower Workouts

In addition to meditating, one of the best ways to build willpower is to incorporate small willpower challenges into your everyday life.[53] You can practice "I will" power by doing small things you don't usually do (such as flossing, if you don't). You can practice "I won't" power by limiting or ending a small habit you usually practice (such as cutting a certain food out of your diet, or controlling your language). These exercises should be small, simple changes that take only a little willpower, and are easy to monitor and do regularly.

Removing Bad Influences

Imagine you have a group of high school kids, all of them fit and studious. All but one. Would you suppose the majority of good habits would rub off on the unfit kid, or would his habits rub off on everyone else? In a study conducted with U.S. Air Force Academy cadets, the least fit cadet at enrollment was the best predictor of the fitness of all other cadets in his unit later on.[54] In a 2007 analysis of the Framingham Heart Study, women with sisters who became obese had a 67 percent increased risk of becoming so themselves.[55] Similar infectiousness was observed with smoking, alcoholism, sleep habits, and drug use.[56] If you're in frequent contact with someone with poor self-control, that person's influence over you can be more powerful than your own long-standing healthy behaviors. Any and all poorly disciplined people in your social circle are threats to your goals. If you can cut them out of your life, you should consider it. If you can't (for example, if they are family members), visit them sparingly, and when you do, take a few moments before you meet them to give yourself a willpower "immune system" boost. Reflect on your goals and remind yourself why you've chosen to behave differently. This will strengthen your resistance to their influence.[57]

Surfing the Urge

One of the points I emphasized in chapter 3 was to stay in your exposures for twenty minutes to allow the adrenaline to drain from your system. There's a similar technique we can use for willpower. When your brain starts to fixate on something it desires, it floods with the neurochemical dopamine. Just as with adrenaline, if you give yourself time to let the dopamine subside, your craving will calm down.[58] Whenever you find yourself feeling a craving, make a deal with yourself: "I will wait fifteen minutes. If I still want it after that, I'll give in." Sometimes that fifteen-minute wait is all that's necessary for you to regain control. Likewise, if you find yourself unwilling to do something, take the same approach. "I'll do it for fifteen minutes, and if I don't want to do it any longer after that, I'll stop." Once you get moving in the right direction, you'll often find you want to keep going.

Chapter Summary

• Willpower is centered in the prefrontal cortex and is correlated with heart-rate variability.

• Eating, sleeping, and exercising well improve willpower. Avoid pollution, stress, and illness.

• Self-shaming, resolutions, morality, and thinking that the future will be easier are toxic for willpower.

• Meditation and small, consistent changes to your behavior are the best willpower workouts.

• Poor lifestyle habits are infectious. People who possess them will undermine your will.

• Waiting fifteen minutes before giving in strengthens your willpower.

Exercises

Exercise 4.1 – Immediate – Consider the Obstacles
Consider the exercises and techniques introduced in chapters 2 and 3. What sorts of obstacles can you imagine getting in your way? When your enthusiasm fails, what rationalizations do you see yourself making for why you don't need to follow through on your plans? If you're coming back to this exercise after finishing *The Hot Guyde*, consider obstacles that may interfere with goals associated with other chapters as well. List these obstacles and rationalizations in your journal.

Exercise 4.2 – Immediate – Try Meditating

Do your first meditation. Set a five-minute timer for yourself and find a comfortable place to sit. Follow the instructions in this chapter. When your mind wanders, return your thoughts to the words "inhale" and "exhale," and focus on your breathing.

Exercise 4.3 – Ongoing – Track Your Willpower Choices
As you commit to "ongoing" exercises, track your "follow through" rate each week. When you intend to go to the gym, how often do you actually go? When you plan an exposure, how often do you do it? Feel free to use the template available at *thehotguyde.com/resources*.

Exercise 4.4 – One Time – Write a Letter to the Future You
The website *futureme.com* allows you to write yourself a letter to be delivered sometime in the future. Use this website to write yourself a letter. Tell yourself what you're doing to make life better for yourself in the future, and what you hope you'll be doing when you receive it.

Exercise 4.5 – Responsive – Practice Dealing with Ineffective Willpower Behaviors
Take a few moments to think about times when you've tried to use shame, resolutions, morality, or procrastination when facing willpower challenges. For the next two weeks, whenever you find yourself making one of these errors, make a note of it in your notebook. Treat it like an undesired automatic thought, and talk back to it with a rational response as we discussed in chapter 2.

Exercise 4.6 – Ongoing – Adopt a Willpower Workout
Choose a daily "I will" or "I won't" willpower workout from the lists below (or one you come up with yourself) and practice it for two weeks. Once two weeks are up, choose another exercise for the following two weeks, preferably from the other list. Continue experimenting with new workouts until you're satisfied with your level of willpower. Monitor your progress with Exercise 4.3.

"I will" exercises:

- Start flossing.
- Do a five-minute workout.
- Draw a picture.
- Clean the kitchen or bathroom surfaces.
- Go for a walk.
- Do one set of pushups to the point of exhaustion.
- Read a random article on Wikipedia.
- Prepare a glass of water before bed to drink immediately when you wake.

"I won't" exercises:

- Cut one type of food you frequently eat out of your diet.
- Stop swearing.
- Perform one everyday task (such as opening a door) only with your nondominant hand.
- Stop slouching.
- Stop using a particular app or website.
- Stop saying "Yeah"—replace it with "Yes."
- Stop watching a TV program you regularly watch.

Exercise 4.7 – Responsive – Surf Your Urges

When you find yourself tempted to fall back into your undesired behavior, "surf the urge." Make a deal with yourself to wait fifteen minutes before indulging, or to practice the activity for fifteen minutes before quitting. After the first time you try it, write in your journal about how it felt.

Chapter 5 – Habits and Cognitive Dissonance

Frank is an extraordinary athlete. He can swim faster and hold his breath longer than nearly anyone who challenges him. He has few vices and rarely struggles to resist temptation. Whatever criticisms you can make of Frank, no one doubts his discipline.

Frank is a good-looking guy, but he struggles in dating. He can carry a conversation, and his abs are chiseled like the ones on a statue of Jesus, but for some reason, women don't like him. Whenever he goes on a date, he fidgets with nervous energy. He doesn't always shower, and when he does, he often forgets his deodorant. His apartment is a smelly mess. He's had a few one-night stands, but when it comes to anything longer than a week, no one is interested. Frank has bad habits, and those habits sabotage him everywhere he goes. Sometimes he'll make an effort to fix his habits, but as the weeks wear on, he always returns to his routine. Frank has an extraordinary will, but like everyone else, he always eventually breaks.

Much of what people consider "bad social skills" and "awkwardness" are actually bad social habits. Holding poor posture, not maintaining eye contact, and other problems we'll discuss in upcoming chapters are things you've learned to practice your whole life. Humans rely on these sorts of habit cues to judge social status, friendliness, and sexual attractiveness because they're the most authentic signals we can read. Good habits are hard to fake, and bad ones are hard to hide. You can control your body language for a while, but just as with Frank's hygiene, your willpower drains, and eventually your true self shines through. Confident body language has to come naturally or you'll send people conflicting signals, which they'll read as "creepy." To change your habits, you need to understand the science behind how habits are made and broken. Knowing this process can also give us a powerful tool for developing confidence and self-esteem, which we'll discuss at the end of this chapter.

What Are Habits?

Deep in the center of your brain, in one of the most primitive, earliest-evolved regions, is a golf ball–sized oval called the basal ganglia. Its primary function is motor control,[59] but it also plays a role in the development of habits.[60]

Habits are an energy-saving mechanism for the brain. When you're learning a new skill, several sections of your brain have to process lots of information and many calculations. When you practice, your brain starts to recognize common sequences that it can group into routines, a process called "chunking." You don't need to calculate consciously how to back out of your driveway or brush your teeth because these sequences have been chunked. The chunks are stored and processed in the basal ganglia, and are the base on which habits are formed.[61]

Habits are never lost, only changed. You've probably noticed that you never completely forget old motor skills you learned, such as riding a bike. Likewise, when addicts see triggers for their addictions, they're always a challenge to resist. Using magnetic resonance imaging, neuroscientists can see old habit pathways lingering in the brain, overridden by those formed in new habit sequences.[62] In this way, though we can change our habits and though we can resist them, they never disappear entirely. Since habits are so low-energy, and since they last forever, we can rely on our habits more than on our willpower—as long as they're working for us and not against us. Master your habits and you'll master your life.

The Structure of Habit

You'll often hear that it takes twenty-one days to set a habit. This number comes from the work of Maxwell Maltz, a plastic surgeon working in the 1950s, who noticed that it took around twenty-one days for his patients to get used to their new faces.[63] This was not true habit formation, so this figure isn't accurate. A study published in the *European Journal of Social Psychology* found that it takes an average of sixty-six days for behaviors to become habits. Subjects showed results ranging from as few as eighteen days to as long as eight months. This study also showed that habit formation develops in a steep curve. The most significant changes happen early on, so it's those first few steps in changing your habits that are most important.[64]

Habits form in a cycle composed of three parts: cue, routine, and reward. New habits form when a cue and a routine become consistently associated with a reward we crave.[65] Most of the time, this is unconscious. We go to the mall, hear the "shopping music" that's playing, purchase merchandise, and feel pleasure. We smell the doughnuts, buy them, and enjoy the sweet flavor. By recognizing the process, we can break bad habits we don't want, and set new ones that will make us happier, healthier, and sexier.

Setting the Cue—Implementation Intentions

The best way to set up a new habit is through a technique called the **Implementation Intention**. Implementation intentions are "if-then" links describing what we do in specific circumstances.[66] They should be broad enough to be common, but specific enough to be realizable. "I will eat fruit" isn't helpful because the parameters are too broad. "When I have breakfast at my girlfriend's, I will have fruit" may be unhelpful because it's too irregular a cue. "When I have breakfast, I will eat a piece of fruit" is the happy medium.

Often, people try to set their habits based on time. "When it's 6:30, I will go to the gym." This tends not to be helpful.[67] Time cues require us to watch the clock, which is itself a new habit we'd need to set (and a stressful one at that). Instead, we want to attach our habits to recurring events in the day, or to another habit we already have.[68] "When I get to work, I will meditate." "When I brush my teeth, I will also floss."

Programming the Reward

There are two kinds of rewards: intrinsic and extrinsic. Intrinsic rewards are pleasures that directly result from the routine, such as the endorphin rush after a workout. Extrinsic rewards are things we shoehorn in with the routine, such as eating a candy bar after studying. Whenever possible, favor intrinsic rewards.[69] Extrinsic rewards can send confusing cues to the primitive parts of your brain. Sometimes candy bars come with studying; sometimes they don't. If you're out of candy bars, you might not study, and sometimes you might have a candy bar even when you didn't study at all. Focus on the intrinsic rewards of the activity and find ways to amplify them. For example, when you finish a difficult exposure exercise, congratulate yourself for a job well done. If all you can use is an extrinsic reward, try to keep it related to the habit, such as a tasty protein shake immediately after a workout.

Breaking Habits

Breaking habits involves reverse-engineering the habit-creation process. To do this, we'll use an approach called **Habit Reversal Therapy.**[70] It involves four steps.

Step 1 – Identify the Routine

This step is straightforward. The routine is the behavior you want to change.

Step 2 – Experiment with Rewards

What itch is your habit scratching? If you're always snacking at your desk, are you hungry or are you bored? Try changing the activity to see if something else will give you the reward you're looking for. Instead of eating, stand up and stretch. Instead of going on Facebook, read a book. Keep track of how satisfied you feel after the alternative. When you find another reward that works, you have a clue to how to change your routine.

Step 3 – Find the Cue

Figuring out the cue to your habit will usually be the hardest part. Pay attention to the circumstances associated with your habit and look for the things that are always there.

• What time of day is it?

• Where am I?

• How am I feeling?

• Whom am I with?

• What did I just do?

• What objects are associated with the habit?

• What physical sensations (such as itching or tingling) am I feeling?

• Is there something I smell, see, or hear?

• Is there a thought I think that kicks it off?

Step 4 – Change the Routine

Changing your habit is simple: create a new implementation intention springing from the cue your current habit is using. "When I feel like shaking my leg, I will stand and stretch instead." "When I feel like breaking eye contact, I will remind myself to hold it for a few more seconds." Make sure not to use a negative implementation intention, such as "When I want to smoke, I will not smoke." All this does is create an ironic rebound effect.[71] Make sure your new habit is a positive action. "If I feel like smoking, I will chew gum."

Change Your World

Sometimes habits are so ingrained that even our best efforts can't dislodge them. In these cases, there is one more measure you can take. You can change your "world."

Major changes to our lives uproot our habits. When you start a new job, you have to learn new skills, which means learning new habits. When you have a baby, you have to accommodate the baby's needs, which means new habits. If you're struggling to make your desired changes, radically changing your environment can help you uproot even the most hardwired routines.[72] Move to a new state or country, or take an extended vacation. Even something less severe, such as rearranging your apartment, can give you the boost you need. Be careful, though. Remember, your old habits don't disappear; they just get replaced. If you return to your old lifestyle, full of all your old cues, you'll feel pressure to return to your "old life" habits. One of the big problems faced by guys who go abroad and make huge changes is that as soon as they return home, they revert to the status quo and lose all the progress they made. If you're going to change your world, leave your old life behind for good, and if you can't, be careful of triggers that will encourage you to return to the way you were before.

Habits and Cognitive Dissonance

In chapter 2, we learned to counter our toxic thoughts with rational ones. In the war on our inner critics, if we think of CBT as our infantry, this next technique is the artillery. Through cognitive dissonance, you can change your toxic thoughts and feelings by leveraging your behavior.

Have you ever been having a conversation and realized that something you believed was completely wrong? How'd it feel? Uncomfortable, right? Humans have a built-in need for mental consistency. When we find ourselves believing two contradictory ideas, it feels wrong and we have to fix it. That discomfort is called cognitive dissonance.

Sometimes cognitive dissonance isn't just about conflicting ideas, but about a difference between how we act and what we believe. For example, let's say you're a young, religious guy who wants to "wait until marriage," but you like having sex with your girlfriend. The difference between your behavior and your professed values causes you to feel cognitive dissonance. There are a few ways you could fix it. You could change your behavior and tell your girlfriend that you can't have sex anymore, but if you're like most people, you'll take the opposite approach and change your beliefs. You might decide "Anal sex is an exception," or "This sex is different from the sex I'll have with my wife." You might even abandon your values completely. By behaving in a way that contradicts your beliefs, you apply pressure to those beliefs, and the more consistently you continue the behavior, the more likely your beliefs are to change.[73]

Remember those self-limiting "nice guy" beliefs we were looking to abolish? By behaving in a way consistent with high self-worth and inconsistent with any "I'm worthless" beliefs you have, you can use cognitive dissonance to systematically reprogram your self-image. The more you practice your new habits, and the more heavily you invest in them, the more likely you'll be to abandon any self-limiting thoughts that contradict them. This approach isn't quite as well established as CBT, but I'm not pulling it totally out of my ass. Inducing this sort of cognitive dissonance has proven effective in treating eating disorders,[74] online gaming addiction,[75] and road rage.[76]

When deciding what habits and hobbies you'd like to adopt, look for compassionate activities that reflect an investment in yourself. Small investments such as flossing, preparing yourself a glass of water before sleep, or giving yourself regular positive affirmations in the mirror all cause cognitive dissonance with any "I suck" beliefs you might have. Hobbies that involve spending a lot of time and energy investing in yourself, such as buying a new wardrobe, going to the gym, or learning to cook healthy and delicious meals, are gold. Every time you practice a gesture of self-love, you chip away at your toxic inner critic's power. Over time, your belief in your worth will affect not only how you treat yourself but how you expect others to treat you and the body language you exhibit.

Cognitive dissonance is uncomfortable, and when you're starting out, acting compassionately toward yourself is going to feel weird. Your inner critic will do everything he can to discourage your changed behavior. He'll tell you "This doesn't work" or "You're wasting your time." "You're being a selfish asshole; try acting for someone other than yourself for once!" he'll say. This is when your habit-forming and willpower techniques are most important. Because you will feel disinclined to continue your compassionate behaviors, the habits keeping them going need to be stronger than the toxic voices in your head encouraging you to stop. To fight back, use everything we've discussed so far. Set implementation intentions for your compassionate behaviors toward yourself. "When I wake up, I will tell myself how awesome I am." Talk back to the toxic thoughts and tell them they're bullshit. Practice your willpower exercises so you can bring yourself to do the behaviors even when your critic's pressuring you not to. As long as you maintain your new habits, self-loving thoughts will gradually overwhelm the self-deprecating ones.

Chapter Summary

• Habits cannot be broken, only replaced.

• Habits consist of a cue, a routine, and a reward.

• We can set new habits by setting an "if-then" routine called an implementation intention.

• We can break habits by identifying the cue, changing the routine, and initiating a reward.

• We should favor intrinsic rewards over extrinsic ones whenever possible.

• If all else fails, you can radically change your life to force habit change.

• By adopting compassionate habits toward yourself, you will cause cognitive dissonance with "I am worthless" beliefs, systematically shifting your thoughts toward confidence.

Exercises

Exercise 5.1 – Immediate – Identify Habit Goals
What are some habits you could adopt today that would help you make the changes you want? What are some bad habits you would like to break? Write about your thoughts in your journal.

Exercise 5.2 – Ongoing – Make Willpower Growth Your New Habit
In Exercises 4.2 and 4.6, we identified two methods for improving your overall willpower. Identify a five-minute slot in your daily routine where meditation could fit, and set a new meditation implementation intention for that slot. "As soon as I arrive at work, I will meditate for five minutes." "As soon as I get dressed, I will meditate for five minutes." Continue this habit for the rest of your life. When planning your "willpower workouts," articulate them as implementation intentions. "When I reach for a door, I will use my left hand." Remember, for your "I won't" exercises,

your implementation intentions must still be worded positively, not negatively. Don't say "When I eat a meal, I will not drink soda"; make it "When I eat a meal, I will drink water."

Exercise 5.3 – Responsive – Set Implementation Intentions to Guard against Willpower Failure

Look back on your answers to Exercise 4.1. Choose the three problems most likely to inhibit your goals and make implementation intentions for the strategies you will use to address them. "When I feel as if I can't go to the gym, I will put on my workout clothes." "When I feel the urge to eat ice cream, I will eat fruit." "When my inner critic tells me I suck, I will tell him to shut the fuck up."

Exercise 5.4 – Ongoing – Adopt One New Compassionate Habit per Month

Have a look at the list below of habits that show compassion for yourself, and brainstorm some of your own. Every month, decide on one new, small, consistent way to show how much you love yourself.

- Start flossing.

- Start going to the gym.

- Cut one unhealthy food (such as soda) from your diet permanently.

- Give yourself positive affirmations every morning. Some suggestions:

    ◦ I am lovable as I am.

    ◦ My needs are important.

    ◦ My mistakes are okay.

    ◦ I am the only person I have to please.

- Learn one new recipe to cook for yourself per week.

- Develop one new skill that requires at least one class per week.

- Write a check to your savings account once per week.

Exercise 5.5 – Ongoing – Break a Bad Habit

Choose one bad habit you would like to eliminate. Carry a

notebook, and use the approach described in this chapter to identify the cue motivating your bad habit and replace it with a healthier one. Do not try to break more than one bad habit at a time. Record your progress in your journal.

Exercise 5.6 – One Time – Romance Yourself
Plan one grand gesture of self-love that you will do for yourself within a month. Take yourself out to dinner, buy yourself a fancy new outfit, treat yourself to a massage, take a day trip (or longer) somewhere nice, or give yourself a gift. Don't tell anyone about what you do.

Chapter 6 – Emergency Techniques

As you start implementing the things we talk about in *The Hot Guyde*, you're going to face some challenges. You will feel nervous about that first date. You will hesitate to write your first online dating message. You will be unsure about reaching for your date's hand, or going in for that first kiss. When you're overwhelmed with nerves and emotions, you won't be able to run back to your journal or do two more months of exposure therapy. When you're in the moment, you need to gain control immediately. In this chapter, we'll talk about techniques for doing just that.

Rewriting Reality

Have you ever heard of the placebo effect? It's a phenomenon in medical research when patients are told a drug will help them. Regardless of the drug's actual effects, because the patients think it will help, they actually experience some positive results. It's a remarkable quirk of humans showing the power of belief, and it's the reason researchers use control groups. Whenever a new drug is tested, some patients will be given the drug while other patients will be given a generic, inert pill in order to make sure any observed benefits aren't just the placebo effect in action. The strange thing is, the placebo effect isn't all about deception. Even when patients know they're receiving a placebo, they still experience the effect.[77] Being told to believe something, even when you consciously know it's not true, can have psychological and physiological effects.

"Our brains are wired first to understand, then to believe, and last to disbelieve. Since disbelief requires additional cognitive effort, we get the physiological effects [of belief] first. And, though this belief may last only a brief moment, it's enough to produce an emotional and physical reassurance, which can change our thought patterns as well as help alleviate the uncomfortable feelings."[78] What William Bosl is saying here is that if we tell ourselves something, even if it isn't true, we'll believe it first and question it second, allowing us to enjoy any calming benefits the lie might bring. If you're hesitating to approach a woman, or you're nervous on a date, and you tell yourself "She's already hot for me," that might be false, but for a little while your brain will believe it, and you'll find it easier to deal with your feelings. I'm not encouraging you to adopt some solipsistic "There is no reality but what I believe" philosophy, and I'm not suggesting that you use this technique regularly, but if you need a quick fix to get over your anxiety, telling yourself a comforting lie can do the trick.

Body Language as a Cognitive Aid

Part of why we're learning so much about self-esteem and psychology is to improve our body language. When we believe good things about ourselves, we project those feelings in how we move. As it turns out, the same is true in reverse. When we take confident postures, they can have a positive effect on how we feel.[79]

Put your hands on your hips, stand tall with a wide stance, thrust your chest out, and put a big grin on your face. How do you feel? Probably great. You're taking the stance of a superhero. No one can stand this way without feeling amazing. Now stand with your body slumped forward, your arms drooping, with a big frown on your face. Try to be happy. You can't. Standing this way will always make you feel bad.

Adopting the body language of the emotion you want

to feel can give you a boost when you need it. If you want to feel confident, assume the superhero pose.[80] If you need to feel warm and happy, make yourself smile or give yourself a hug. It's not a permanent fix, but if you need a boost before meeting that woman on your first date, it'll help you out.

Eat

Willpower depends heavily on how much sugar you have in your blood. If you're hungry, you'll be more irritable and impatient, and are far more likely to give in to willpower challenges. If you're feeling crappy or you're in a bad mood, eat something! Keep a pack of granola bars in your car or carry one in your pocket. When you're stressed out, chow down.

Slow Your Breathing

If you find yourself growing anxious, another quick fix is to slow your breathing to six breaths per minute. Doing so activates your prefrontal cortex and raises heart-rate variability.[81] It will cut off your panic and put your rational mind back in control.

Visualization

Just as visualizing a scary exposure can provoke a fear response in us, imagining happy things can flood us with positive feelings. Before you do something stressful, imagine yourself being wildly successful. The woman you're dating blushes and kisses you. The crowd cheers for your performance. Your interviewer smiles, shakes your hand, and tells you how excited she is to have you joining the company. This imagery will fill your brain with happy chemicals, calming you down long enough to take the first step toward facing whatever is stressing you out.

Music

Music can have a powerful effect on our emotional states.[82] In one study, the song "I Know It's Over" by the Smiths ameliorated depressive symptoms in some participants.[83] Listening to Mozart has been found to improve spatial reasoning abilities.[84] Experiment with different types of music and make a series of playlists that provoke different emotions in you. When you need a boost, play the right song for the moment.

Chapter Summary

• We believe before we disbelieve. Telling yourself a comforting lie can relieve short-term stress.

• Assuming confident and happy postures will cause you to feel those emotions.

• A quick snack can restore your willpower.

• Slowing your breathing to six breaths per minute can put you back in control.

• Visualizing success will flood you with happy chemicals.

• Inspiring music can motivate you.

Exercises

Exercise 6.1 – Immediate – Try Out the Techniques
Experiment with each of the techniques listed in this chapter in a safe, nonthreatening environment. See how each of them makes you feel.

Exercise 6.2 – Responsive – Use the Techniques in Your Next Exposure Exercise

During your next exposure, try out one or several of these techniques immediately before you face your fear. Does this make the experience any easier? Write in your journal about how things go.

Exercise 6.3 – One Time – Make a Motivational Music Playlist

Think about the music you like to listen to, or explore the songs listed below. Make a motivational playlist for yourself when you're looking to inspire yourself to face a new challenge.

- "Ascension," a/k/a the "Super Saiyan 3" theme from *Dragonball Z*
- "Lux Aeterna," a/k/a the theme from *Requiem for a Dream*
- "Dies`Irae" from the Verdi *Requiem*
- The "O Fortuna" section from *Carmina Burana*
- "Big Battle" from the soundtrack to *Dune*
- "Eye of the Tiger" by Survivor
- "Gonna Fly Now" (the *Rocky* theme) by Bill Conti

Part II: Social Skills

Chapter 7 – Listening, Sensitivity, and a "Feeling of Importance"

Rahul steps aboard the elevator of his skyscraper apartment building, joining an attractive neighbor. The ride to the twentieth floor is a long one, and after a bit, his neighbor speaks up. "Ugh, these elevators are so SLOW!" Looking to be helpful, Rahul explains how the hydraulic system of the elevator works, and how this speed of ascent is optimal for safety and convenience. The rest of the ride is silent. On the twentieth floor, as the woman steps out, she mutters "Asshole" just loud enough for Rahul to hear. Rahul's reply has pissed her off, but he can't understand why.

People crave connections. We all want to share ourselves and let others know how we're feeling. When Rahul's neighbor shares her frustration about the elevator, she isn't looking for Rahul to explain why the elevator travels at the speed it does; she wants him to acknowledge her feelings. Because he doesn't do that, she feels frustrated and dismissed, so she calls him an asshole. Rahul had heard her comment, but he wasn't listening for what she truly wanted.

Some of us are slow to pick up on the underlying messages people give us. We might not know what to look for, or we could be so concerned with getting other people to accept us that we never think they might be looking for us to accept them. Good listeners go beyond simply hearing a speaker's words. They connect. They suspend their agendas and make the speaker a priority. When the speaker talks to them, he or she feels "felt." If you can be one of the few who recognizes when others need you to listen, and do it well, you'll be powerfully loved.

Actions People Mistake for Good Listening

Waiting for the Speaker to Finish

One of the most common habits you'll find in conversations is listeners who "politely wait" as others speak. They're aching for the moment when they can shift attention back to themselves, but they know interrupting would be rude, so they sit quietly and bide their time. Good listening isn't silent. It's interactive. It takes energy. Showing receptive body language, interjecting with acknowledgments such as "Yeah" and "Uh huh," and asking follow-up questions are all actions that go further than you might think. You want to show the speaker that you care about what he or she is saying. If you're silently tolerating the speaker's noise until you can take over the conversation, you'll be perceived as an asshole.

Giving Advice

You're chatting with a friend when she starts to complain about her boyfriend. Looking to be helpful, you give her suggestions about what she could do. She gets annoyed. What the hell?

Most of the time, people can solve their own problems. When they come to us, they're not necessarily coming for help; they're coming for empathy. They want to share their feelings and have those feelings acknowledged. By offering solutions, you aren't acknowledging their feelings; you're focusing on the problem. Even with the best intentions, you wind up ignoring the speakers. When people come to you with problems, assume they're just looking for empathy, and give advice only if they ask for it.

Reassuring

Your best friend just failed her exam. Hoping to comfort her, you say "You can make it up on the next one." She doesn't feel any better.

It hurts to see our friends and loved ones upset, so it's natural to try to comfort them. Unfortunately, as with advice, reassurance focuses attention on the problem rather than on their feelings. Giving them a hug, or simply saying "I'm sorry. You want to talk about it?" won't fix the problem, but it will let them know they're not alone. This reassures them more than any other words you could say.

"I Know How You Feel"

Isn't empathy when you feel the same feelings as another person? What could be more empathetic than letting people know you understand them? Telling them you know how they feel looks like empathy, but it's the exact opposite. By saying this, you imply that talking about their feelings would be a waste of time. Since people need to share their feelings, this dismissive statement isn't helpful. If you know how another person feels, you know that you'd want someone to be there and listen to you. So do it.

Telling People How to Feel

"Don't be scared." "You don't have to be sad!" Telling people how to feel doesn't change their feelings; at most, it makes them feel guilty for having them. Instead, ask them what's troubling them. If there's a solution, help them find that solution. "See, there's nothing under the bed!" If there isn't a solution, just let them know that you're there for them. Sometimes that's all you can do.

Sharing Anecdotes

Your buddy tells you that his girlfriend has cheated on him. You, in turn, share your story about the time your girlfriend cheated on you. Your friend gets pissed off.

Sharing anecdotes isn't empathy. Yes, you're trying to relate to your friend, but that's not what your friend needs. He wants you to listen to him and bear witness to his struggle. Sharing anecdotes just shifts attention away from your friend and toward you. A simple "Fuckin' hell man, I'm so sorry. You wanna tell me about it?" will always help more than any version of "Me too."

How to Be a Good Listener

Listening Empathetically

Being a good listener isn't complicated; it's a matter of showing that you care about the speaker's feelings. There's a simple, guaranteed way to do that, and it's called an empathetic response. It has two pieces:

1. Acknowledge the person's feelings.

2. Encourage further explanation.

"I slept awfully last night." "That sucks. What happened?" "I can't figure out what to wear." "Yeah? What are you dressing up for?" Anything that shows you recognize the emotion is sufficient for the first step. It can be anything from "Uh huh" to "Gross!" to "That's great!" or "That blows." The second piece just asks for more details. Dig into the emotions. "What did you feel like saying to her?" "Geez, what the hell was he doing there?" The more specific and emotional your question, the better. If you don't understand what the speaker's saying, ask for clarification, and once you think you've got it, paraphrase it in a sentence. "So you're not sure if the green top's too loud with that skirt?" This lets the person know you're listening and that you care, and if he or she winds up asking you for advice, you'll be in a better position to give it.

Avoid "Zoning Out"

Half the battle of helping people "feel felt" is paying attention to what they're saying. If you're looking for a quick fix, focus on holding eye contact. Look directly into their eyes and try not to be the one to look away. Not only will this help you pay attention, it has positive body-language connotations. You will come across as more confident and likeable.

Paying attention is nothing more than a willpower challenge. Everything we discussed in chapter 4 will help, and you can directly apply your lessons from meditation. When you're meditating, you practice returning your mind to your breath. In the same way, when you're in a conversation, practice returning your mind to the person who's speaking. Adding your "Uh huhs," nods, and follow-up questions not only helps your speaker know you're listening; it helps you pay attention.

Sensitivity

Imagine you're a parent and your teenage son comes home, slams the door, and runs to his room. You ask him what's the matter and he shouts "Leave me alone! I don't want to talk about it." An empathetic listener would recognize that something is wrong, and might chase his son to uncover the problem. A respectful listener would heed his son's words and leave him alone. What's the right thing to do?

Just because someone isn't being forthright doesn't mean that person doesn't need your empathy. Many people think it's rude to be direct about their feelings. Others are simply too overwhelmed to talk to anyone in that moment. Sometimes you'll find yourself in a struggle between respecting someone's express wishes and fulfilling what you sense the true wishes to be. In these situations, don't force the issue, but make it clear that you care. "Okay. If you need an ear, I'm here for you." People need to know that you will listen to them, and that includes listening when they say they don't want to talk. They need you both to respect them and to stay on their side. Show them they have your support and you'll be giving them what they need.

This skill is called sensitivity, and it comes with

experience. It's the ability to recognize what a person's deeper feelings are and respond with empathy. The better you know someone, the more you'll be able to recognize the cues. Until you know that person well, the best you can do is imagine yourself in his or her shoes. Ask yourself, "What sorts of things would make me behave the way she's behaving right now?" "How would I want me to behave if I were feeling the way he is?" You won't always be right, but asking yourself those questions will always help. Listen to people's words—what they are, how they're spoken—and note the body language that accompanies them. If all else fails, just make it clear you're on their side and that they can ask if they need anything. Beyond that, don't pressure them. If you follow this policy, people will find you sensitive and respectful most of the time.

A Feeling of Importance

In 1936, Dale Carnegie published *How to Win Friends and Influence People*, the first, and one of the greatest, self-help books ever written. Among his lessons, there's one that stands out:

> *"There is one all-important law of human conduct. If we obey that law, we shall almost never get into trouble. In fact, that law, if obeyed, will bring us countless friends and constant happiness. But the very instant we break the law, we shall get into endless trouble. The law is this: Always make the other person feel important."*[85]

In addition to solid listening, the quickest way to build rapport with strangers is to show genuine appreciation for what they do. The guy who shows up to the party with a guitar wants compliments for his music. The co-worker who gave the presentation wants recognition for her work. When you see someone doing something praiseworthy, give praise. Your appreciation should be genuine; don't manufacture cheap compliments, but when you like something, let people know, and share your praise lavishly. Nothing shows people that you're on their side better than recognizing their hard work.

When you're sharing your compliments, be specific. Highlight the details about someone's performance, appearance, and the like that you appreciate most. Whenever possible, favor things that took effort to do. Saying "I like your dress" will never compare with "I like how you put together your outfit. The way your dress contrasts your earrings echoes your skin and eyes. Are you a designer?" When you're specific, you'll intuitively focus on the thought and effort that was put into the work, rather than just the end product. And if you're talking to exceptionally talented people, see if you can recognize something besides their prominent talent; most people will appreciate those compliments more than if you appreciate the things they're always complimented for. The old saying "Tell the smart girls they're pretty and the pretty girls they're smart" has some truth. Appreciate the things people work at, not just the things that come easily.

How to Remember Names

A final point, and one we're also taking from Carnegie, is the importance of knowing someone's name. "A person's name is to that person the sweetest and most important sound in any language."[86] You'll have a hard time showing people that they matter if you can't remember their names. Here are some pointers to help you out.

1. When you meet people, repeat their names back to them. "I'm David." "Hi, David; good to meet you."

2. Use the name at least twice more in the conversation. It enhances your long-term memory.[87] "So David, tell me what you do all day." "It was great chatting with you, David."

3. Associate the name with something memorable—a mnemonic device, preferably one you can associate with a physical feature: "Jaguar Jackie"; "Khakis Kevin."

4. Excuse yourself for a moment and write down the names of everyone you've just met. A short description helps too. "Bill—gray shirt, Rebecca—headband, Stacey—curly hair."

Chapter Summary

• Listening is the ability to suspend your agenda and prioritize the speaker.

• Make empathetic responses that acknowledge people's emotions, and ask for details.

• Hold eye contact and practice "returning your mind" to the speaker to avoid zoning out.

• When people give you mixed signals, remind them that you're there for them, and don't push.

• Recognize people for the things they do for social approval, and give genuine compliments.

• Make your compliments as specific as possible, and recognize people's less obvious talents.

• Remember names by repeating them, using them in conversation, making memorable associations, and writing them down.

Exercises

Exercise 7.1 – Immediate – Recognize Unempathetic Replies
Read through the following conversations and critique the responses. If you don't think the responder replied empathetically, describe what was done wrong and write an alternative reply that would have been more empathetic.

1. "I can't stand working on group projects." "Yeah, but they're important! You need to learn how to work with others."

2. "I feel sick." "Here, have some cold medicine."

3. "I haven't been sleeping well lately." "Well, maybe if you didn't stay up watching TV all the time, you'd sleep better."

4. "My boyfriend just dumped me." "Oh my god! Are you all right? You want to talk about it?"

5. "I've been feeling depressed." "Yeah, I know what you mean. I've been feeling down too."

6. "I got fired." "That sucks."

7. "I couldn't find my favorite necklace." "Did you try your purse?"

8. "My boss really chewed me out today." "He tell you to work harder again?"

9. "My dog died last night." "Well, she's in a better place now."

Exercise 7.2 – Immediate – Practice Empathetic Responses

Write an empathetic response to each of the following statements.

1. "God, it's the fourth rainy day we've had in a row."

2. "I don't know what to wear."

3. "I did more work on the project than anyone. I feel as if they're taking credit for my work."

4. "My book sucks. I'll never be a published writer."

5. "My dog peed on the carpet again."

6. "I can't seem to get this portrait right."

7. "I've been through it a thousand times! What the fuck is wrong with my code?!"

Exercise 7.3 – One Time – Practice Not Zoning Out

Go on YouTube, or another service of your choice, for university lectures. If you need a suggestion, MIT posts several on its channel: *https://www.youtube.com/user/MIT/*. Look for lectures longer than twenty minutes on topics you're not excited to learn about. Watch and listen to a lecture. Notice when your mind wanders and practice bringing it back to the lecture just as we practice in meditation. Do not take notes. After you've watched the video, write a one-paragraph summary of the lecture. If this is a struggle for you, consider making this an ongoing exercise.

Exercise 7.4 – One Time – Be the Speaker

The next time something is bothering you, try sharing your feelings with various people in your life. Pay attention to how they listen. What did you like about how they listened? What didn't you like? How did you feel about each of their responses to your feelings? Write in your journal about these experiences.

Exercise 7.5 – Ongoing – Practice Face Memorization

Find a face memory game online to practice associating names with faces. One is available at *thehotguyde.com/resources*. If you struggle, consider making this an ongoing exercise.

Exercise 7.6 – Responsive – Find the Interesting Thing

Every time you go out to a place where you'll be meeting strangers, go with the following goal: "For at least one person, I will learn his or her name and the most interesting thing about that person." You can uncover those interesting things however you like. Some possible techniques: encourage people to brag, ask them what they're proud of, or ask them what they do when they're not at work. In your journal, document what you learn about these people. Write down their names and the interesting things, and highlight them.

Chapter 8 – Talking

Will arrives at his friend Ruby's twenty-ninth birthday party. He takes off his coat and grabs a drink, and before long he is chatting with Vanessa, Ruby's twenty-seven-year-old co-worker. "So, what do you do?" "I'm a legal assistant with Ruby." "Oh yeah? How long have you been doing that?" "Three years." "Did you study law?" "Yes." "Where'd you study law?" "Northeastern." For two more minutes Will peppers the young attorney with questions until she excuses herself to use the restroom. When she comes out, she spends the rest of the night avoiding Will at all costs.

The way most people talk to strangers is what I call "the interview." One person, the "rapport seeker," or the person more interested in pleasing the other person, asks a list of fact-based questions that elicit one-word replies. None of the facts is important; the two people don't build rapport, and they sure as hell don't build chemistry. The person on the receiving end feels consumed, and before long will be looking for a way to escape.

Introductions

The first thing you say when you walk up to a group of strangers depends on the situation. Are you out meeting people for fun, or do you want something specific? Is it a social atmosphere or a place where people don't want to be disturbed? We'll touch on the other cases, but most of the time, we're going to be approaching people in social atmospheres while we're looking for fun, so that will be our focus.

In any given social setting, your opening move is pretty

straightforward: walk up to a group, genuinely compliment them, and ask permission to join. "My friends haven't shown up yet and you guys seem like fun; mind if I join you?" "You guys seem like the coolest people here; can I chill with you?" Unless there's something about you that creeps them out, most folks will at least be polite. They're out to have fun, and when you're a cool guy who's making them feel good (with the compliment, for starters), they'll usually welcome you in. If they turn you away, assume they have their reasons — probably nothing to do with you — and move on. Remind yourself that their reaction has no bearing on your worth, and there are plenty more people to relax with.

If you're in a place where social interaction is taboo (a library, the grocery store, the street), you're in what I call a cold venue. People are busy. They're not looking to be social and they probably won't like your interruption. You're a stranger approaching them in a place you're not supposed to; that's violating social norms. What else are you willing to violate? These are the sorts of thoughts that will be running through their heads, and the colder the venue, the more uncomfortable and freaked out they'll feel. We'll discuss how to approach people in these sorts of venues in chapter 21, but as a general rule, I don't recommend it. There's something to be said for overcoming the fear of approaching a stranger and striking up a conversation, but as a way of meeting dates and making friends, I don't think it's an optimal way to do it. When you're filling your lifestyle with activities that introduce you to hundreds of people, it simply isn't necessary.

Small Talk

After introductions, most people break into "small talk." Small talk is unthreatening, superficial conversation about generic topics. "Sure is crazy weather we've been having." "How's school going?" "Good." "Yeah, doing well?"

"Yeah." It isn't about connecting; it's about relieving awkwardness. It's the sort of conversation people have when they're thrust together involuntarily in an elevator or at a funeral. Silently ignoring each other would be rude, so they relieve the awkwardness with polite, but distance-maintaining, chitchat. Unfortunately, since this is the only way most people interact with strangers, lots of folks fall into this mode at social gatherings as well.

If you're looking to connect with people, it's best to avoid small talk. If you have to use it, stick to safe topics: weather, sports, the immediate environment, clothing, or how slow your mode of transportation moves. If you're acquainted, family members, pets, school, work, a recent major life event, or a known hobby or talent can be considered fair game. If you want a relationship with this person that will last longer than two minutes, avoid this mode of conversation like the plague and switch to banter as soon as you can.

Banter

While small talk is about reducing awkwardness and keeping distance, banter brings you together. It's the start of trust and friendship. When done right, it's lighthearted and full of laughter. Flirting is essentially banter plus sexual tension.

Unlike small talk, banter delves into topics unique to the person you're talking to, rather than generic things everyone has in common. "So what do you do for a living?" "Where did you go to school?" "Where are you from?" These questions are the bread and butter of how most people banter, but are actually the worst examples of banter you'll find. Even though the topics are more personal, since the questions are factual and since they can be answered with a single word, they're still a little distancing, and they don't build much rapport. The key to good banter is to connect on an emotional level, and when you're conducting a survey, that's not going to happen.

Another dynamic to consider in your banter is the value you're providing your listener. Think of value as "stuff people want," which in social contexts usually means interesting information, good feelings, and social validation. The best conversations are between people who are constantly exchanging value, and the more they talk, the better they both feel. You want to give your listener things to respond to and have feelings about, and you want to show that you care and have feelings about what they're saying as well.

Here's a way to think of this. Imagine we have an actor, Joe, who's improvising a scene on stage. Joe moves around an imagined kitchen, interacting with an invisible stove, sink, and pans. Fred, a second actor, comes on stage, walks through the invisible stove, and shouts, "What are you doing?!" How does it feel to be Joe in this situation? Not good. Fred has put all the pressure on Joe to come up with something funny to entertain the audience. The scene lives and dies on what Joe says next. If, instead, Fred had said, "What the hell is that pig doing on the counter?!" he's given Joe something to work with. Fred's question has information and an emotional context Joe can react to. "This here pig ate my prized corncob collection!"

When you're chatting with a stranger, it's the same idea. We don't want to put pressure on the other person to provide all the value. We want our questions and comments to have emotional meaning and informational usefulness, and to offer an easy direction to take the conversation. At the top of this chapter, Vanessa became irritated with Will not because he did something offensive, but because nothing he was saying provided her with any value. He saddled her with the job of providing all the interesting and emotional content in the conversation, and she didn't appreciate it.

Turn Your Questions into Observations and Guesses

A quick way to provide some value early in a conversation is to share your emotional impressions of the people you meet. People love to learn about themselves, especially when it's good news. You know all those "interview questions" we're trying to avoid? Take those questions and turn them into guesses. "Where are you from?" can become "You seem like a New Yorker." "Where'd you go to college?" can become "You seem pretty smart; you a Harvard grad?" "You come here often?" can become "You seem to know this place pretty well." If you're right, they'll be amazed at your insight. If you're wrong, your guess is its own topic of conversation. Keep your guesses genuine (don't tell everyone you meet that they seem as if they're from New York), but try to keep the observations flattering. If your question or guess implies an insult, your first impression will be sour.

Turn Your Questions into "Open-Ended" Statements

If you can't think of an observation to share, reword your question so it starts with "Tell me about." "So tell me about where you grew up." "Tell me about what it was like to live in Germany." Wording things this way still calls upon your partner to provide most of the value, but it offers a broader canvas to work with. Talking about "living in Germany" can mean anything, and this kind of suggestion encourages people to focus on the topics they like talking about most. Did they like the food, the culture, or the people they dated? All of those will be more engaging and emotional than an answer to "Where are you from?" Encourage people to talk about themselves and their passions, and as long as you're an eager listener, they'll love it.

Ask Emotional and Open-Ended Questions

There's nothing wrong with asking questions, but your

other two options will tend to be stronger. When you do ask questions, try to keep a couple of things in mind. First, if your question can be an emotional response to something, make it so. "Holy crap, you're an amazing singer. You do this professionally?" "I love your accent. Where are you from?" Compliments and excitement are always strong, so use them often. If you don't have some strong emotional reaction to the person, ask whatever you like, but try to keep it open-ended, preferably on an emotional topic. "What do you do for fun?" "What makes you, you?" or "What do you do that's not for money?" These sorts of questions all provoke interesting and emotional replies, and once you have those, you can employ the next technique to keep the conversation going.

Threading

The most common question I get about social skills is "How do I know what to say?" Here's the answer: look for "free information."

Free information is anything someone tells you beyond the direct factual answer to your question. "Where are you from?" "I grew up in Maine, in the woods by a lake." The factual answer is "Maine." Everything beyond that is free information. You can ask more about the woods, or the lake, and if you're really insightful, you can try to read into why those things in particular were chosen. Is the person into nature? Water sports? Go ahead and ask. "You must've gotten to do lots of water sports." "You ever get to go camping up there?" By paying attention to the free information your conversation partner gives you, you can avoid ever running out of things to talk about. If we think of conversations as "threads," free information is the "knot" that connects those threads. When we move from topic to topic, connected by these knots, we call this "threading."

Let's say you're talking to a woman and she says, "I

just got back from visiting my uncle in Florida." In this case, the new potential threads are "visiting," her "uncle," and "Florida." Generally, the best thread to follow is whichever one has the most emotional significance and is most relevant to the person you're talking with. In this case, the topics from best to worst are probably: "uncle," "Florida," and "visiting." While Florida might be the easiest for us to relate to, her relationship with her uncle probably has more meaning for her. If it turns out not to be a good topic, you can always choose another thread.

Brevity

"Brevity is the soul of wit." Shakespeare wrote this line ironically in *Hamlet,* but that doesn't make it any less true. When we were in school, especially college, most of us were trying to meet page requirements, and we learned to write as verbosely as possible. In the real world, especially in conversations, this is a waste of time. Good conversations are value-dense. If you're in the habit of using lots of unnecessary words to express yourself, people will learn to take you less seriously when you speak, and they'll be more comfortable interrupting you. One of the points we'll discuss in the chapter on vocal tonality is that slower speech tends to sound more confident, but that's true only when your words are dense with value. Since we eventually want to adopt that confident, slow speech pattern, we need to learn how to say more with less.

Take Time to Assemble Your Sentences

Some folks are in the habit of starting their sentences before they're sure what they're going to say. They compensate with "filler words" to give themselves the time they need. "You know what I was thinkin'? I was thinkin' that if we want to do paintball Saturday night, we oughtta stop by the shop tomorrow morning to pick up gear." Compare this with "Hey, if we're paintballin' Saturday, you guys wanna pick up gear in the morning?" Taking just a half-second pause before you start talking can make the difference between sounding like a dumbass and speaking like a confident leader. The more you can talk like the latter, the more people will learn to shut up and listen when you do.

Silence Is Better Than Tics

Instead of "filler words," some of us resort to tics: "umm," "so," "like," "uh," "aaaaand," and so on. These tics tell our listeners that we haven't thought through what we're saying and it's probably not worth listening to. If you find that people tend to interrupt you, or their attention tends to wander, you might be surrounded by assholes, but you might also have bad verbal tics. If this sounds like you, consider your tics a bad habit, as discussed in chapter 5. Monitor your use of verbal tics in conversations in your notebook. Count how many times you use them per day. Notice the situations where they arise most often. When you take your pause before speaking, consciously remind yourself to slow down your speech and avoid your tics. With practice, they should go away.

Storytelling

Telling a good story is one of the most important banter skills you can learn. Just like good listening, quality storytelling relies heavily on empathy, so the most important elements are imagery and emotions. The art of good storytelling lies in helping your listeners imagine themselves experiencing what you're describing. If the details don't serve that end, they're not worth adding.

The Hook

The first words of your story are the ones that pull in your audience. We call them the "hook." The hook should give your audience a reason to care, and the best hooks tend to be a powerful emotion, a superlative, or something related to the listener. "I was euphoric." "Here's the weirdest thing that ever happened to me." "You ever been hopelessly lost in a city?"

Sensation and Emotion

"This morning I took my dog for a walk in the park. On the way, I passed one of my favorite bakeries, so I grabbed a blueberry muffin. While I was sitting at the table, a bird flew down and took a bite out of my muffin. I wasn't sure whether it was safe to keep eating, so I threw it out."

You probably don't find this story engaging. Not only doesn't it have a hook, it's a list of facts. "X happened, then Y, then Z." There aren't any emotions or sensations to help us project ourselves into the story. Let's see if we can change that.

"I hate birds [emotional hook]. I was going for a walk with my dog today. Beautiful morning, 74 degrees, no clouds, perfect weather for taking her out. We're walking along, she's sniffing everyone who goes by, the usual, when the smell of fresh-baked bread hits me. I can't resist, so we stop in the bakery and I grab a muffin. We're chilling outside, I'm munching away, when *out of nowhere* this bird swoops down and plants its beak right in the muffin. It pulls a big ol' hunk out and flies away. My muffin's in ruins. I'm sitting there pissed off and flabbergasted, and my dog gives no shits. Wound up throwing out the rest of the muffin. Fuckin' birds, guys."

This still isn't the best story, but it's a big improvement. Notice how it adds imagery and feelings. "Beautiful morning, no clouds, big ol' hunk, muffin's in ruins." You get a much clearer image of what's going on. "I hate birds" is emotional and begs for an explanation, and the story provides it. The profanity serves only to highlight the emotions. When you're telling your story, feel free to indulge in your descriptions, remember to hit all five senses, and bring in emotions whenever possible.

Structure

When you're bantering, you don't have to have a firm structure for a story to work, but it helps if you keep a few things in mind. Every major event that happens in your story is called a "beat," and the beats should happen in a logical succession. You start with your hook, some rising action builds up the plot, you hit your climax, there's some fallout from the climax, and then you do your close. You should be able to connect every beat in your story with a "but" or a "therefore," never "and then."[88] "I was eating my muffin, but a bird bit it; therefore I threw it out." This will keep your plot in motion. If you have to use "and then" to connect the events, it's probably because that beat isn't necessary for the narrative, and you'll be wasting your audience's time.

The Close

The ending of your story should invite others back into the conversation. The simplest way to do this is to invite everyone to comment. "Something like that ever happen to you?" The other option, and the one I tend to prefer, is to connect the story to the present in some way. Perhaps you learned a lesson, or maybe that story is important to you for some reason. "Fuckin' birds, guys" implies the lesson "You can't trust birds." Other examples could be "That's how I met Sasha" or "That's why I drink cider instead of beer." Once you've closed, stop talking. You've contributed plenty of value. Let other folks share their reactions or move on to another topic.

A Word of Warning

A good story will let your listeners imagine themselves experiencing the things you're telling them. If you do it right, it can have a powerful effect on the tone of the conversation. If your story's funny, energetic, or inspiring, people will feel uplifted. If it's creepy or gross, they'll feel creeped and grossed out. If everyone's having dinner, don't share the story about the time you ate that cockroach.

Keep in mind that any story you tell will be associated with you. Even if the story's about your buddy, your audience will still project you onto your protagonist, so if the story's about an asshole, you might not want to tell that story. Save your weird and morally questionable stories for people who know you well.

Conversation Topics to Avoid

A lot of people commit social suicide by bringing up the wrong topics. You know that guy who's always trying to argue about politics? Or your family member who brings up that time someone cheated? Talking about serious issues is important, but in a social environment where people are trying to have fun, it's a buzzkill, and people will hate you for it. For most purposes, there are two topics that are always off limits and several that you're better off avoiding.

The Bad Qualities of Other People

People don't like to be judged. If you're judging people in your stories and banter, your audience will see you as someone to keep at arm's length. Conversations are supposed to bring you closer, not give people cause to avoid you. In general, don't judge—but if you do, don't talk about it.

Women You've Slept With

A lot of guys like to brag about their sexual

"conquests." They may talk big, but the only reason for them to act that way is to assuage their insecurities. Don't be one of those guys. Approval-seeking isn't healthy behavior, and even if you want that kind of validation, don't brag about it; live it. Earn your reputation by flirting with women you like, not by telling tales.

The main reason for this rule is a matter of sensitivity to your lovers. You might have nothing but positive opinions about sex, but not everyone thinks the way you do. Slut-shaming is a real thing. Your lack of discretion can have social consequences for the women you sleep with, and they'll resent you for it. If a woman nearby was thinking you were cute, but overhears you bragging, she'll probably find herself a lot less inclined to join you. Don't talk about your sexual partners—but if you do, keep them anonymous.

Topics Better Avoided

The following topics aren't banned, but they can be alienating, polarizing, or mood-killing. If you bring them up, some people will be upset, so do so with caution.

• Politics

• Religion

• How to raise children

• Ethics and morality

• Sex

• Finances

• Divorce

• Death

• Abortion

• Family problems

Talking by Text and Phone

Body language is one of the most important ways we express our feelings. Talking on the phone deprives us of that whole resource. The second most important way we express our feelings is through tone of voice. When texting, we lose that too. When you're using these media, both you and your partner will be more prone to misinterpretations. Emoticons help, but can carry their own negative connotations; for example, using too many "smiley" emoticons tends to suggest a need to please. You have no control over how the other person will read your text, and you don't have any body language in front of you to help you interpret the feelings. What you meant as flirty and cute can easily be read as creepy without the right context. The more you chat over text and phone, especially if that chatting is flirtatious, the more risks you're taking.

Texts and phone calls also present problems in terms of timing. Texting is a "low priority" medium, so it's socially acceptable to take forever to respond. If you're in a fight, or asking someone on a date, waiting for a reply can be nerve-wracking. Texts also allow for plausible deniability; people can say they never received your texts at all, leaving you hanging indefinitely. The more emotionally invested you are in the conversation, the more painful these media can be.

For these reasons, use phone and text as little as possible, and try to use them only to work out logistics: when and where you're meeting your date. Leave the declarations of love for when you see her in person. As a rule of thumb, use as few words as possible. Your grammar doesn't have to be perfect, but don't write like a moron. "Hey karaoke Saturday wanna come" is adequate, "how r u" is not.

Chapter Summary

- In social situations, approach a group with a genuine compliment and ask permission to join.
- Turn "interview questions" into statements to give them energy.
- Keep your questions emotional and open-ended.
- Look for free information in every sentence, and ask about the most-emotional topics.
- Keep your sentences short, and take a few extra seconds to form them before speaking.
- Emphasize emotions, imagery, and sensations in your story above facts.
- Give your story structure with a hook, rising action, climax, falling action, and close.
- Every beat in your story should connect with a "but" or a "therefore," never "and then."
- Don't talk shit about people.
- Don't brag about sexual encounters.
- Try to avoid communicating by phone or text. When you do, keep it brief and limited to logistics.

Exercises

Exercise 8.1 – Immediate – Turn "Interview Questions" into Statements

Read through the following cliché "interview questions." For each one, come up with a statement you could use that implies the same question, but is more energizing. For example, "Where are you from?" could become "You're from Boston, aren't you."

1. What do you do for work?
2. Where did you go to school?
3. What did you study in school?
4. Did you grow up around here?

5. Do you come here often?

6. What's your favorite food?

7. What's your favorite sports team?

8. Are you looking forward to the weekend?

9. Do you have any pets?

Exercise 8.2 – Immediate – Identify Threads

Read the following replies to "What's up?" and identify the "free information" available in each sentence. Identify the most emotionally relevant topics and come up with empathetic responses or other comments you can make in reply, for example "Just got back from playing Frisbee golf with my Ultimate team." Free information: she likes Frisbee, she's part of an Ultimate Frisbee Team. "That's fucking awesome, I've always wanted to try that out. How'd it go?"

1. "Been camping all weekend. The weather was beautiful."

2. "Was just taking my dog for a walk."

3. "Just finished practicing for the Super Smash Brothers tournament."

4. "Finally finished my damn history essay."

5. "Learned a new dance; think I'm going to teach it at the next rehearsal."

6. "Had to visit my mom in the hospital."

7. "My pen exploded all over my face and shirt. Had to walk around like that all day."

8. "No one at the party was cool. It sucked."

9. "Not much. Just spent the day with my cat."

Exercise 8.3 – Immediate – Convey Thoughts in Fewer Words

Read the following sentences. Rewrite each one such that it conveys the same message in fewer words.

• Hey, if you happen to be available on Saturday, I was thinking we could go bowling together.

• I wanted to let you know that I'm having a party this evening, and I'd be thrilled if you came.

• Would you be okay with me grabbing a glass of milk out of your fridge?

• As far as anyone's been telling me, there are more than 500 people coming to this concert tonight.

• Would you happen to be available this weekend to help me move a few boxes?

• I was hoping we could have spaghetti this evening.

Exercise 8.4 – Immediate – Critique Stories

Read through the following three stories. Identify what the speaker is doing wrong. Rewrite each of these stories in your own words, adding sensations, emotions, and imagery.

"On my last day as a camp counselor, the kids played a prank on me. I was pulling the last canoe up the beach when they came at me from all directions and sprayed me with super-soakers full of lemonade."

"I was eating my sandwich when I noticed there was a bug inside. I almost threw up."

"Last Halloween, these four women dressed as vampires were hitting on me in this bar. They kept rubbing their hands all over my chest. Then one of them bit me, and it hurt. I think they might have been real."

Exercise 8.5 – Responsive – Practice Brevity

For the next week, whenever you're about to say something, take an extra second to think before speaking. When you forget, make a mark in your notebook. At the end of the week, write in your journal about any changes you've noticed in your speech.

Exercise 8.6 – One Time/Partner – Write Your Own Story

Think of a story that's happened in your life. Think of the individual beats that happened in your story. Connect them with a "but" or a "therefore," discarding any plot elements that can be connected only with "and then." Write your story using plenty of sensations, emotions, and imagery. Read your story aloud to a trusted friend.

Exercise 8.7 – Ongoing – Use Wristband Reminders

Purchase two bright wristbands of different colors. Each wristband will serve as a reminder. The one on your right wrist is saying to you "Don't talk shit about people." The one on your left wrist is saying "Don't talk about women you've slept with." Wear these wristbands for one week, or until you no longer do either of these things. When you screw up, make a note in your notebook.

Exercise 8.8 – Immediate – Rewrite Text Messages
Read the following text messages. Identify what (if anything) is wrong with them, and rewrite them in a more confident way. Note that the best way to fix some of these messages might be to not send them at all.

1. "Hey I had so much fun the other night! Would you like to get together tomorrow?"

2. "Hey there ;) ;)"

3. "Hi I was thinking about you just now and I hope you're doing good"

4. "Hi, tomorrow afternoon some friends and I are going to the arcade. Would you like to join us?"

5. "My dog just jumped over the fence!!!!"

6. "wana cum ovr"

7. "Hey :) Thanks for hanging out last night. You want to have dinner Saturday? :)"

8. "Hi"

Exercise 8.9 – Immediate – Watch Films with Good Banter
With your notebook in hand, watch the following films: *Before Sunrise* (and anything else by Richard Linklater), *Shakespeare in Love,* and *Casino Royale.* Pay attention to the flirting and banter. What do the characters talk about? How emotional are the conversations? What makes these conversations seem real? What helps them flow? Take notes as you're watching, and record your conclusions in your journal.

Exercise 8.10 – Partner – Practice Bantering with a Partner
Invite a friend to read this chapter and explain what skills you're looking to practice. Engage in a conversation with a

focus on emotional topics. Try to offer plenty of free information in your replies and encourage your friend to do the same.

Exercise 8.11 – Ongoing – Practice Opening
Go to a bar, club, or party. Find a group of people and ask to join them. "Hey, you guys seem cool, can I hang out with you for a bit?" Banter with them for as long as you like. If this is scary for you, treat this as an exposure exercise and incorporate it into your exposure schedule, approaching a group no less than once per week.

Chapter 9 – Reading Body Language

If you take a class on sales or public speaking, you'll hear that only 7 percent of what we communicate is verbal, 55 percent comes from body language, and 38 percent comes from vocal tonality. These figures are misinterpretations of the work of Albert Mehrabian, whose research found that subjects could identify emotions conveyed by a woman's single spoken word best through photographs, second-best through tone, and least of all through text.[89] While this is not nearly so dramatic as the evangelists of the "7 percent rule" insist, Mehrabian's research does teach a valuable lesson: if you want to know how someone's feeling, body language will tell you best.

Most of us learn to read body language intuitively. If an aggressive cop walks up to your car, you don't need an education in nonverbal cues to feel anxious. You just do. If you want to turn your intuition into a real social skill, you need to become consciously aware of these cues and what they mean. In this chapter we'll discuss the gestures most valuable for dating and making friends, focusing on those that show discomfort, hostility, friendliness, and sexual attraction.

The Limitations of Studying Nonverbal Communication

Finding peer-reviewed research on body language isn't easy. Due to its contextual nature, scientific analysis of nonverbal communication is extremely difficult to do,[90] and few reliable studies exist. There is, however, a sort of body language "lore" out there, studied in sales, law enforcement, and other fields where being able to read people is valuable.

Although it's difficult to quantify, it seems useful enough on a practical level to help people's social abilities significantly. The ability to recognize nonverbal cues is associated with high social competence and status[91] and workplace competence.[92] I've also found it helpful in everything from recognizing sexual interest to avoiding liars. I've found this "lore" reliable enough to be worth sharing here, but make sure to take it with a hefty dose of skepticism.

Gestures come in clusters, and the meaning of a gesture will change depending on its context. Holding eye contact is usually a sign of friendliness, but if it's accompanied by crossed arms, it can mean hostility. A man who's hiding his hands in his pockets might be self-conscious, but he could also just be cold. The meaning of gestures also changes from culture to culture; for example, doing "horn fingers" in the USA is a rock-and-roll signal meaning "Rock on," but if you use that gesture in Argentina, it means "You're being cuckolded." We'll be discussing body language from an American point of view. Most of these insights will apply all over the world, but if you're not American and anything I mention seems off to you, you're probably right. Be careful of your interpretations and never stop looking for other indicators.

Signs of Discomfort

People aren't always forthright about letting us know they're uncomfortable. When they make the following gestures, asking them how they're feeling, or backing off, can put them at ease.

The Tight-Lipped Smile
The tight-lipped smile stretches the lips across the face, hiding the teeth. It is especially common among women trying to hide their dislike for someone. Specifically, it's an indicator that there's something they want to say, but they're holding it

back.

The Frown
The corners of the mouth turn downward, indicating strong displeasure.

Biting One's Lip
The teeth are visible and bite down on the lower lip. It is a comforting gesture for anxious people, and is usually clustered with other gestures on this list.

Crossed Arms
Any and all barriers people form to protect their vital organs are signs of discomfort and anxiety. The most common is interlocking one's arms and resting them just below the chest. If the crossed arms are accompanied by arm-gripping or fists, the discomfort and hostility are greater. Self-hugging (wrapping your arms around your body but without interlocking them) is also a sign of discomfort, but less hostile.

Disguised Arm Crosses
People who don't want to communicate their defensiveness will avoid crossing their arms, but they still feel the urge to do it. They'll usually invent excuses to cover their vital organs with their arms without making it obvious. Examples include adjusting their cufflinks, playing with their watches, looking in their wallets, holding folders against their chests, holding their cups in two hands, clutching their purses, or positioning their cups on the opposite side of the table from their dominant hands, necessitating a reach-across. If you see people making such gestures, they might be anxious.

Clenched Fists
Clenched fists suggest defensiveness and anger. The whiter the knuckles, the more hostile they feel.

Rubbing/Covering Eyes and Ears
When people see or hear something they don't like, their eyes or ears will itch, which motivates the people to touch them.

Children exaggerate this, often covering their eyes or ears completely to "keep out the bad." Adults are subtler, usually rubbing their eyes or scratching their ears. It could always be a coincidence, but if you see people rubbing their eyes or ears after you've said something, they probably didn't like it.

Darting Eyes

When you're standing face to face with someone and that person's eyes are darting around the room, he or she is looking for a way to escape the conversation. Let them.

Leading Foot Pointing Away

The farther a body part is from the brain, the less conscious control we have over it. Since the feet are the most distant, they reveal our hidden desires more than any other body part. If someone's front foot is pointing toward an exit or a path away from you, that person wants to get away.

Ankle Lock

When people lock their ankles, they are protecting their vulnerable areas in much the same way as when they cross their arms. If these gestures are combined, such people are extremely uncomfortable.

Extended Blink

When a blink lasts for several seconds, the blinker is attempting to erase an image from the mind. If the look is directed at you, the person may be annoyed or otherwise unhappy that you're there.

Gripped Hands behind the Back

When people grip their hands behind their backs, it's a sign of frustration. The higher up the arm the grip is (such as at the forearm or elbow), the greater the frustration. If the hands are relaxed behind the back, and not gripped, this is a sign of confidence, not frustration.

Picking at Imaginary Lint

If someone is picking imaginary lint off of clothing, it means that person disapproves of something that's been said, but is uncomfortable saying so. Consider asking what's on his or her mind.

Signs of Dishonesty

Detecting when someone is lying can be invaluable, both to protect yourself and to discover why someone feels the need to lie in the first place. Unfortunately, cues for deception are faint, and they aren't always accurate.[93] Give people the benefit of the doubt, but if you see these signals, especially together, it might be worth some extra probing.

False Smiles
True smiles are almost always signs of honesty, but fake smiles are the opposite.[94] A genuine smile will be symmetrical and involve a crinkling of the eyes. False smiles come quickly, are held longer, and will be more exaggerated on the left side of the face than the right.

Hiding Hands
People who are feeling open and honest tend to keep their hands visible, with their palms outward. Liars hide their hands.

Touching the Face, Especially the Mouth
In the same way we cover our eyes and ears when we see and hear things we don't like, we cover our mouths when we say things we don't like. Again, children are less subtle about it than adults. Adults will fake a cough, rest a finger over their mouths, or stroke their chins.

Swallowing
When lying, our throats get dryer, encouraging us to swallow.

Rubbing below the Nose
According to research done at the University of Granada,[95] lying causes an increase in temperature around the nose; this is called the "Pinocchio effect." This change causes discomfort,

encouraging the liar to touch his or her nose for relief.

Pulling the Collar

According to body-language researcher Desmond Morris, lying causes a slight rise in body temperature, leading to irritation in the sensitive skin along the shirt collar, encouraging the liar to pull the collar to cool down.[96] This gesture, especially combined with related indicators like sweating and flushed cheeks, is a sign of deception.

Foot Motion

Because they have less conscious control over their feet than over other parts of their bodies, liars tend to shuffle their feet.[97]

Incongruence

Since people often try to control their body language while lying, any contradictory gestures, especially discrepancies between what the feet are doing and the expression on the face (least controlled vs. most controlled), are signs of deception.

Contraction of Pupils

When we're looking at someone we like, our pupils expand. When we're looking at someone we dislike, they constrict. If someone has constricted pupils when looking at you, but seems to be acting in a friendly way, that person may have ulterior motives.

Frequent Blinking

Rapid blinking is another adult manifestation of the "hide the evil" response. Such blinking while speaking suggests that the speaker is uncomfortable with the words and may be lying.

Signs of Friendliness

Vertical or Palm-Up Handshakes

Revealing the palm of one's hand shows friendliness or submission. If people reach for your hand with their palms up, they're asking for you to take the lead in the relationship.

Laughter
People laugh to create rapport. If someone is laughing at everything you say, that person wants your approval.

Touching
Any form of physical contact is a sign of fondness. If people don't like you, they'll go out of their way to avoid touching you.

The Eyebrow Flash
The eyebrow flash is a quick rise of the eyebrows, usually from across the room. People do it only with people they like, or people they want to like them.

Standing at an Angle
When people stand directly across from one another with their feet pointing straight, this is a sign of exclusive attention, due either to strong intimacy or to hostility. When people turn their feet and bodies to an angle of 45 degrees or greater, it's a posture that encourages friendly, casual banter. They are also inviting others to join them. When you're looking for groups to be social with, look for people standing at angles to one another.

Mirroring
According to research performed by T. L. Chartrand and J. A. Bargh, when people like each other they unconsciously mimic each other's gestures, a behavior called the "chameleon effect."[98] Listeners imitate poses adopted by speakers, and may even imitate each other's accents and intonations. The highest status person in the group tends to be the one most imitated.

Signs of Domination, Confidence, and Hostility

The Palm-Down Thrust
Just as the palm-up thrust into a handshake suggests

submissiveness, its opposite, the palm-down thrust, expresses an intent to dominate.

Steepled Hands

If someone pushes the tips of the fingers upward in the shape of a steeple, it is a gesture of extreme confidence and self-assurance. If the steeple is pointing downward, it's a sign of introspection and thought.

Displaying Thumbs

Thumbs are associated with self-assurance. The "cowboy stance," in which a man tucks his fingers into his belt or pockets and lets his thumbs point at his dick, is a strong display of confidence. If the thumbs are on display while the arms are crossed, the person is feeling both confrontational and self-assured.

Spread Legs

Spread legs take up space and communicate both comfort and ownership of territory. That stance displays the genitals, showing a lack of concern for any threats anyone else might pose. It's a dominant gesture, and a rude one, especially when space is limited.

The American Figure Four

The figure four involves reclining in one's seat and resting one leg's ankle on the knee of the other leg. It communicates extreme comfort and confidence. If the hands are placed behind the head with the elbows pointing outward (like a catapult), the gesture is amplified. If the person is gripping his or her top leg, however, that's a sign of discomfort.

Straddling a Chair

Straddling a chair with the chair's back against one's chest is an aggressive posture. The chair acts as a shield in the same way crossed arms do, except this posture leaves the arms free to attack.

Hands on Hips — the "Superhero Pose"

The superhero pose involves putting one's hands on one's hips and projecting the chest outward. It's a sign of extreme confidence and self-assurance.

Leaning

Leaning on objects implies ownership of those objects. Leaning on someone's office door frame, sitting in someone else's chair, or using someone else's property without permission are all strong impositions of dominance.

The Upward Nod

Nodding upward is a greeting that exposes the jugular. Between friends, it means "Good to see you; I trust you," and tends to involve a smile. When done to strangers, it shows a lack of concern for their presence. Essentially, it means "Yeah, I see you there, bitch."

Signs of Sexual Attraction

In Both Sexes

Dilated Pupils

When couples stare into each other's eyes, they're looking for pupil dilation. The larger someone's pupils are when looking at you, the more attracted to you that person feels. If a stranger tries to hold eye contact longer than is normally socially appropriate, that is also a sign of attraction.

The Forward Foot

Just as the front foot points to an exit when we want to escape, it points toward the people we desire. When someone's chatting in a group, the foot holding less body weight will point at the person the speaker finds most attractive or important.

Preening

When noticing an attractive person, members of both sexes will brush themselves and adjust their clothing, even — or especially — when it's not necessary.

Proximity
When attracted to someone, members of both sexes will consciously or unconsciously stand close to the people they like. Sometimes this will take the form of "finding an excuse to stop" while walking around the room. They may adjust their makeup, look at their phones, or pretend to be interested in something nearby. In truth, they're trying to get the attractive person's attention.

Touching
People find excuses to "accidentally" touch people they find attractive. They might brush against them, bend over and bump them, or back into them. When they aren't attracted, people avoid touching as much as possible.

Licking Lips
Members of both sexes lick their lips around people they find attractive.

Straightening Posture
Both men and women subconsciously straighten their posture when walking near someone they find attractive.

The Crossed Leg
When people are sitting together on a couch or bench, if they find a companion attractive, they will cross their legs with the top foot pointing toward the person they fancy. If there is no attraction, the top foot will point away.

In Women

The Face Platter
When a woman makes the form of a bridge with her hands and rests her chin on it, it creates a "frame" for her face as if to say "Look how cute I am." It's a flirtatious gesture and thus indicates attraction.

Lowering Eyes and Looking Up

When a woman tilts her head down while looking up with her eyes, it's meant to be seductive.

Exposing Her Neck
When a woman finds a man attractive, she will find excuses to expose toward him her vulnerable, intimate regions, one of which is her neck.

Looking over a Raised Shoulder
With her back turned to the attractive man, when a woman looks over her raised shoulder as if she's peeking over a hill, this is a flirtatious gesture.

Revealing Wrists
As with the neck, women reveal their vulnerable wrists to men they find attractive. This is most common among women who smoke, as they'll display their wrists while holding their cigarettes. You may also see it in how women hold their purses, if the bags are small enough.

Stroking a Cylindrical Object
When women are thinking about sex, they'll subconsciously stroke cylindrical objects. This is most common with the stems of wine glasses, cigarettes, pens, and fingers.

Penetrating Circular Objects
A woman who is thinking about sex will penetrate objects with her fingers or feet. She may finger a ring or slide her foot in and out of her shoe.

Touching and Flipping Hair
Around men they find attractive, women—even those with short hair—will flip and adjust their hair to get the men's attention.

Crossing and Recrossing Legs
Women will cross and recross their legs around men they find attractive. This is an especially strong indicator of attraction when combined with the following gesture.

Showing of Calves' Muscle Tone

When an attractive man is nearby, a woman will cross her legs and press her calves into each other in order to accentuate her muscle tone.

Exposing the Armpit
Armpits, like necks and wrists, are intimate and vulnerable places, and exposing them shows attraction to a nearby man. It also spreads a woman's scent.

Holding Her Handbag Close to Him
A woman's purse is an intimate possession and functions almost as an extension of her body. When standing in a group, she will hold her purse closest to the person she likes most.

Knee Pointing
Just as we point our feet at the people we find attractive, when women are seated they will point one or both knees at men they fancy.

The Fleeting Glance
When a woman sees at a distance a man she likes, she will stare at him until he looks in her direction. She will hold his gaze for a few seconds, then look away. The longer she holds the gaze, the more pronounced an invitation it is for him to come talk to her. Women often need to attempt this several times before men take notice.

Chapter Summary

• Body language is the most reliable way to read a person's emotions. Learn it.

Exercises

Exercise 9.1 – Immediate – Take Some Body Language Tests
I've linked to several body languages quizzes at *thehotguyde.com/bodylanguage*. Visit the page and try out the

quizzes listed. Record how you did in your journal.

Exercise 9.2 – Ongoing – Go People-Watching
Over the next several weeks, schedule four visits to public places where you can people-watch. One of these locations should be a bar and one should be an outdoor space, such as a park. The other two may be wherever you choose. Observe the body language of everyone there. Can you tell who is attracted to whom? Can you tell who don't like each other? Who can you predict will go home together? Were you right? Write about your experiences in your journal.

Chapter 10 – Social Status

Mark is the kind of guy everyone seems to like. When he steps into a bar, people turn their heads. As he walks through a venue, women check him out. When he approaches strangers, they greet him warmly and remember his name. When he speaks, people listen, and he's rarely interrupted.

Julien's a lot like Mark. He's about as good-looking, comes from a similar family, and works at a similar job. Despite the similarities, though, Julien's social experiences are quite different. He has friends, but when he tries to organize events, they tend not to show up. When he tries to talk to strangers, they ignore him, and service at bars is always slow. When he proposes ideas at work, people don't take them seriously. Why don't people treat Julien as well as Mark?

The last several chapters have focused on the "warm" side of social skills, the sorts of things you'll find in most books on how to be good with people. Sensitivity and genuine appreciation are important elements of charisma, but they aren't everything. Rock stars don't have panties thrown at them because they're so damn friendly. Charisma is what you have when your personal warmth is combined with status.

What Is Status?

Status is the influence, deference, and attention someone commands in a community.[99] For our purposes, we're not concerned with status conferred through rank, as in the military or in politics. When it comes to dating and relationships, that sort of status plays a role, but it's less important than what we're interested in. When you put twenty strangers in a room together, who's most important?

Who will be a good leader? How do they decide? The processes underlying this sort of spontaneous social arrangement are harder to understand, but they have much more to do with sex and attraction than institutional rankings do. It's the difference between the boss you obey because you have to and the co-worker you listen to because you want to.

The way social status works is similar to the way prices are set in a market. Lots of people bid the price of something up and down until they reach a "going rate." Similarly, we figure out how we and other people in a group rank based on how they behave toward us and toward each other. Are they eager for rapport? Do they not care what we think? Do they tolerate being treated like crap? These cues play into our subconscious judgments of ourselves and others, influencing our self-esteem and how we treat other people.

When you're meeting strangers, the biggest determiner of your social status is you. No one knows anything about you except what you reveal through your nonverbal communication and the way you behave. There are five major cues people look to for status. In order of importance, they are:

- Behavior toward others

- Body language

- Vocal tonality

- Reactions of others

- Clothing/accessories

The first three are by far the most important, with behavior toward others having the most influence. No matter how confident your body language and voice, and no matter what you're wearing, in any interaction the less emotionally reactive person will usually be perceived as possessing higher status. If you're getting angry and the other person is staying calm, people will assume the calm guy is both higher status and in the right. If you're a "nice guy" trying to please everyone you meet, and other people aren't trying to please you, anyone watching will instinctively assume you're the lower-status party. The difference between a high-status but friendly guy and a "nice guy" is subtle, and mostly a question of intent. How to communicate high status through all of these cues — except for the reactions of others, since those are out of your control — will be the topic of the next several chapters.

The Two Types of Status: Dominance and Prestige

When I told you about Mark, I was illustrating a specific kind of social status, one that projects magnetism and respect. When Mark wants to get a bartender's attention, he does it by making eye contact and smiling. There's another type of status you may have encountered, one practiced by Ted. When Ted wants a bartender's attention, he gets it by pushing the other customers out of the way.

According to the work of Joey Chang and Jessica Tracy, there are two main approaches to achieving social influence: dominance and prestige. Dominant leaders achieve rank through coercion and fear.[100] When the police officer pulls you over, or your boss threatens to fire you, that's dominance in action. People defer to dominant leaders not because they want to but because they're afraid of what will happen if they don't. Dominant leaders tend to be aggressive, disagreeable, narcissistic, and manipulative.[101]

The other path to status, the one we'll be focusing on, is prestige. Prestigious leaders tend to be agreeable and conscientious, and they possess high self-esteem.[102] Instead of using fear, they attract followers by demonstrating skill and success.[103] While dominant leaders prioritize their own gains over those of the group, prestigious leaders tend to be concerned with the common good.[104] The bulk of men's dating advice focuses on developing dominance, mostly because it's easy to understand and straightforward to achieve. Since we're interested in achieving not only social status but positive relationships with other people, *The Hot Guyde* will focus on prestige, but we'll touch on dominance a bit first.

Understanding Dominance

For better or worse, dominance works. Coercion and threats can earn you influence in the right contexts.[105] People who bully, are rude, and behave in an antisocial manner tend to be the most influential members of their relationships.[106] Dominance is the most robust predictor of leadership, outperforming conscientiousness and intelligence.[107] It predicts the emergence of leaders in the military,[108] in focus groups,[109] in college frats,[110] and in peer-rated evaluations of leaders' skills.[111] People see dominant leaders as more competent, even when they're not.[112]

There are five main nonverbal characteristics that successfully predict dominant personalities:

- Size[113]

- Strength[114]

- Masculine features[115]

- Low voice[116]

- Open posture (taking up space)[117]

If you're big and manly, you'll have an easy time being dominant. It's a primitive mode of hierarchy common to many animals,[118] so it makes sense that it depends heavily on genetic, rather than learned, traits. We can develop some of these qualities by changing how we talk, altering our body language, and working out, and we'll discuss how to do all three. The question is, how much do we want to?

The Advantages and Disadvantages of Dominance

Since dominance is based on nonverbal, cross-culturally effective cues, dominant behavior will raise your social status in nearly all contexts. Furthermore, because dominant qualities are mostly inherent, if you have them you're not likely to lose them.

The advantages end there. Dominance relies on intimidation, so when you grow weak, or someone stronger enters the picture, you'll lose your appeal. Leading through dominance can also evoke a sense of injustice in subordinates. You'll make enemies, and if your followers have the chance to leave, they usually will. Social status is worthless if no one will be social with you.

Dominance also doesn't transfer well to other areas of your life. Coworkers and friends don't appreciate being bullied, and as we'll discuss in chapter 27, it's a strong predictor of unhappy relationships and divorce. Though some women might find dominant guys preferable to "nice guys,"[119] dominance isn't attractive,[120] and it pales in comparison to how hot most women find prestigious men.[121]

We can use dominance in a limited way and avoid most of the negative consequences. The passive elements of dominance, such as deepening our voices and practicing open body language, aren't harmful, and they will encourage some degree of baseline deference from others before they get to know us. For this reason, I consider these behaviors worth adopting, and we'll discuss how to do so in the next two chapters.

Prestige

Prestige is the bread and butter of how we think of social status. It's the charm possessed by rock stars, actors, and Casanovas alike, and in humans, it's the more influential of the two paths to high status. It is, however, more complicated than dominance. People admire others for having traits they find valuable, but what traits are deemed valuable varies from person to person.[122] In a group of musicians, the best composer might be the leader. In a group of mercenaries, it might be the best marksman. No matter how much of a leader you are in a circle of friends, you can be an outcast in another.

Successful prestigious leaders share two main attributes: they appear to possess skills central to a group's goals and challenges,[123] and they're willing to use those skills to help others.[124] The problem with prestige, and the reason dominance sometimes wins out, is that it isn't always obvious who the most skilled people are. If you were to talk to ten scientists in a field you're not familiar with, how would you figure out who the most knowledgeable one was? You wouldn't be able to. Since people lack practical expertise when choosing leaders, they have to rely on competence cues,[125] such as confident body language,[126] certainty in speech,[127] expressions of pride,[128] social deference from others,[129] and generosity.[130] When choosing which scientist to listen to, you'd probably pick whichever one seemed most certain about what he or she was saying. Is that confidence appropriate, or is the scientist a charlatan? You won't know that for a while. When it comes to first impressions, social status comes from being confident and self-assured — but if you want to maintain your status, you need to deliver.

There are thus three essential steps to developing prestige in a social circle:

• Adopt confident body language and behaviors (for first impressions).

• Develop mastery of the skills the social circle values.

• Share those skills with that social circle.

None of those is easy, and that's the point. Confidence and generosity are difficult to fake. If you don't believe in yourself, your nonverbal cues will give you away and no one will take you seriously. This is the reason for part I of this book. People who love themselves project behaviors and cues that encourage others to love and respect them too. People who think they're worthless do the opposite.

Universal Prestige

Since prestige is deference based on the mastery of skills, it's situational. You might be the natural leader of a team of computer programmers, but that doesn't mean you'll have any prestige on your soccer team. If I were to teach you the perfect way to become the leader of your local Goth scene, your status wouldn't translate to the local hippies. Wouldn't it be nice if there were skills we could develop that were universally desired, incredibly valuable, and rare — ones that would command prestige no matter whom we talked to? As it turns out, such skills exist: social skills.

Just as the mastery of technical skills can generate prestige in relevant settings, mastery of social skills attracts prestige in social settings. Notable ones to focus on include:

• Being a source of fun

• Speaking and listening well

• Sexual attractiveness

• Networking

• Helping people get what they want

Bartenders and DJs almost always have high status in their venues because they're sources of fun. Attractive women get into clubs for free because the clubs know they'll bring in dozens of men. Both of these are types of prestige. Since most people are worried about their own social status, and since associating with high-status people raises it, having high status is itself a source of social value, and thus raises your prestige when shared. This is why being "popular" is difficult to achieve but relatively easy to maintain. Status, both high and low, is self-reinforcing.

The fastest way to improve your general prestige is to improve your social skills. Work on your sense of humor, your listening skills, and your banter. Get comfortable introducing people to one another. Organize events. Anything you can do to make people feel good about themselves gives you social value. Those friends you make while rock climbing at the gym? Invite them to hang out with your friends from your dance class. Take them all out for laser tag, karaoke, bowling, or the local festival. Create Facebook events or Meetup events, or just send invitations by text. Talk to new people at your venues, introduce them to your friends, and start inviting them to events as well. Suddenly you're a source of fun and a networker of people. You're the reason your friends hooked up. You helped your buddy find his new job. You are valuable.

When you're doing this right, the benefits should be enormous but effortless. Most of these are activities you'll want to be doing anyway. These skills are rare and valuable not because they're hard to acquire, but because for most people, they're scary. Being social requires putting yourself out there and risking rejection. Because most people are too caught up in their own shame to do this, it doesn't take much to become better than average. Since this is one area in which people suffer so much, and from which they long for release, they'll always appreciate you for helping them.

The Paradox of Prestige

There is a hazard to prestige that the dominance-pursuers don't have to face. Imagine you're talking to some guy who invites you to a party. He introduces you to his female friends; he buys you a drink, and gives you some useful advice on your clothes. Then he asks you, "So do you like me now?" The answer is probably "Yes," but how did that question make you feel? Two seconds ago, you thought the world of him. Now, you realize that everything he did was just to butter you up.

Prestigious leaders don't do the things they do to earn status; they do them because they're ends in themselves. If the reason you're planning all these events and helping all these people is that you're looking for social validation, you're not acting like a prestigious leader; you're acting like a manipulative people-pleaser. Your generosity has strings attached, and therefore it's not generosity at all.

This is the paradox of prestige. People who want prestige repel it, and people who achieve prestige don't care. In order to earn prestige, you can't be worrying about your social status. It's nice to have, but it's not something you ever actively pursue. You devote yourself to your hobbies because they're worth doing for their own sake. You share your skills with others not because you want people to like you but because you enjoy seeing them succeed. Over time, you'll notice that your life is full of cool people and admiring fans, and all you had to do was live well, do interesting things, and share those experiences with others. The prestigious man's reputation is built over hundreds of small interactions in which he helped people out. He's coming from a place of abundance, and he doesn't see life as a zero-sum game. Everyone's success just adds to his. Humility costs him nothing; in fact, it will make him even more admired and appreciated. In short, you earn prestige by living an interesting life, learning to be comfortable with yourself, practicing confident body language, and being generous with what you have. If you can do those things, you will possess more social status than the hulking, aggressive douchebags delivering backhanded compliments ever will.

Chapter Summary

• Social status is the influence, deference, and attention one commands in a community.

• A person's status is determined spontaneously through nonverbal consensus among observers.

• People evaluate status based on a person's behavior toward others, body language, vocal tonality, appearance, and the reactions of others.

• Dominance is status taken through intimidation. Prestige is status earned through admiration.

• Size, strength, masculine features, a low voice, and open postures encourage dominance.

• Dominance can lead to social and relationship problems, and though it's preferable to submissiveness, it is unattractive to most women.

• Prestigious leaders possess skills central to a group's goals and are willing to share those skills.

• Since competence is difficult to measure, groups rely on competence cues, including confidence, certainty, pride, generosity, and deference from others.

• Because social skills are universally valued, developing them can lead to universal prestige.

• Improving one's humor, one's listening, bantering, and networking skills, and one's ability to help others, serves this end.

• Trying to earn prestige is antithetical to prestige. Practice and share your skills because it's worth doing, not because you want attention.

Exercises

Exercise 10.1 – Immediate – Write about Leaders You Know
Think about two people in your life you would consider leaders: one who leads through prestige, one who leads through dominance. Write a paragraph on each describing them, including examples of how they exercise their

leadership. Next, think of two examples from fiction, one of a prestigious and one of a dominant leader, and write similar paragraphs about them.

Exercise 10.2 – Immediate – Observe High-Status Behavior in Marketing

Look for five music videos starring male pop stars. What have the directors done to communicate to viewers that the pop star has high status? How do women react to the star? How do men react to the star? How is he dressed? Where is he? How does the music video communicate each of the five status cues? Write about your findings in your journal.

Exercise 10.3 – Ongoing – Add Social Status Cues to Your People-Watching

In Exercise 9.2, you went to social venues to observe the body language of others. In this exercise, visit two more venues to people-watch, and this time, pay special attention to status. Among groups of friends, can you identify which person stands out as the leader? Who gets fast service at the bar? Who seems to command respect and who seems to invite disrespect? What behaviors and body language do you see these people exhibit? What are they wearing? Write about your experiences in your journal.

Chapter 11 – Expressing Body Language

In this chapter and the next, we'll discuss how to modify our nonverbal modes of expression to communicate dominance, prestige, and goodwill toward others. While learning about desirable body-language habits, keep in mind everything you learned about habits in chapter 5. Transforming your old, low-status body language into confident gestures will likely require a few months of habit reversal therapy. Doing so will help you project confidence, people will treat you as higher status by default, and you'll provoke cognitive dissonance with any self-deprecating beliefs you might have. It will take time, but it's worth it.

Posture

There's only one rule when it comes to posture: open is better. Open postures are inviting, and they simultaneously project dominance, warmth, and confidence. Closed postures encourage people to stay away. They communicate defensiveness, and thus read as insecure, threatening, and generally low status, which is why low self-esteem is so often attached to seeming "creepy." When adopting new posture habits, you'll want to favor open palms, held-back shoulders, a fully extended neck, and a wide, comfortable stance.

Much of the clinical research on posture explores correcting it as a means of relieving pain. Since poor posture is not usually the true cause of pain,[131] medical research has not developed much in the way of posture-correcting therapies. Fortunately, there is sufficient information out there to help us. We know that the majority of posture problems come from living a sedentary lifestyle,[132] so anything that gets you up and moving will help. There are also some specific techniques developed by professional posture experts that we can incorporate into our habit-reversal therapy.

Things That Don't Work

Willpower

As we discussed in chapters 4 and 5, trying to change our habits through force of will doesn't work. Willpower is limited; habits are eternal. You might make progress for a little while, but it's not a long-term solution.

Stretching

It's popularly believed that poor posture is caused by tight muscles. This myth claims that our muscles are like elastic bands, and when they're not flexible enough they collapse inward. Researchers looked into this and found that stretching does not help to correct posture.[133] Poor posture is not a physiological problem; it's a psychological, habit-based one. Since those advocating stretching misunderstand the problem, it's no surprise that it doesn't work.

Things That Work

Movement

Human bodies are not stacks of books. The center of gravity in your head is not positioned along a straight line to your chest, hips, or knees. Our bodies operate in a system of dynamic equilibrium, keeping themselves upright through constant tiny adjustments made by our muscles. When we're in motion, our muscles trade off the work of holding us up, so no single muscle group gets too tired. When we're sitting or standing still for a long time — for example, at a desk job — the same muscles work constantly until they're exhausted. This causes us to slump in our chairs and let our necks sag. The more time we spend sitting and staring at computer screens, TVs, and books, the more the slumped posture becomes our default position.

The single best way to reverse this process is to live a lifestyle that resembles what our bodies have evolved to do. Get out and move. Adopt hobbies that require you to run, bend, and use your body in ways you don't usually use it. All sports qualify, but parkour, gymnastics, and martial arts stand out. Dance classes are excellent too, especially solo dance: jazz, tap, ballet, hip-hop, pole dancing, whatever you like. When you're spending ninety minutes or more a week in a room surrounded by mirrors, feeling and watching yourself move, you won't be able to help but improve your posture.

Ergonomics

Another simple solution to bad posture is to fix the environment that's triggering your bad habits in the first place. Is your computer monitor too low for your eyes? Does your chair give poor support to your back? Investigate the places where you spend most of your time and try to determine what's contributing to your posture problems. Is there anything you can change that will encourage better habits? Perhaps you can stack some books under your monitor, or find a chair with a headrest to support your head properly. Some people have success when they switch to standing desks. Talk to your boss about solutions, or consider investing in them yourself.

Alexander Technique

When your posture is right, your whole body should feel comfortable and light. Your head should almost feel as if it's floating on your neck, and it should rotate effortlessly. You should think of your weight as being carried by your skeleton, not your muscles. When you stand against a wall, your heels, your butt, and your shoulder blades should all lightly touch the wall, and maintaining this position should feel effortless.

If you find that moving more and improving your ergonomics aren't enough to achieve this, you might need to address your problems directly. For this, we will base our approach on one employed by singers, dancers, and actors to correct their posture: a method called **Alexander Technique**.

The first step in using Alexander technique to correct posture is to figure out what you need to change. Find or create a space with several full-length mirrors (or a video camera) to observe yourself from several angles, sitting, standing, and walking, to identify undesirable postures. You can also ask a friend to take photos of you from different angles and positions, sitting and standing. Study your image in the mirror or on camera. Do you have a bit of a hunchback? Does your head hang? Are your shoulders too far forward? Write down any and all issues you find.

With the problems identified, your next step is to figure out what's causing them. Are you unnecessarily tensing muscles or are you failing to engage muscles you need to? Since you can't be staring at yourself in the mirror 24/7, you'll need to learn what proper posture feels like, so you can tell, even when you're not watching yourself, whether you're standing correctly or falling into your old habits. You need to know what "right" feels like.

To this end, we're going to use a yoga pose called the **semi-supine position**. Place a book that's about two to three inches thick on the floor. Lie down on your back and rest your head on the book. The book should be just thick enough to maintain the natural curve of your spine without tilting your chin up or down. If you need a thinner or thicker book, use it. Bend your knees and pull your feet in until they rest flat on the floor. Rest your hands on your belly button and let your elbows drop comfortably to either side of your torso. In this position, all of your muscles are completely relaxed. This is what your body feels like without any unnecessary tension, and when you're practicing proper posture, it should feel similar.

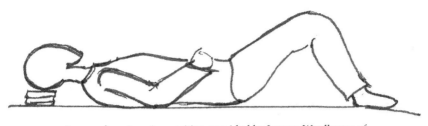

Image of semi-supine position provided by Jeremy Woolhouse of
PoiseAlexanderTechnique.com, used with permission, available at
http://www.poisealexandertechnique.com.au/articles/2014/10/9/guide-to-semi-supine-practice[134]

Compare how your muscles feel in the semi-supine position to how they feel when you're sitting, standing, and walking. Do you notice unnecessary tension in your shoulders, neck, or elsewhere? Does any of this tension correspond to the posture problems you identified in your photos, videos, or mirror notes? Watching yourself in the mirror, and focusing on one muscle at a time, try to relax any improperly tensed muscles. Imagine there are soft hands massaging and pressing your muscles in the direction you want them to go. You aren't forcing yourself to relax; you're allowing the soft hands to do their work. When you release the tension, how does it affect your posture in the mirror? If it has a desirable result, take note. I've found this approach effective for curing hunched shoulders and "claw hands."

For problems that involve straightening your body, you need to do more than just release tension. Imagine there's an invisible string pulling your body in the direction you want your posture to adopt. If you tend to jut your neck forward, imagine there's a string lightly pulling on the top of your scalp, pulling your skull upward and straightening your neck. Remind yourself that you don't need to tense any muscles to adopt the right posture. The string is already suspending you; all you need to do is stop resisting. Let your neck and back lengthen upward until they've gone as high as they can go. How does this feel? Try turning your head left and right. Do you feel how effortless it is? Try this several times and notice how the tall, "string" posture feels different from how you stand normally.

If you hunch your back or roll your shoulders forward, a combination of the string and "soft hands" approach works best. Imagine there are soft hands lightly pushing your shoulders back. As the hands are pushing your shoulders, imagine that a string attached to the center of your chest is lightly pulling upward at a 45-degree angle. Your shoulders should rest comfortably back as your chest projects outward. Trust the string and the hands to support you. Don't resist them. Remember, you're not trying to hold the right posture; you're relaxing into it. You are disengaging your old, tense habits and allowing your body to adopt its comfortable, natural, balanced posture. When holding the position is effortless and your muscles feel at ease, you're doing it right.

Setting the Implementation Intention

When you have a solid idea of what changes you need to make and what the right posture feels like, the next step is to set implementation intentions to train yourself in your new habits. "When I am sitting, I will imagine the string pulling up on my head." "When I am standing, I will imagine the string pulling up on my chest." You may also want to set a timer to remind you to practice. Whenever the timer goes off — say, every thirty minutes — take a moment to relax your muscles and visualize the strings. When the new posture starts to feel more natural than the old, you can stop using the timer.

Walking

If you want to learn to walk with confidence, the best teachers are runway models. Take a moment to go online and find some footage of male fashion models walking the runway. Pay attention to the following:

• **The Stride.** Models' strides are large—not so large that they look unnatural, but large enough to take up space and make the models appear self-assured.

They step with the full length of their legs, and when they lift their feet, they kick them back, making their strides seem even longer.

• **The Gaze.** They focus their eyes directly ahead, never looking up, down, or to the sides. This gives the impression of purpose.

• **The Posture.** They stand up straight with their arms relaxed comfortably at their sides.

• **The Shoulders.** Female runway models walk with one foot almost directly in front of the other, which shifts their hips with each step. Male models keep their legs shoulder-width apart, which doesn't shift their hips. Instead, they move their shoulders slightly with each step.

• **The Pace.** Models walk at a fast but comfortable clip. They do not waste time, but neither are they rushing. This further communicates resolve.

Find a hallway or large room, ideally with mirrors, and experiment with walking like a runway model. Step with a long stride, fully upright, at a decent pace, and focus on a point directly ahead of you. Notice how walking this way makes you feel. Do you feel powerful? Does it feel unusual? Practice walking this way in public. You'll probably notice people moving out of your way more than usual. When you walk this way, you're communicating high status, and people adjust themselves to you accordingly.

The Handshake

The first handshake you share with another person is your best opportunity to make an impression. It's the first socially acceptable moment when the two of you breach the touch barrier, and it sets the tone for how physical interactions between you will go. One study found it to be one of the most important elements in determining the outcome of a job interview.[135] It's a big deal, especially in a potentially sexual relationship. If it goes well, you'll be friendly. If it's awkward, you'll be cold.

Handshakes to Avoid

The Dead Fish – This handshake involves a limp hand with a limp wrist. The shaker doesn't truly grasp the other person's hand so much as allow the shaker's own hand to be grasped.

The Palm-Down Thrust – We've discussed this and its passive sibling in chapter 9. The palm-down thrust is the hallmark of a douchebag, implying a desire for domination.

The Palm-Up Thrust – This handshake is a sign of submission; anyone who shakes hands this way is inviting the other person to lead the relationship.

The Knuckle-Crusher – This is the only handshake ruder than the palm down-thrust. It conveys extreme insecurity and the need to cause physical pain to others in order to dominate. Your handshake should be firm, but you should not hurt your partner.

The Fingertip Grab – As the name implies, with this handshake the shaker accepts only the fingertips of the other person rather than the whole hand. It's a hallmark of insecure people, designed to keep the other person at a distance and maintain personal space.

The Politician – In an effort to appear more sincere, the shaker uses both hands to encapsulate the partner's. Instead of supported, the receiver feels trapped.

A Proper Handshake

A good handshake is firm and loving, like a hug. If you're seated, stand up. Look the other person directly in the eyes. Smile. When you present your hand, keep all four of your fingers together and stretch your thumb upward. Point your hand directly forward so your fingers are vertically aligned at a right angle to the ground. Keep your palm flat, not cupped. When you take the other person's hand, press the taut skin of your thumb against the other person's and immediately wrap your fingers around his or her hand. Drop your thumb down over the top of your partner's hand and grip it strongly. Shake from the elbow, not from the wrist or the shoulder. Maintain eye contact throughout the shake. After several pumps, release the hand and let your arm fall casually to your side.

If you would like to flirt with your handshake, keep holding her hand a few moments after you finish the pumps. The longer you hold hands, the more intimate the moment will be. If she scratches the inside of your hand, this is a secret signal that she wants to fuck. It's far more common between homosexual men, but if you ever meet a woman who uses it, it's a fair bet that's what she means. Invite her to chat somewhere private.

Smile

There's a contingent of body-language experts who say, mostly based on studies of chimpanzees, that smiling is a submissive gesture. If you're smiling because you're uncomfortable, in a context in which you might let out some nervous laughter, sure, that might be submissive, but coming to that conclusion beyond that context doesn't seem right to me. When Han Solo offers his signature lopsided grin, people don't read that as submission; they read it as cocky. Most smiles are friendly and joyful. They show that you're happy and relaxed. A genuine smile isn't submissive, so don't listen to the naysayers. There are many women who will find it your most attractive feature.

When a smile is a genuine response to joy, it's symmetrical and accompanied by a crinkling of the eyes. This is called a Duchene smile. If you're someone who struggles to smile genuinely (perhaps because you think your smile is ugly, or you learned not to show it because you were embarrassed about your braces in middle school), you might have to remove the stigma you associate with smiling. The easiest way to do this is to practice. Stand in front of your mirror and think about happy and funny things. Let your smile erupt. Feel your eyes crinkle, let your dimples dimple, and show your teeth. Get used to this image and remind yourself that it's okay to share. No one's going to hate you for your smile. It's up to you whether you show both rows of teeth or just the top. Most celebrities favor the latter. Practice smiling every morning in front of a mirror for a couple of minutes a day, and try to remember to show your full, toothy smile in your daily life. As with any habit, when you do it consistently, it will gradually replace any tight-lipped or otherwise inauthentic smile you've learned. When you love how you look and feel when you smile, and maybe even start to get compliments for it, you'll know you're doing it right.

Lean Back

The next time you go people-watching, look for a couple on a date at a restaurant and watch their body language. You'll notice that the person who is leaning forward (usually the guy) will come across as the more eager party. Leaning forward is a rapport-seeking gesture. We do it when we want people to like us, thus conveying lower status. The person who is leaning back conveys higher status and comfort.

You shouldn't hide your interest on your dates, and I don't think you should totally do away with leaning forward, but be mindful of it. It's mostly a problem for taller guys who learn to lean forward habitually because it's the only way they can hear and talk to people shorter than they are. Your stature gives you some dominance, but your habitual leaning tells others that you see them as higher status than you. Instead of leaning, ask people to speak up, or consider sitting down. When you're sitting in a group, remind yourself to lean back in your chair and listen more closely instead of leaning forward. If you break this rule, it's not a big deal, but be aware of it, and try not to make it your default position.

Fidgeting

Fidgeting suggests anxiety and poor self-control. It suggests low social status and it's distracting. When you feel the need to shake your leg, play with a pen, rub your hands, or whatever your tic might be, prepare an implementation intention with an alternative. Remind yourself to relax the relevant muscles, practice compassion toward yourself, think soothing thoughts, or engage more directly in something relevant to the conversation. Do it consistently enough and the habit will break.

Eye Contact

We've mentioned eye contact several times already, but no chapter on charismatic expression would be complete without reiterating its importance. Eye contact is everything. It conveys trustworthiness, confidence, compassion, and sexual interest. It is the most powerful expression you can use. Make eye contact, make it often, and never be the one to look away. If you do break eye contact, break it by looking to the left or right, never down, as looking down communicates submissiveness and insecurity. The more eye contact you can make, the greater the impact you'll have.

Chapter Summary

• The most effective way to fix your posture is to get out and move.

• Adjust the ergonomics of your work and play spaces to prevent poor posture habits.

• Relax unnecessarily tense muscles to address tension-induced posture problems.

• Imagine strings and soft hands pulling and pushing your body into your desired posture.

• Set implementation intentions and reminders to practice your new posture exercises.

• Walk with a long stride at a fast pace, look forward, and keep your feet shoulder-width apart.

• Use a firm, vertical handshake that feels like a warm, loving hug.

• Smile genuinely and often.

• Lean back when you sit.

• Don't fidget.

• Make plenty of eye contact, and don't break it by looking down.

Exercises

Exercise 11.1 – Immediate – Try the Semi-Supine Position
For five minutes, lie on the floor in the semi-supine position as described in this chapter. How does it feel? Make notes in your journal.

Exercise 11.2 – One Time – Identify Posture Problems
Set yourself up with mirrors, stand in a room with mirrored walls, or use a video camera, and observe your posture from several angles. Are your shoulders hunched? Do you jut your neck forward? Do you stand at your full height? Do your shoulder blades, butt, and head touch the wall without adjustment? Make note in your journal of all the posture problems you would like to correct.

Exercise 11.3 – Ongoing – Move!
Choose an active hobby you can adopt, such as a sport or dance. Several suggestions are available in chapter 15. Commit to practicing this hobby once per week for no fewer

than three months. At the end of the three months, check your posture in the same way you did in Exercise 11.2. Write in your journal about any changes you've noticed.

Exercise 11.4 – One Time/Ongoing – Improve Your Ergonomics

List the three places where you spend most of your time. Examine the way you sit or stand in these places. In what ways do these environments encourage poor posture habits? What changes could you make to improve the posture these environments encourage you to adopt? Can you give a chair a headrest? Raise the level of your monitor? Get creative, and use the Internet for help.

Exercise 11.5 – Ongoing – Set Implementation Intentions for Posture Correction

Choose one posture correction you'd like to make based on your findings from Exercise 11.2. Using the information in this chapter, determine what approach would help you correct your posture problems. Do you need to relax your shoulders? Project your chest? Straighten your neck? Set an implementation intention to make the necessary change. "When I am sitting at my desk, I will imagine a string lightly pulling on the top of my head." Set a timer to go off every thirty minutes to remind you.

Exercise 11.6 – One Time – Look up Videos of Male Runway Models

Search on YouTube or other online video services for videos of male runway models at fashion shows. Watch how they walk, and take notes.

Exercise 11.7 – One Time/Ongoing – Practice Walking Like a Runway Model

Find a long hallway or dance studio full of mirrors. Practice walking like a runway model as you observed in the videos from Exercise 11.6. Keep your eyes forward and walk with a long and comfortable stride. If you like, ask a trusted friend to watch and help you. Notice how this style of walking feels different from how you normally walk. Try walking this way down a public sidewalk and notice how other people react to you. Write in your journal about your experiences.

Exercise 11.8 – Partner – Practice a Proper Handshake
With a partner, experiment with different handshakes. Each of you should perform each of the "bad" handshakes described in this chapter. Notice how it feels to deliver such a handshake, and to receive it. Then practice delivering a "good" handshake as described in this chapter. Think about how the good handshakes feel different from the bad ones.

Exercise 11.9 – One Time – Apply the Proper Handshake
The next five times you go out, whether for social or business purposes, make a conscious effort to perform an excellent handshake within seconds of meeting everyone. How did the interactions go? Were they different from usual? Write in your journal about the experiences.

Exercise 11.10 – One Time/Ongoing – Practice Smiling
Go to a mirror and imagine something that makes you happy, or a funny joke you heard. Watch yourself smile. Is there anything you don't like about it? Does it look fake? What would you change about it? Experiment with different ways to smile. What looks most handsome? When you're out at your next social event, as you're practicing your handshakes, practice looking in people's eyes and smiling.

Exercise 11.11 – Partner – Practice Eye Contact
With a partner, practice staring into each other's eyes for several minutes. Notice when it feels uncomfortable, if you feel compelled to laugh, and how your feelings toward your partner change. After this, have a conversation. Hold eye contact while your partner is talking and while you speak. Watch how many times your partner breaks eye contact with you, and ask your partner to watch for when you break eye contact. If you want to make it a game, the person who breaks

eye contact more buys the first round of drinks.

Exercise 11.12 – One Time – Make Eye Contact with Strangers
Go to a public area—a park or a busy sidewalk—and walk around. As you pass people, make eye contact with them. Once you've made eye contact, you are not allowed to break it. They must be the ones to do so, no matter how big or attractive they are. Feel free to do this exercise more than once.

Chapter 12 – Vocal Tonality

There's a reason Barry White was a sex symbol, and it wasn't his looks. An attractive voice is a huge turn-on. Learning how to use your voice well can be as important and powerful as improving your body language, and it's a skill few understand.

A Charismatic Voice

Measuring what makes a voice charismatic is challenging, but one thing we're pretty sure of, at least in men, is that deeper voices read as more powerful. Dominant leaders speak in lower tones,[136] listeners rate deeper voices as stronger and more masculine, and men who see themselves as stronger deepen their voices in competitive contexts.[137] Women also tend to prefer men with deeper voices, at least when the women are fertile.[138] If you can speak with a deep, resonant voice, people will take you more seriously — and most women will find you sexier.

Studies of how subtle vocal adjustments can affect the way people see us are harder to come by, but many vocal experts agree on at least one point: The inflections we use when we end our sentences affect how people hear what we say, perhaps even more strongly than our overall tones. If the tone of your voice rises at the ends of your sentences — what linguists call a "high rising terminal" — you will come across as insecure.[139] Linguist Robin Lakoff calls it a speaking style that signals subordination.[140] Alternatively, when your tone drops, you'll come across as dominant. If confidence is your goal, it'll usually serve you better to lower the pitch at the ends of your sentences or keep it level, rather than raising it.

Developing a Charismatic Voice

Step 1 – Breathe

Below the lungs is a muscle called the diaphragm. When we inhale, the diaphragm drops down, expanding the lungs and pulling air inside. Many of us don't use our diaphragms well. We breathe primarily with the tops of our lungs, a habit called clavicular breathing. It's shallow, and if that's the way you breathe, it can leave you easily winded from exercise and force you to speak in shorter bursts.

At the bottom of your rib cage is a pair of ribs that stick out from your sides a little further than the rest. These are your "floating ribs." To fix clavicular breathing, stand with your hands just beneath these ribs so that your thumbs and index fingers straddle your sides. Bend over at your waist so your body is parallel to the floor and inhale deeply through your nose and mouth. Imagine the air rushing into your back, and think of using your lungs to push your hands outward. Feel that expansion with your hands and repeat the exercise several times. When you breathe in this way, you engage the intercostal muscles, which are the muscles running along the ribs responsible for expanding the lungs. Since your intercostal muscles have more nerve endings than your diaphragm, it's easier to feel when you're using them correctly, and when you're using them, your body automatically engages the diaphragm. Though many voice teachers tell their students to think of "breathing into the belly" to induce diaphragmatic breathing, practicing engaging your intercostals will give you a better sense of the correct sensation, and is thus what I suggest. When you can feel the muscles in your ribs expanding outward, you're doing it right.

While you're practicing this diaphragmatic/intercostal breathing, see if you can keep your breaths silent. Slow them down and move your mouth into an "oo" shape as if you're inhaling through a straw. The silent breaths ensure that nothing in your mouth or throat is obstructing the airflow.

As you're breathing, slowly start raising your torso upright. Keep your hands on your ribs and try to maintain the same feeling of expansion into your back and hands. If you lose that feeling, bend over until you find it again and try a second time. The goal is to become capable of this intercostal and diaphragmatic breathing while standing, and to do it naturally in place of your clavicular breathing. If you're able to keep the feeling, practice this daily, and move on to the next step.

Step 2 – Relax the Throat

Many of us tense up our throats when we speak, which can limit our volume, make us sound unhealthy, and cause vocal damage. The "nerd accent," as imitated by the character Napoleon Dynamite in the movie of the same name, is a symptom of a tight throat. If you have this problem, do the following:

While using the breathing technique from step 1, practice letting out a soft sigh. The sigh should be breathy, like a pop star's singing voice or an impression of a cheesy sex hotline. Let far more breath run through your vocal cords than you need to make a sound. Do this several times until you're used to the feeling.

Step in front of a mirror and watch your throat as you sigh; then start to increase the volume. Think of moving the breath through your vocal cords faster and faster. You might feel the urge to "squeeze" or "clamp down" with your throat. Try to resist this urge. To increase volume, instead of clenching your throat, think of accelerating your breath faster. On every sigh, stay relaxed but try to get louder and louder, and watch your throat in the mirror. You should not see any muscles tensing. If you do, quiet down a bit and think of relaxing those muscles. Eventually, you should reach a point where the air is flowing freely, you feel no tension, and the tone is no longer breathy. This is what singers call a "supported tone," and it's the voice you should be speaking with. It will sound healthy, free, and appropriately loud. Don't worry if you don't get this the first time. It may take several days of practice. When you think you have the hang of it, practice speaking sentences, sometimes with the breathy tone and sometimes in full voice. After a few days of practice, it should feel natural.

Step 3 – Open Your Mouth

If people often tell you that you mumble, try the following. Watch yourself speaking a sentence in the mirror. On each word, open your mouth as wide as possible, taking extra time to say each word as needed. Imagine you're trying to help a lip-reader a hundred feet away understand what you're saying. Our goal is to increase your range of comfort in how wide you can open your mouth so enunciating doesn't feel so strange. If you can articulate more than necessary, you can articulate as much as necessary. Repeat this exercise several times. When you've grown comfortable with the exaggerated motions, practice speaking with mouth movements about halfway between your normal habit and the exaggerated exercise. Practice every morning in the mirror, and set an implementation intention to speak in this way during every conversation from now on. Feel free to wear a colored wristband to remind you to do so, or track your progress in a notebook.

Step 4 – Train a Deeper Voice

The voice you have is the voice you have. There is little you can do to make it higher or lower after you've hit puberty. However, knowing that deeper voices tend to be more charismatic, you can make the most of what you have by speaking in the deepest part of your range.

Review the "sigh" exercise we used in step 2. Employing the same sort of breathy, relaxed tone, try giving a sigh that spans your whole vocal range, starting with the top of your range (high pitch) and dropping down gradually to the bottom. You'll know you've hit the bottom when you enter your "fry tone," which is a quiet, "gravelly" part of your range.

Our voices have two (perhaps three) registers, named for where the sound resonates in our bodies. Lower notes resonate in the chest and are called "chest voice," while higher notes resonate in the head and are called "head voice." (The third register, the falsetto, also resonates in the head, and is caused by pulling the vocal folds tighter than normal.) You might notice a "crack" between these two registers while you practice your sigh. When you're speaking, you want to be in the area of your voice below that crack, and you should always feel a soft rumbling in your chest when you speak. When you do the sigh, try to listen for the switch into the chest voice, and observe when your sound produces vibrations down there instead of in your head. Feel for the range just above the fry tone, and try speaking a few sentences around those pitches. You might not have much volume there at first, but it will grow stronger with practice. Try speaking in your lower range for several minutes a day. Read aloud plays, books, or whatever you like, just to get yourself used to speaking in this range.

Step 5 – Eliminate Nasality

Some of us are in the habit of pushing our voices up into our noses, giving them a "buzzy" quality. Steve Urkel from the TV show *Family Matters* comes to mind. This sound is caused by a drooping soft palate, and most people think it's ugly. If you have a nasal voice, try the following:

Run your tongue along the roof of your mouth. Toward the back, you'll feel a spot where it switches from a hard surface to a soft, fleshy one. The fleshy area is your soft palate. To raise it up, practice yawning. Yawning naturally raises your soft palate to its maximum height. If you've ever tried to talk while yawning, you'll notice your voice has a "domey" quality. We don't want to go that far, but we want it to be higher than it usually is. Stand in front of a mirror, start to yawn, and feel your soft palate go up. If you're having trouble feeling it, try using some peppermint mouthwash or eating something minty. It will make your mouth feel "cool," and your soft palate will be more sensitive to the motion of the air.

When you have an idea of what the "yawn" feeling feels like, try speaking as soon as you feel the soft palate rise. After you've had a few successes, practice holding your nose while speaking. A proper speaking voice shouldn't change when you pinch your nose.

If the "yawn" technique doesn't help you, try experimenting with impressions while holding your nose. Think of doing a Steve Urkel impression, and then think of doing the polar opposite. Experiment with different ways of speaking until you find one that doesn't change when you hold your nose, and then see if you can talk that way without holding your nose. When you've found a way to ditch the nasality, that is your new speaking voice.

Step 6 – Speak Slowly

To practice speaking slowly, imagine yourself having a conversation, but slow your speech to an absurdly slow pace. Think of Eeyore from *Winnie-the-Pooh* (minus the depression), or a slow Southern drawl. In ordinary conversation, consciously think of cutting your rate of speaking down by half, and err on the side of too slow. It's easier to speed up than slow down, and when you're nervous you'll tend to speed up anyway. When you're comfortable with speaking uncomfortably slowly, feel free to set your pace however you like. As with the other exercises, the goal here is to increase your freedom and comfort with all rates of speech.

Step 7 – Drop Ending Tones

In front of a mirror, practice speaking several sentences twice, first with an upswing in pitch at the end and then with a downswing. Notice how your up-swinging sentences sound unsure of themselves while the down-swinging ones seem confident and commanding. For the next couple of days, carry a notebook or electronic device and monitor how often you raise your pitch at the ends of sentences. Practice lowering the pitch at the ends of your sentences, even when you're asking a question. If you notice any changes in how people treat you, write about them in your journal.

Step 8 – Don't Laugh at the Ends of Sentences

Some of us are in the habit of closing our sentences with nervous laughter. "Yeah, I just went to the grocery store, hehe." It's a dead giveaway of low self-esteem. The simplest way to address this habit is to monitor it just as you monitor your inflection. Every time you laugh at the end of a sentence, make a mark in your notebook, and make a conscious effort to resist the habit. Within a week, it should be noticeably reduced.

If you're having trouble understanding these exercises, head over to *thehotguyde.com/voice* for an accompanying video lesson. Most of these techniques are easier to understand when you see them demonstrated.

Chapter Summary

• Breathe into the bottom of your lungs using your intercostal muscles and diaphragm.

• Relax your throat so air flows across your vocal cords freely and without tension.

• Open your mouth wide enough to articulate the words you say.

• Speak in your chest voice.

• Raise your soft palate to avoid a nasal tone.

• Speak slowly.

• Drop the ending tones of your sentences to convey confidence.

• Don't laugh at the ends of your sentences.

Exercises

Exercise 12.1 – Immediate – Try Out These Vocal Techniques
Review the vocal exercises described in this chapter. Try them out in front of a mirror.

Exercise 12.2 – One Time – Identify Vocal Faults
Make two recordings of yourself speaking. In the first recording, read a paragraph of text. In the second recording, paraphrase the paragraph of text you just read in your own words. Listen to the recordings and identify issues you would like to address. Is your voice too high? Too nasal? Do you have a rising inflection? Note that it is a peculiar trait of humans to hate the sound of our own voices on recordings. Don't lament if your voice seems "ugly" to you; focus on specific problems to solve. If you'd like, share this chapter with a trusted friend and ask for suggestions on what to work on.

Exercise 12.3 – Ongoing – Correct Your Vocal Faults
Rank your vocal faults in order of importance. Each month, practice the relevant vocal exercise to correct your most significant fault every day in front of the mirror, and try to apply the lessons of the exercise in your everyday life. Don't try to fix all your problems at once. One fault per month is a reasonable pace.

Chapter 13 – Assertiveness

Remember Jeremy, the "nice guy" from chapter 1? He's changed a lot. He's spent hours poring over books on psychology and social skills, and with a lot of effort, he's solved most of his problems. He's learned to talk back to his self-defeating thoughts. The friends he's made through the gym and tango lessons are cool people, and they treat him well. But there's one nagging problem Jeremy still has. Whenever he talks to his old friends and family, they're able to unearth his shame and manipulate him. He can't say "No" to anyone who knew "old Jeremy." He learned how to stand up to his inner demons, but he can't figure out how to stand up to other people.

When we're young, being assertive is natural. No one-year-old in human history has felt bad about demanding attention, and every three-year-old's favorite word is "No." We lose our assertiveness because people teach us it's wrong. Sometimes we learned by example through role models who never learned to be assertive themselves. Sometimes we learned through experience, when asserting ourselves resulted in punishment or our loved ones withdrawing their affection. Obedience was what we traded for love. In this chapter, we'll talk about how to reclaim your assertive side. You'll learn how to say "No," how to ask for what you want, and how to stand up to manipulators and bullies.

The Three Toxic Social Strategies

The Passive Style

Lex is finishing up his day at work. After weeks of

fourteen-hour days and exhausting weekend jobs, he is finally ready to take his vacation. "Hey, Lex," comes the boss's voice from across the room, "we closed a deal and are getting a big shipment in on Tuesday. Mind coming in after all?" "Oh…yeah, of course, not a problem."

Like most "nice guys," Lex practices the "passive style," one of the three toxic approaches frequently adopted by people who have never learned to be assertive. Everyone in Lex's life, from his boss to his wife to his friends and family, knows that Lex will always give in as long as they push.

The passive style is born of fear. We're afraid of conflict, so we give in to unreasonable demands, never say anything that would make others upset, and rarely give criticism or feedback. At the root of the passive style are beliefs such as "Other people are more important than I am" and "If I assert myself, I'm selfish." Generally, passive people learn this approach early in life, either through family members who never respect their boundaries, never ask them to do things they don't want to do (and thus never let them practice saying "No"), or respond to assertiveness with violence. Passive people have never seen healthy assertiveness, so they have no idea how to use it.

The Aggressive Style

On the opposite side of the toxic-personality spectrum is the aggressive style. People with aggressive personalities feel fear just as strongly as do passive people, but while passive people shut down, aggressive ones get angry. On the surface, this tactic seems more effective. People bother you less, they acquiesce when you push back, and it feels righteous and justified. In the long run, though, it's toxic. People start to avoid you; they shut up instead of compromising, and since you're so easy to provoke, you're more likely to get in trouble.

Aggressive men usually have learned their aggression

from their parents. They tend to have low self-esteem and see all obstacles as threats to their self-worth that must be overcome with rage. They have distorted beliefs such as "If I don't flip out, I'll never get my way" or "When I attack, I'm just being honest." Many aggressive people see the world as a zero-sum game: if you're not the winner, you're the loser.

The Passive-Aggressive Style

The passive-aggressive approach is usually a fallback position for situations when people-pleasing and outright intimidation can't work. Users of this style are manipulators, looking to control people through subtlety. Instead of getting angry, they hide their frustration and attack in small, hardly detectable ways. They'll do their work badly, break things, spread rumors, or feign illness. The passive-aggressive style is a mixture of anger and powerlessness. These people want control, but fear the consequences of taking it by force. The distorted thinking behind passive aggression is directed outward, with thoughts such as "Other people aren't considerate enough." They see themselves as perpetual victims and use this perspective to justify their secret, cruel behavior.

Unassertive people make use of all three of these strategies, but most people have a favorite. "Nice guys" are usually passive, but will shift into passive aggression when it suits them, and turn aggressive during their "victim vomit" tantrums. You might be thinking that assertiveness is the middle ground between aggression and submission, but in reality, it works on a whole different plane.

The Assertive Style

The strategies above have something in common: they're about controlling other people. All three aim to make others do what you want them to do. The passive person tries to please people into compliance. The aggressor intimidates. The passive aggressor uses shame and frustration. Assertive people aren't interested in controlling others; we're interested in retaining control over ourselves. We tell people what our expectations are and where our boundaries lie; it's up to them to act accordingly. If they cooperate, we both benefit. If they don't, they suffer the consequences of their actions. "If you don't pay your part of the utilities by Wednesday, I'll need to cancel the account and sue you for what you owe me." "If you ever hit me, that will be the end of our relationship." You are responsible for taking care of yourself, and others are responsible for taking care of themselves. They can choose to disrespect your boundaries, but if they do, there will be consequences.

Dealing with Manipulators

The biggest threat to your well-being and self-esteem will come from aggressive and passive-aggressive manipulators. With aggressors, you will almost always have to cut them out of your life, which we'll discuss later. You can deal with passive aggressors by insulating yourself from their tactics and setting clear boundaries.

The big weapon of the passive aggressor is shame. When your mom said to you "You haven't cleaned your room in two weeks," she wasn't just stating a fact; she was appealing to your sense of shame. The power of her words lay not in the fact but in the implication: "People who don't clean their rooms are bad." Through this implication, she established herself as a legitimate judge of your character and informed you that cleaning your room would increase your worth in her eyes. Instead of being honest and assertive, perhaps by saying "It makes me uncomfortable when your room's so dirty," your mom shifted the debate to "You are a bad person if you don't obey me." This manipulation has power only if you believe she is a legitimate judge of your moral worth. If that's not something you believe, it won't work, and you'll force her to try something else.

This sort of gambit is used more often than you probably realize. Here are some of the most popular ways people shift the debate from a difference of opinion to a difference of "goodness":

- Demanding that you provide reasons for your behavior
- Criticizing you for changing your mind
- Refusing to accept "I don't know"
- Accusing you of "not caring"
- Implying that it's essential that you please them
- Claiming that your desires are not "logical"
- Appealing to religious teachings
- Adopting a critical tone of voice

All of these are variations on a theme: "I have the right to judge you, and I don't approve." It's all bullshit. Your desires don't have to "make sense," and you don't owe anyone an explanation. There's nothing wrong with changing your mind, and it's unreasonable for someone to expect you to know everything. You don't have to care about other people, and it's not your responsibility to solve their problems. If someone wants something from you, it's reasonable for you to expect that person to ask for it directly. You are not responsible for reading minds. Any time people try to shame you, ask yourself if they're using one of these techniques, and remind yourself that you don't have to accept their manipulative premises.

Assertive Techniques for Dealing with Manipulation

"No"

When someone is pressuring you to do something you don't want to do, all you have to say is "No." You don't need to make excuses, apologize, or defend yourself. You don't need to ask permission to say "No" — for example, by saying "Would it be okay if I didn't?" — and that person doesn't have to accept your refusal. Unless you've agreed to something ahead of time and the other person has held up his or her end of the bargain, you are under no obligation to do anything for anyone. If you're a passive person, watch yourself for these tendencies and make an active effort to block them. Say "No, thank you," and leave it at that.

The "Broken Record"

Sometimes people won't accept your "No," especially if they're accustomed to manipulating you successfully. These sorts of people succeed because they persist. As long as you're willing to say "No" one more time than they're willing to ask, you'll win. Repeat your position calmly and unemotionally until the other person accedes to your request or you find a compromise.

"I'd like to talk with you about life insurance." "I'm not interested in life insurance." "Have you considered what would happen to your loved ones if you were to die?" "I have, and I'm not interested in life insurance." "A responsible husband and father would get life insurance." "Whether that is so or not, I'm not interested in life insurance." "Are you aware of how inexpensive life insurance can be?" "No, and I'm not interested in life insurance."

As we discussed in chapter 10, the less emotionally reactive person will tend to command higher social status. Use the methods in chapter 6 to keep control of your emotional state. If you can relax and avoid feeling scared, ashamed, or angry, you will have more power, and the manipulator's morale will plummet. Keep your tone even and direct, and repeat your position.

"Fogging"

When a passive aggressor tries to shame you, the easiest and most effective way to assert yourself is to agree with the information but not the implication of what was said. The power of passive aggression lies in the unspoken moral implications behind the words. If you don't acknowledge that the unspoken implications exist, you force the passive aggressor to ask for what he or she wants directly.

If someone comes up to you and says "Your shoes are ugly," think about what that person is trying to do. Does that person really care about your shoes? No. He or she's trying to dominate you. When you're insulted, what's your instinctive response? You get defensive. "No they're not!" "I think they look fine." "I don't care!" All of these responses give the manipulator power. You've been provoked into fighting on that person's terms. By defending yourself, you've implicitly agreed that the ugliness of your shoes is a legitimate basis on which you should be judged. By becoming emotional, you've shown to your manipulator, yourself, and everyone watching that you care what your manipulator thinks. Even when you shout "I don't care," everything about your behavior suggests the opposite, and people will believe your nonverbal cues more than your words.

Instead of defending yourself, what would happen if you agreed with the manipulator? By agreeing with the literal meaning of the words, but not acknowledging the moral implication, you show that you don't care about your manipulator's judgments. "I suppose my shoes could be better." By replying this way, you're saying "You may be right, but how you judge my shoes is irrelevant to my worth," or in other words, "I give no shits what you think." When someone shames you, look for any truth in the words used and agree with that truth. If the statement is totally true, agree completely. If it's probably true, say it's probably true. If there's a principle you can acknowledge, agree with the principle.

• "You haven't cleaned your room in two weeks!" "Yeah, it's been a while since I've cleaned my room."

• "If you don't clean your room, it will smell." "You're right. If I never clean my room, it will probably start to smell."
• "Don't you want your room to look nice when you bring guests over? If you don't clean your room, they'll think it's gross." "You're right, I don't want my guests to be upset. When I feel the need to clean my room, I'll be sure to do it."

Each of these acknowledges the truth behind the statement but doesn't acknowledge the implication that people who don't clean their rooms are bad people. It also reinforces your position that cleaning your room is your responsibility and your decision. By being assertive, you force your manipulator to be honest about his or her position. In this case, maybe your mom thinks your room reflects poorly on her parenting. Maybe she's embarrassed when she has guests come over. Whatever the reason, you've demonstrated that shaming you won't get her what she wants. She has to appeal to your self-interest, or at least your empathy, if she wants you to change anything. Manuel Smith calls this technique "fogging" because it's comparable to creating a fog bank.[141] People can hurl their criticisms all they want. You'll absorb them, and they won't affect you.

Inquiry

Sometimes passive-aggressive attacks aren't easy to agree with — for example, when someone says "You're an asshole." You could fog and say "I could probably be a better person sometimes," but there's a stronger alternative. In these cases, the best approach is usually to ask for clarification. "What makes you say that?" Don't be indignant or critical in your responses. Keep them factual and unemotional. Genuine curiosity puts manipulators on the defensive. They have to justify their aggressive attacks, which they probably can't do. "Your shirt looks like shit." "Yeah? What makes you say that?" "It has stripes." "All right, then." As long as you make it clear that the manipulator's opinion is worthless to you,

you'll maintain your status and composure, and the insults will only dig them a deeper hole.

Inquiring isn't just a defensive strategy. It can also help you out when talking to passive people. Since such people think sharing their wishes is immoral or dangerous, finding out what they want can be like trying to crack a nut with Play-Doh. If you notice they've adopted some anxious body language, or they've said passive-aggressive things, ask about them. "You seem upset; anything on your mind?" "That seemed like a backhanded compliment. Is there something bothering you?" Asking directly can mean the difference between fixing a problem and months of quiet resentment.

Asking for What You Want

There's another side to assertiveness besides saying "No": asking for what you want. You can't control other people, and you shouldn't try to, but you can let them know how you're feeling. No one can read your mind. Just as you enjoy making other people feel happy, and you dislike pissing them off, most people feel the same way. Asking for what you want lets people know how they can improve their relationships with you.

Describe, Express, Specify, Outcome (DESO)

There are four steps to an assertive request — describing, expressing, specifying, and stating the outcome.[142] Describing means telling the other person what's going on. "You didn't show up to our date last night." Expressing means sharing what emotions you felt because of it. "I was pretty upset." Specifying involves stating exactly what it is you want to change. "If we're going to keep planning dates, I'd like you to show up, or at least give me notice if you can't." The outcome sets forth the consequences. "Otherwise, I'm moving on." Hitting all four of these points helps people empathize with you and gives them a "right way" to go. If you know you're going to confront someone, try writing out a script. It will help ensure that you're understood, and it can help you clarify your own thoughts.

Focus on Behavior

Let's say you're dating a woman and she's consistently late to your dates. A lot of guys in this situation get fed up and react aggressively, saying things like "You don't care about my time!" Attacking the other person's character is a feature of the aggressive style. It reveals that the other person's gotten to you, puts that person on the defensive, and makes you look like an asshole. Instead of attacking, try to focus on the specific behaviors you want to change. "The last few times we've gotten together I've had to wait half an hour [describe]. It made me feel pretty crappy [express]. I'd feel a lot better [outcome] if you could meet me as planned from now on [specify]."

Emphasize the Positive

Critical feedback is sometimes necessary, and when it is, you shouldn't shy away from it. However, it's a lot easier to deliver if it's been cushioned with lots of positive feedback. Try to maintain a three-to-one ratio between positive and negative feedback. Whenever someone does something you like — such as your date from the last example showing up on time — let her know. Show her how happy you are to see her when she shows up. Mention past examples when the person acted in the way you liked. For example, let's say you were tired of planning everything and you'd like your girlfriend to take over once in a while; you could say "I had a blast that time you suggested we go to the Renaissance Faire. Anything else you've been wanting to check out?" When you've given lots of positive feedback, the difficult conversation where you say "Sometimes I feel you're expecting me to plan everything, and I get frustrated when you shoot down my ideas. Would you be open to offering some suggestions sometimes?" will go a lot more smoothly.

Use "I" Statements

The "I" statement is an approach to conflict developed by psychologist Thomas Gordon in the 1960s.[143] When you're expressing your feelings, try to start your sentences with "I" instead of "you": "I felt anxious when you insisted," as opposed to "You made me feel scared." It shows that you're taking responsibility for your own feelings and it keeps you from attacking the other person. It also keeps the conversation grounded in facts.

Rewards Are Better Than Punishments

When you bring up the outcome in your DESO speech, try to mention rewards instead of punishments. "I'll feel a lot better" or "Things will go more smoothly" will tend to serve you better than "If you don't do it, we're finished." We're all the centers of our own universes, and most people think they're justified in how they behave. If you're threatening punishments, the other person will probably resent it. Sometimes it's necessary to do so, but it should be a last resort.

Compromise

Assertiveness doesn't mean "My way or the highway." If you're always delivering ultimatums, something is wrong. Respecting yourself and making your wishes known is important, but you're not the only person in the conversation. When two assertive people disagree, they're not looking to part ways; they're looking for a compromise.

Compromise means finding the best solution—one that meets everyone's desires as far as possible. Just ask: "What would you be comfortable with?" "What would make this easier for you?" "I can't do what you're asking, but maybe I can do something else. What could I do to help?" As long as you're listening and considering their side of things, most people will be willing to compromise. If they're not, there's nothing you can do. Their behavior is their responsibility, and if it's harming you, you have to get them out of your life.

Dealing with Resistance

As you start asserting yourself, some people will react badly. They'll get angry, redouble their shame attempts, threaten consequences, or become needier. In the face of most resistance, mixing an empathetic response with the "broken record" will get you the best results. "C'mon man, I'm desperate. I need you to spot me $500." "I see that you're frustrated, but I will not give you money." "But if you don't give me money I can't make my rent!" "I understand that you're worried about your rent, but I will not give you money." "What the hell kind of friend are you?" "I know this is hard for you, but I will not give you money." "Our friendship is done." "If that's how you feel, that's a shame, as I like being friends with you, but I will not give you money."

Just because your boundaries upset someone doesn't mean they're wrong. People need to learn to take care of themselves without violating you. If refusing to let them exploit you means the friendship is over, you were never friends, and in the long run you're doing them a favor.

Ending Relationships

As you persist in your assertiveness, your relationships will start to be transformed. People who didn't respect you will change their tunes. People who exploited you will go away. Your social circle will change from a cluster of needy manipulators into a group of high-achieving, respectful individuals.

A small number of people, usually relatives and old "friends," will persist in their efforts to control you. Some will be emotionally abusive, and some of those situations could get physical. In these cases, you'll have no choice but to remove them from your life.

How you do this is up to you, but here are a few points to keep in mind. You don't owe such abusive people anything—not even an explanation. If you want, you can cut all contact with them and never speak again. It's not the most sensitive approach, but it's within your rights, especially if you think they'll be violent. Alternatively, you can explain your feelings. "I don't appreciate how you treat me. I've told you I don't like it and you haven't stopped. You've given me no reason to expect you'll change. I don't want you in my life anymore. Please don't talk to me again." You aren't being critical or emotional. You're stating the facts and your wishes. You've provided the abusive people with a chance at closure and ways they can improve, which is more than they deserve. Maybe they'll change their tune, but whether they do or not, it's not your concern.

You Don't Have to Be Assertive All the Time

When you're visiting your grandmother and she offers to make you a cup of tea you don't want, you have the option of saying "No," but you don't have to. Your self-esteem isn't going to collapse because you take a few sips of Granny's weird tea. Assertiveness is a skill, and you use it, just like sensitivity and banter, when you need to. When people are hurting you, you shouldn't be afraid to say "No." When you want something, you shouldn't be afraid to ask for it. Not being afraid to do it doesn't mean you have to. It's fine to put another person's interests before your own, as long as you're doing it on your terms.

There are moments when assertiveness is probably the wrong choice. If you're talking to someone who's upset, it's probably a good time to turn down your assertiveness skills and turn up your listening and sensitivity. If someone has a gun pointed at you, "No" is likely not the right thing to say. Temper your assertiveness with sensitivity and use your judgment in the moment. If you can pull off being both assertive and compassionate, you'll have the most universally attractive personality science has found.[144]

Finally, when you're learning this skill, don't assert yourself with everyone at once. Doing so will create a united front against you, and since your willpower is limited, this will maximize your chances of failure. Break your social circle into groups and assert yourself with one group at a time. For example, start by asserting yourself with acquaintances, then with friends, then with family, and then at work. You'll have a much easier time making your transformation piecemeal than all at once.

Chapter Summary

• You are the only legitimate judge of your worth.

• People will try to shame you by turning their personal preferences into moral "truths."

• Be a "broken record." Unemotionally repeat your position until the manipulator gives in.

• Agree with any truth a manipulator says without acknowledging the implied moral judgment.

• Ask for details about criticisms. This shows you aren't emotionally fazed by them.

• Describe, Express, Specify, and Outcome: use all four when asking for what you want.

• Find ways to compromise.

• When people resist your responses, empathetically acknowledge their positions, but be a "broken record."

• Cut out of your life those who repeatedly disrespect your boundaries.

• Temper your assertiveness with sensitivity.

Exercises

Exercise 13.1 – Immediate – Identify Personality Styles

Think back on the four social strategies described in this chapter: the passive style, the aggressive style, the passive-aggressive style, and the assertive style. For each style, think of one person in your life who practices that style regularly. What does that person do that makes you think so?

Exercise 13.2 – Immediate – Practice Fogging

Write out a "fogging" response that would be appropriate for each of the following manipulative statements. For example, the response to "Good boys clean their rooms" might be "Yes, I suppose it would be good to clean my room once in a while."

1. "A real man would pay for the date."
2. "If you loved your mother, you'd call her more often."
3. "If you were a competent employee, you wouldn't complain."
4. "If you really cared, you wouldn't say 'No.'"
5. "If you were smarter, you'd do your homework."
6. "Only bad husbands don't plan vacations for their wives."
7. "A dad who loves me would buy me a cell phone."
8. "A real man would be willing to fight for me."
9. "A real friend would help me move."

Exercise 13.3 – Immediate – Practice Inquiry

Write out an assertive inquiry for each of the following manipulative statements.

1. "You're an asshole."
2. "Your grammar sucks."
3. "You're ugly."
4. "You're creepy."
5. "You're a worthless piece of shit."

6. "You don't care about me."
7. "You disappoint me."
8. "You're a retard."
9. "You're a pussy."

Exercise 13.4 – Immediate – Practice Writing DESO Scripts

Write a DESO script for each of the following situations. Keep in mind the suggestions from this chapter: focus on behavior, emphasize the positive, use "I" statements, and favor rewards over punishments.

1. You want your boss to give you a raise.

2. You want your roommates to pay their part of the utilities on time.

3. You want your girlfriend to start splitting the cost of your dates.

4. You want the department store to accept your returned, defective merchandise.

5. You want your parents to stop shaming you for not practicing the piano.

Exercise 13.5 – Immediate – Identify Manipulators in Your Life

Identify five people who passive-aggressively manipulate you in your life. Provide examples of times each of them has done so. What would happen if you were to say "No" to their manipulations? Write out a DESO script in which you ask one of these people to stop behaving this way.

Exercise 13.6 – Partner – Practice Saying "No"

Have one partner make a series of requests, such as "Will you go out with me?" "Will you help me move?" "Would you pass me that box of tissues?" The questions can be as serious or as ridiculous as you like. The other partner practices saying "No." Switch roles after ten questions.

Exercise 13.7 – Partner – Practice the Broken Record

Partner A will try to convince Partner B to do something. It can be painting a house, buying a drink, lending money—whatever. Use any means short of violence to get your partner to acquiesce. Include all the manipulative tactics described in this book—shame, intimidation, bargaining, and whatever else you can think of. Partner B must then be assertive and say

"No" in any fashion necessary to stop Partner A. Perform this exercise six times, alternating roles each time, so each partner plays each role three times.

Exercise 13.8 – Ongoing – Put a Moratorium on the Word "Sorry"

For one month, you are not allowed to use the word "sorry." If there is a pressing need to apologize to someone, you must find a way to apologize that does not involve using that word. Carry a notebook or wrist counter to monitor your uses of "sorry" each day. After the month has elapsed, you may use "sorry" again, but only in the context of genuine sorrow. You may not use "sorry" to apologize for the behavior of other people, for random misfortune (such as bad weather), or for any reason other than that you have directly wronged another person. Write in your journal about how this goes.

Exercise 13.9 – Partner – Trade Compliments

Exchange compliments with your partner. When your partner compliments you, accept it graciously. "Your presentation yesterday was fantastic." "Thank you; I worked hard on it." Offer ten compliments each, alternating roles each time. Do not switch roles until your partner has graciously accepted your compliment.

Exercise 13.10 – Ongoing – Accept Compliments

For one week, pay special attention to positive feedback that comes your way. When it does, you are not allowed to downplay or dismiss it. Accept all compliments by saying "Thank you." For example: "That shirt looks fantastic!" "Thank you, I think it looks good too!" Carry a notebook; document all compliments you receive, and how you respond to them.

Exercise 13.11 – One Time – Write and Apply DESO Scripts

Write a DESO script for each of the following:
• Requesting a table reservation at a fancy restaurant
• Returning a product to a department store

• Asking a family member or roommate to take on a new chore
• Asking your girlfriend or wife to change a behavior

If being assertive scares you, give each of these activities an exposure rating from 1 to 10 and work them into your exposure schedule. When the time is right, execute each of them. Make a reservation at a restaurant (and cancel it later if necessary). Purchase a product and return it two days later. Ask a family member or roommate to take over a chore. If you have a significant other, the next time an opportunity arises, ask her to change a behavior you dislike.

Exercise 13.12 – Ongoing – Ask for Something
Once per month, ask one person to do something for you. Ask a friend to teach you a new skill. Ask someone on public transportation to trade seats with you. Ask someone to proofread your cover letter when you apply for a job. People don't have to acquiesce, but you have to ask. If they help you, thank them graciously. You don't owe these people a return favor, but the next time you're planning something fun, remember how cool they were.

Chapter 14 – Humor

Have a look at these three words: **Tooth, Potato,** and **Heart**. These words have something in common. Can you figure out what it is? If you can't, no worries. Fewer than 20 percent of people are able to. How about this one: **Wet, Law, Business**. Any better luck there? If not, try this last one: **Cottage, Swiss,** and **Cake**. On this last one, 96 percent of people in a study conducted at Northwestern University[145] were able to recognize the connecting factor among those words as "cheese." The first one was "sweet," and the second was "suit."

This study was an investigation of human insight—our ability to pull solutions to problems out of thin air by searching through everything our brains can dig up. When we find a solution, something extraordinary happens. We smile. Solutions to problems give us pleasure. As psychologist Alison Gopnik puts it, "Explanation is to theory formation as orgasm is to reproduction."[146]

When you were trying to figure out "tooth, potato, heart," "sweet" was probably not the first thing you thought of. I kept thinking of "ache," even though I knew it was wrong. When we set our brains to work on these sorts of insight problems, MRIs show that we don't just probe our memories; we activate everything. Some regions of our brains produce helpful results and some do not. Near the center of your brain, between the two hemispheres, is your brain's "overseer," a little module called the anterior cingulate cortex. When looking for proper solutions, the anterior cingulate is the part that holds back some of the most potent, but wrong, responses. If you've ever taken a Stroop test, that's basically an anterior cingulate workout. (The Stroop test involves reading the names of colors when they are printed in text that's a different color from what they are named: for example, seeing the word **BLUE** in red type. It requires forcing your brain to ignore the sensory input of color and focus on the meaning of the text.)

What does this have to do with being funny? In 2007, Karli Watson and her colleagues at the California Institute of Technology conducted an MRI study of how our brains process humor. Subjects were asked to look at a series of cartoons, some of which had the punchlines removed. In the funny cartoons, two parts of the brain showed more activity: the anterior cingulate and the reward system.[147] The funnier the joke, the bigger the reward and the more the anterior cingulate got involved. Just as with our "tooth, potato, heart" problem, humor is a kind of insightful discovery.

What Is Funny?

If you peruse the countless books on humor on the shelves of your local bookstore, you'll find a wide range of opinions about what makes something funny. Some of the biggest contenders include surprise, pain, timing, exaggeration, truth, and "anything that makes us laugh." While all of these are factors in humor, none of them is the answer in and of itself. I could start talking about spoons and you might be surprised, but it wouldn't be funny. I can make an exaggeration: "There are trillions of letters on this page," and while it might be ridiculous, you're not laughing.

Even laughter isn't a reliable indicator of humor. People laugh for all sorts of reasons, and according to research, 80 percent of laughter has nothing at all to do with humor.[148] We laugh when we feel uncomfortable,[149] when we find someone attractive,[150] and to build rapport.[151] In 1962, in an episode known as the Tanganyika Laughter Epidemic, laughter was so contagious that a thousand inhabitants near the village of Kashasha in Tanzania suffered uncontrollable fits of it for six months.[152] They weren't reacting to the funniest joke in history; they laughed because other people were laughing, and for no other reason.

Even more confusing are the sorts of things we find funny. We don't tend to think of the annihilation of our species as a joking matter, but in the context of *Dr. Strangelove*, it's hilarious. We make jokes about everything from annoying bosses to dead children. Even the mundane can be funny. In a study conducted by Swedish psychologist Göran Nerhardt, when subjects were asked to organize weights, they laughed out loud when handed one that was much lighter than the ones that came before.[153] Why would such a simple thing be funny to so many participants? Because the new weight created an implicit joke. Jokes are what happen when our expectations are shattered in a way that makes rational sense. Humor is the pleasure we take when we find unexpected, but correct, resolutions to problems.

The Three Stages of Humor

According to cognitive neuroscientist Scott Weems, there are three stages to humor: constructing, reckoning, and resolving.[154] Constructing is the "insightful" stage. It's when our brains start looking for solutions to the joke's "problem." It's the setup: "Why did the chicken cross the road?" In the reckoning stage, we discover that the expectations we built in the constructing stage were wrong, and we start looking for alternatives. The punchline introduces a solution we hadn't thought of. The more novel the solution, the more pleasure we get out of it, and that pleasure comes out as laughter.

"The other day a guy told me he hadn't had a bite all day. So I bit him."

Here's a classic joke. When we read the setup, "The other day a guy told me he hadn't had a bite all day," we assume he's using "hadn't had a bite" in the colloquial sense. He's saying he's hungry. The obvious resolution is to say "So I bought him a sandwich." If the joke ends that way, no one will laugh. It isn't funny because our expectations are fulfilled, not shattered.

The success of the joke lies in interpreting the meaning of "bite" in an unexpected way — in this case, literally. "So I bit him." Our expectations are shattered, but the solution we're given still makes sense because of the double meaning. We find it funny, and we laugh.

A Way that Makes Sense

"The other day a guy told me hadn't had a bite all day. So I drove him to Texas." In this version, we have shattered expectations, but the resolution doesn't make sense. In order to be funny, the punchline has to offer a legitimate solution to the problem the joke creates. A punchline to a joke must be different from our expectations, but still appropriate in context. The more unexpected the resolution, and the more satisfactorily it resolves the problem, the funnier the joke. This is the challenge of comedy. It calls on us to think of stuff that no one else thinks of, but still works. It takes a keen intellect and an ability to "think outside the box," which is why being funny is rare, and so prized.

The Rule of Threes

The first step in telling a joke is to set up your audience's expectations, and a simple way to do this is the **Rule of Threes**. If I start listing things — yogurt, cream, butter, and cheese — you get the idea that I'm listing dairy products. If I add another item, "toe cheese," it turns into a joke. Introducing two or more related things creates a trend in your audience's minds. When you introduce another thing that breaks that trend, you have the makings of a joke, and that joke will be funny to the degree that the punchline departs from, but still sort of makes sense in, that list.

"I don't get modern technology. Can't seem to figure out computers, iPhones, or deodorant."

"I'm trying to learn drums from the greats: Buddy Rich, Ringo Starr, and Animal from *The Muppets*."

Rule of Threes jokes are just about the simplest jokes you can make. Try inventing a few yourself. They don't have to be hilarious; just follow the structure and see if you can come up with something that brings a chuckle. Start with two things that have an obvious relationship — expensive cars, beautiful women, famous politicians, whatever. When you have your two things, create an introductory line that makes their relationship clear. "My dad always insisted on luxury cars. The garage had nothing but a Mercedes, an Aston Martin, and..." For the punchline, experiment with things that relate to the previous category, but depart in a fundamental way: "a Pinto," "an M1 Abrams," "Fufu the riding dog."

Not every joke will follow this format. After all, a noisy fart in the office can be a lot funnier than any Rule of Threes joke. But if you can understand why this is funny, you'll understand the makings of humor, and it will be your foundation for practicing and for building more-complicated jokes.

The Comic Premise

One popular way to think of shattering expectations is to imagine two realities — actual reality, and then the joke's reality. The difference between them creates the incongruity that sparks the humor. In comedy circles, we call the alternative reality the *comic premise.*

"I had an apartment and I had a neighbor, and whenever he would knock on my wall I knew he wanted me to turn my music down and that made me angry 'cause I like loud music...so when he knocked

on the wall, I'd mess with his head. I'd say "Go
around! I cannot open the wall!" — Mitch Hedberg

Mitch spells out the two realities. In actual reality, the knock meant "Turn it down!" In comic reality, it meant "I want to come in." Since everyone knows knocking on the wall means "Turn it down," Mitch's alternate interpretation is funny.

Another way to think of this is to see how comedy writers use this technique in film. Writers create expectations and shatter them by giving their funny characters a *comic perspective.* They create a gap between the way a character sees the world and how the world actually is. Sheldon Cooper of *The Big Bang Theory* sees everything as perfectly logical and unemotional. When he misunderstands emotional and social cues from his friends, the gap between his interpretation and how things really are makes us laugh. Austin Powers believes he's a sex god from the sixties. When his antiquated behavior clashes with the norms of the nineties, we laugh. Our expectations are built by our everyday experiences, and those expectations are shattered when we discover the character's interpretation of those experiences. Whether you're writing a sitcom or telling a joke, the funniest jokes will often be those that manufacture gaps between the premise and the normal experiences of your audience. If you can do that consistently, you'll have the tools for great comedy.

Exaggeration

"My dad always insisted on luxury cars. The garage had nothing but a Mercedes, an Aston Martin, and a Ford."

This punchline's not so funny as "a Pinto." Why not? The Pinto is a Ford car, so why isn't saying "a Ford" just as funny?

A joke's humor is proportional to the size of our shattered expectations. There are two ways to make the "shattering" bigger: by making our expectations stronger and by exaggerating the resolution. Generally, our most clever jokes will be funny because of their strong expectations, but if we can't strengthen the expectations, exaggerating the punchline works fine. "Ford" isn't so funny as "Pinto" because a car famous for erupting into a ball of fiery death is a bigger departure from "luxury" than a generic middle-class brand.

Any time you tell a joke, take it to the extreme. "He said he hadn't had a bite all day, so I bit him" wouldn't be so funny if I just "told him I'd bite him." Actually biting someone violates social norms, so it's less expected and more extreme. The more ridiculous the resolution, the funnier discovering it will be. It wasn't a bird that crapped on your head; it was a demonic sky bomber of shit. You weren't happy; you were cheerier than an orgasm on speed.

Comic Timing and Tone

Teaching good delivery would be hard as hell if we were working together in person, much less through text on a page. There isn't a universal rule. Robin Williams sped up his punchlines. Steven Wright slows them down. What works for you is going to depend on your mannerisms and style. Ultimately, you're going to have to learn this through experimentation and by studying other people telling jokes. That said, I have a few pointers that will keep you out of the worst trouble.

Put the Punchline at the End

Comedians have ruined many a great joke because they kept talking after the damn punchline. The setup is there to give the audience all the information it needs to establish expectations. The setup builds what we call "comic tension." If you keep talking after the punchline, you rob your audience of permission to laugh, and your joke dies.

> "A guy hires a hooker and brings her back to his place. She looks him in the eye and says 'Honey, for $300, I'll do anything you want.' He looks back at her and says, 'Okay, paint my house,' and puts $300 on the table."

This joke sucks. We've spoiled the punchline with the additional content. All the necessary information should have come before the punchline. "A guy hires a hooker and brings her back to his place. She looks him in the eye and says 'Honey, for $300, I'll do anything you want.' He slaps $300 on the table, stares into her eyes, and says 'Okay, paint my house.'"[155] Always put the punchline at the end and you'll avoid this amateur mistake.

Brevity Is Still the Soul of Wit

Any superfluous material we have leading up to our punchline will reduce its impact. Jokes should have the smallest amount of content possible to set the audience's expectations. It's why we have the "Rule of Threes" and not the "Rule of Nineteens." Two points is all you need to set the trend. If your words aren't either establishing expectations or exaggerating, they shouldn't be in the joke.

Universality

"Is it solipsistic in here, or just me?" If you're a philosophy major, you probably liked that joke, but for most people this isn't funny. In order for audiences to set expectations, they need to understand the joke's references.

There's a reason why comedians tend to talk about the same handful of topics: sex, dating, marriage, parenting, work, school, food, aging, weather, being a kid, politics, celebrities, religion, race, sports, and music. Most people have enough background in these areas to understand the setup. Comedians also tend to focus on the pain involved with such subjects. Everyone understands pain, so even if you don't get the references in the joke, you know what it's like to be frustrated, annoyed, or hurt. It's emotional, it's memorable, and it feels empowering to laugh about it. If you want to find the richest source of comedy in your own life, think about the stuff everyone experiences that causes you the most pain.

Specific Techniques

Wordplay

"Support bacteria — they're the only culture some people have." —Steven Wright

Wordplay jokes shatter our expectations by exploiting implicit incongruities in the language. This usually involves words with double meanings or words that sound similar. Any time you find such a word, it's a possible joke. The more unusual the word, the better the joke will be.

Sarcasm and Satire

"Something is wrong here. War, disease, death, destruction, hunger, filth, poverty, torture, crime, corruption, and the Ice Capades. Something is definitely wrong. This is not good work. If this is the best God can do, I am not impressed. Results like these do not belong on the resume of a Supreme Being. This is the kind of shit you'd expect from an office temp with a bad attitude." —George Carlin

Society is full of arbitrary social norms that are taboo to question. Since no one talks about them, pointing out how ridiculous they are can be funny. Simply talking about taboo topics shatters expectations, and a little exaggeration can make them hilarious. If the taboo topic is a secret source of pain for the audience, that will amplify the humor even further. Just keep in mind that it's inherently subversive, so if there are folks in your audience who believe in the stuff you're criticizing (or can't tell that you're being sarcastic), they might get upset.

Callbacks

A callback is when you make a reference to something funny that happened earlier. It's frequently used in sitcoms (*Archer* uses them well), and some standup comedians work them into their acts. For casual purposes, a callback can be a joke you made earlier that day, or a funny memory. Bringing it up at a relevant moment can be all it takes to provoke a chuckle, but don't use the same one too often or it'll lose its impact.

Humor Amplifiers

Anything unusual or unexpected about the way you deliver your jokes will add to the humor. Unusual numbers (such as 37), the letters "K" and "Q," unusual words, caricatured voices, and unusual facial expressions can all give your comedy more power. In their own way, each of these things shatters our expectations. Think about the way you're delivering your jokes. Sometimes a change in your tone of voice, just to let your audience know "this is funny," is all it takes to evoke laughter.

Incorporating Humor into Everyday Life

Chances are, you're not looking to become a comedy writer or a standup comedian. This is a book on dating. We're looking to use humor as a social lubricant.

There's no clear-cut way to add humor into your social interactions. I'd be doing you a disservice if I said "Always tell this joke in XYZ situation"; frankly, that won't work, and if it did, it would work only once. The easiest approach is to just incorporate humor into how you see the world and live your life. Look for the humor in everything you do. That couple's making out. What jokes could I make? Today was a bad day at work. What about my pain is so ridiculous that I can turn it into humor? Write in your journal about these things. The world offers a limitless supply of setups waiting for punchlines. If you can make thinking humorously a habit, you'll never want for jokes when chatting with your friends.

If you want some specific advice, try to incorporate more simile, metaphor, hyperbole, and (some) profanity into your speech. Don't say "It's been a while"; say "Bro, the last time I saw you, it was, like, Pangea." "It's been a rough week" can be "I've been busier than a cucumber in a women's prison." This is the quickest, easiest way to add some humor into your speech, but don't do it too often. There's a line between being the funny guy and being the guy who's trying too hard to be funny. You want your humor to be spontaneous. As with everything else in this book, do it because it's fun and worth doing, not as a means to win approval.

Chapter Summary

• Humor consists of shattered expectations resolved in a way that makes sense.

• The stronger the expectations, the funnier the shattering.

• The bigger the shattering (via exaggeration), the funnier the joke, as long as it still makes sense.

• Keep your jokes short and keep your punchlines at the end.

• Your audience must understand your joke to find it funny. Keep references universal.

• Always look for the humor in your life.

Exercises

Exercise 14.1 – Immediate – Deconstruct Jokes

Yes, explaining jokes is a social taboo, but understanding why funny things are funny is the fastest way to become funny yourself. Read through the following jokes and explain what makes them funny. Look for the expectations established in the setup and how the punchline resolves them in an unexpected way. Take note of anything else about the joke that makes it effective (word choice, intonation, universality of topic, positioning of the punchline, and so forth).

Example: "My father died fucking. He did. My father was 57 when he died. The woman was 18. My father came and went at the same time." — Richard Pryor

Explanation – The joke is a double entendre. Pryor uses the double meaning of "came" and "went" to refer to orgasm and death. It also deals with the fear and pain of our parents dying.

1. "My mother was real cheap. Okay, practical. She would never pay a bill on time. 'If they ain't cutting it off, I ain't paying.' She would say, 'The first bill is a suggestion. If they really want you to pay, then they'll come and tap on your window.' Her whole philosophy of life was: if you die owing money, then you've won." — Chris Rock

2. "A bear and a rabbit were taking a shit in the woods. And the bear turns to the rabbit and says, "Excuse me, do you have problems with shit sticking to your fur?" And the rabbit says, "No." So the bear wiped his ass with the rabbit." — Eddie Murphy

3. "You can figure out how bad a person you are by how soon after September 11th you masturbated, like how long you waited...and for me it was between the two buildings going down.... I had to do it; otherwise they'd win." — Louis C.K.

4. "Beer commercials usually show big men, manly men, doing manly things. 'You've just killed a small animal. It's time for a light beer.' Why not have a realistic beer commercial, with a realistic thing about beer, where someone goes, 'It's 5 o'clock in the morning. You've just pissed on a dumpster. It's Miller time.'" — Robin Williams

5. "I never got along with my dad. Kids used to come up to me and say, 'My dad can beat up your dad.' I'd say 'Yeah? When?'" — Bill Hicks

6. "I'll tell you what I like about Chinese people — they're hanging in there with the chopsticks, aren't they? You know they've seen the fork. They're staying with the sticks. I'm impressed by that. I don't know how they missed it. A Chinese farmer gets up, works in a field with the shovel all day…shovel…spoon…come on…there it is! You're not plowing forty acres with a couple of pool cues." — Jerry Seinfeld

7. "[Sesame Street's] got a character on there named Oscar, they treat this guy like shit the entire show. They judge him right in his face, 'Oscar you are so mean! Isn't he kids?' 'Yeah Oscar! You're a grouch!' Its like 'BITCH! I LIVE IN A FUCKING TRASHCAN!'" — Dave Chappelle

8. "I saw the movie Crouching Tiger Hidden Dragon and I was surprised because I didn't see any tigers or dragons. And then I realized why: they're crouching and hidden." — Steve Martin

9. "One night I come home. I figured, let my wife come on. I'll play it cool. Let her make the first move. She went to Florida." — Rodney Dangerfield

Exercise 14.2 – Immediate – Write Some "Rule of Threes" Jokes

Refer to the "Rule of Threes" section in this chapter. Brainstorm a variety of generic topics — smartphones, computers, football, whatever comes to mind. Choose five topics and come up with three "Rule of Threes" jokes for each topic. Pick the three funniest jokes you come up with and write them in your journal.

Exercise 14.3 – Immediate – Play "Sex with Me"

Brainstorm several professions, objects, celebrities, or any nouns you like. Choose five and come up with three jokes each using the following form:

"Sex with me is like _____; [punchline]."

Here are some examples:

"Sex with me is like hacking; it involves digital penetration."

"Sex with me is like a highlighter; how the fuck did it get in your hair?"

"Sex with me is like Tom Brady; women can't talk about it without bringing up the deflation incident."

Exercise 14.4 – Ongoing – Watch Comedy

Over the next month, make it a point to watch stand-up or improvisational comedy acts. Watch several episodes of *Whose Line Is It Anyway?* Look up the comedians mentioned in Exercise 14.1, any of the comedians mentioned in this chapter, or any others you would like and find videos of their routines on YouTube or another service. Watch them and take notes. What jokes get the best laughs? What makes those jokes especially funny? Go to some live performances, including at least one amateur open mic night. What goes well? What doesn't? Write in your journal about your experiences.

Exercise 14.5 – Ongoing – Take an Improvisational Comedy Class

Look online for improv comedy classes near you and attend for at least a month. Write in your journal about your experiences.

Exercise 14.6 – Ongoing – Perform Comedy

For several weeks, carry a notebook in your pocket. Every time something happens that's painful, ironic, strange, or otherwise a potential joke, write it down. Try to come up with several dozen jokes. Practice delivering them in front of a mirror and, preferably, for a few friends. Ask them which ones they think are best. Memorize them and practice delivering them as a full routine in front of your mirror. After four to six weeks, find an amateur open mic night and perform. If you have an opportunity to perform through your improv comedy classes, that qualifies for this exercise too.

Chapter 15 – Lifestyle

At this point, you know everything you need to be a socially adept dude. You can make friends, be the life of the party, and meet dates. You're brimming with potential. The question is, how are you going to apply your knowledge? I have some suggestions.

1. Make a list of things you'd like to get better at.

2. Make a list of things you've always wanted to do.

3. Make a list of things you suck at, whether you want to do them or not.

Pick one item from each list. These three activities are your new hobbies, and through these hobbies, you will get out of your comfort zone and start meeting new friends and dates. You don't have to adopt all three hobbies at once, but over the next three months, you must get started on all three. Devote at least three hours per week to each of them. At the end of each month, you can stop one hobby, and you can choose another, but no matter what, you must be working on at least two hobbies in any given week.

Suggested Hobby Ideas

Take a look at the ideas below. The "individual" hobbies listed are ones you can pursue on your own, while "social" hobbies are ones that inherently involve other people. Individual hobbies can be social hobbies, but you'll need to put in some extra effort to find clubs that practice them.

Individual Hobbies

Painting	Sculpture	Photography	Fiction Writing	Philosophy
Math	Astronomy	Programming	Bodybuilding	Pottery

Singing	Baking	Cooking	Swimming	Electronics
Sewing	Knitting	Musical Instrument	Nonfiction Writing	YouTube Channel
Skiing	Snow-boarding	Scuba Diving	Skydiving	Scrapbooking
Glassblowing	Wood-working	Meditation	Fishing	History
Foreign Language	Travel	Drawing	Running	Reading
Free Running	Gardening	Car Restoration	Metalworking	Geocaching
Model Building	Leather-working	Archery	Hiking	Rock Climbing
Piloting	Magic	Brewing	Bicycling	Sailing
Birdwatching	Horseback Riding	Jewelry Making	Pole Dancing	Spelunking

Social Hobbies

Animal Welfare	Cosplay	Baseball	Improv Comedy	Standup Comedy
Theater	Card Games	Board Games	Dungeons and Dragons	Volunteer Work
Soccer	Ultimate Frisbee	LARPing	Salsa	Social Dancing
Group Dance	DJing	Volleyball	Badminton	Yoga
Martial Arts	Obstacle Courses	Dog Walking	Bowling	Gymnastics
Chess	Camping	Karaoke	Billiards	Paintball
Laser Tag	Fencing	Golf	Historical Reenacting	Squash
Watching Movies	Filmmaking	Go-Carts	Parkour Classes	Religion

Top 10 Hobbies

If you're looking for hobbies conducive to your self-improvement and dating pursuits, here's my Top 10 list for those purposes. I've included ratings for each one on how well they'll keep you fit, how effectively they can introduce you to women, and how well they'll help you improve your psychological health.

#10 Rock Climbing
Fitness: 5/5
Meet women: 3/5
Psych: 4/5
Overall: 4/5

Climbing is incredible. It's simultaneously gratifying and humbling. The more you do it, the stronger you'll get and the greater the challenges you'll face. If you're looking for an activity that works your brain as well as your body, there are few better.

#9 Music
Fitness: 1/5
Meet women: 4/5
Psych: 3/5
Overall: 3/5

Any kind of music will do—singing, guitar, piano, sax. The benefit and hazard of music is that it requires ridiculous amounts of practice. Your willpower will skyrocket, but it takes a lot of time. Once you start performing, you'll often be the center of attention, and you'll be inherently high status at your venues. If you're looking for a hobby that gets women to approach you, this is a good one.

#8 Martial Arts
Fitness: 5/5
Meet women: 3/5
Psych: 5/5
Overall: 4/5

A good martial arts school will teach you more than how to fight. It'll teach you to meditate, how to focus, how to establish habits, how to use your body, and how to assert yourself against threats. As with dance, you'll be watching yourself in the mirror for a few hours a week, and you won't be able to help but make friends with your sparring partners. Be wary; some martial arts schools are run by people who get off on dominating. You don't need them in your life. If you can find one with defensive, rather than aggressive values, it's gold.

#7 Parkour/Gymnastics
Fitness: 5/5
Meet women: 4/5
Psych: 4/5
Overall: 4/5

Parkour and gymnastics are like rock climbing. You will never run out of challenges. You will face your fears, you'll get in shape, and they're second only to solo dance as a means of improving your posture. There are plenty of women in these sports as well, especially gymnastics, and they're smart, ambitious, and physically attractive. If you get into slacklining, you'll find a great social community there too.

#6 Cooking
Fitness: 4/5
Meet women: 2/5
Psych: 3/5
Overall: 3/5

Being a good cook is invaluable. You can feed yourself, your dates, and others. If you're dieting for muscle growth or fat loss, meal planning gets a lot easier if you can prepare your own food. Cooking or baking together also makes a great date.

#5 Reading
Fitness: 1/5

Meet women: 2/5
Psych: 4/5
Overall: 3/5

I assume you already do this to some degree, since you've made it this far in this book. Reading is a cheap way to learn and improve yourself. If you do it a lot, your intelligence will skyrocket. It's the most cost-effective way to improve your mental strength.

#4 Weightlifting
Fitness: 5/5
Meet women: 3/5
Psych: 5/5
Overall: 4/5

The benefits of weightlifting are extraordinary. It's almost as effective as CBT at fighting depression. Your body will become more attractive. You will live longer and look younger. You will be stronger. There's a reason "bros" answer every problem by asking "Do you even lift?" While it's not the answer to everything, there's hardly anything it can't help with. As a guy looking to improve himself, you can't afford not to do it, which is why it has its own chapter in this book.

#3 Improv Comedy
Fitness: 1/5
Meet women: 4/5
Psych: 4/5
Overall: 4/5

Improvisational comedy is the single best "cross-training" for social skills. It teaches you to talk, listen, be funny, tell stories—and do it all under pressure. The closest substitute is acting classes, and they don't do the job as well. If you're lacking in social skills, this is your #1 choice.

#2 Dance
Fitness: 3/5
Meet women: 5/5

Psych: 4/5
Overall: 4/5

Any kind of dance will do. Social dancing is the single easiest way to meet women. Individual dancing will develop your bodily awareness and posture faster than any other practice, and women in those classes will outnumber you ten to one. What improv does for speaking, dance does for your nonverbal skills.

#1 Travel
Fitness: 2/5
Meet women: 5/5
Psych: 5/5
Overall: 5/5

This is the most expensive suggestion on this list, though with proper hostel planning and a willingness to visit Third World countries, it's not so daunting as you might think. I'm not talking about vacations in beachy resorts. Travel means visiting places with radically different cultures and lifestyles, and immersing yourself in them. Eat the local food. Learn the local language. Make foreign friends. Travel is unequaled as a tool to change your life, both for the lessons you will learn and for the opportunities to change your habits. You will grow in ways you can't imagine.

Love to Suck

When you start a new hobby, you're going to suck. The main difference between extraordinary performers and failures is that the extraordinary performers keep trying. Yes, there are sometimes differences in natural talent, but talent gets you only so far. We all eventually have to practice and push beyond our limits, and since people who suck have been working hard all along, sometimes it's easier for them than it is for the "geniuses."

Just as we want to divorce our self-esteem from the

approval of other people, it helps if we separate it from "success" at our hobbies. Are we taking risks? Are we getting out and trying? As long as we can say "Yes" to those questions, we're successful. If we can improve on how we were last week, cool. If we win competitions, also cool, but our worth doesn't depend on either. If we screw up, it's not failure; it's an opportunity for reevaluation and learning. When you're thinking this way, sucking is good. It's a sign that you're taking yourself out of your comfort zone, which is something most people never do. Be proud.

Building a Social Circle

Social circles are created when you combine social hobbies with all of the social skills we've discussed in this book. People like to spend time with other people, especially people who make them feel good. As long as you're meeting people, appreciating them, sharing with them something of value, and showing that you value their friendship, you will make friends. If you don't have a lot of social hobbies, you can still meet friends by looking for clubs centered on your individual hobbies. Look for rock-climbing clubs, book clubs, or events that focus on your other interests. People like people who are into the things they're into. When it's an activity that requires trust, such as anything team-based, it's even easier, since people who help us achieve our goals are natural allies. If you're not making friends in these settings, review the other chapters in part II, and consider asking someone what you're doing that's turning everyone off.

Once you're out and being social, don't stop. Keep going to the same groups and events at least once a week. Seeing the same people over and over again encourages everyone involved to like one another. It's called propinquity,[156] and it also plays a major role in sexual attraction. Ever notice how in high school people within a clique always seem to date one another? That's propinquity in action. We tend to like, and feel attracted to, the people we interact with most. If you're not making friends and finding dates, chances are it's because you're not seeing the same people often enough.

Finding Clubs and Activities

The Internet is an incredible resource for finding clubs and activities. If you're at a university, your school directory should have information about student groups. Otherwise, use Google. The website *meetup.com* is full of people trying to make friends and hook up. Find a group that interests you and go. You can start your own group if you want, though I'll warn you that running it will be a difficult and thankless job.

Setting Your Schedule

Part of the challenge of changing your lifestyle is fitting all this new stuff into your schedule. It isn't always easy, and your natural tendency will be to do nothing. Chapters 4 and 5 will help, but a little commitment and planning will make it easier. You need to prioritize and to budget your time.

Start by dividing your schedule into four categories:

• **Obligations** – stuff you have to do that's scheduled by other people (work, school)

• **Responsibilities** – stuff you have to do that's scheduled by you (sleep, eating, chores)

• **Social** – stuff you don't have to do that involves other people (clubs, sports)

• **Personal** – stuff you don't have to do that involves only you (video games, reading)

We want to keep the first category to a minimum. Cut as many obligations out of your life as you can. This may require heavy use of the assertiveness skills discussed in chapter 13. Negotiate shorter hours, change jobs, and say "No" to things you don't really want to do. Take whatever measures you can to maximize your unobligated time.

Next, whenever you can, automate your responsibilities. You want them to be as infrequent, simple, and low-energy as possible. If it takes a lot of time to pay your bills, see if you can automate them with your bank's "automatic payment" system. If your bank doesn't have one, change banks. Wash your dishes as you cook so you don't have a big pile to do after you eat. Anything you can do in less than five minutes, do immediately. If there's something you don't know how to automate, Google for advice. Someone else might have found a way. If you have more than eighteen hours per day of obligations and responsibilities after this cutting (including work and sleep), review your efforts. You may be able to cut more.

With that done, look over your schedule and take an inventory of your free time each week. Schedule at least one full evening (or equivalent) per week to do absolutely nothing. This time is yours, and it's non-negotiable. Use it to rest, sleep, and pamper yourself. This is your "I love me" time. Once you've dealt with your obligations, this needs to be the highest priority in your week.

The rest of your week is open for whatever activities you'd like. Block out time for your three hobbies and keep a couple of evenings per week open for spontaneous activities such as dates, visiting friends, or extra rest. Maybe Mondays and Wednesdays you have two-hour martial arts classes. Saturdays, you do one three-hour climbing session. On Thursdays, you have a salsa class, followed by two hours in the club. This leaves you with Tuesday evenings for dates, Friday and Saturday evenings for fun, and all of Sunday for "me time" and chores. Schedule things however they work for you, but make sure you have a plan. If you're working a normal 9–5, Mondays through Wednesdays are often best for your hobbies, and Fridays and Saturdays are best to leave open, since those are the evenings when other people tend to plan things. Thursdays can go either way. Here's what my daily routine looks like:

5:15 a.m. – 5:45 a.m.– Wake up, eat pre-workout meal
5:45 a.m. – 6:00 a.m. – Leave for gym
6:00 a.m. – 6:45 a.m. – Lifting
6:45 a.m.– 7:15 a.m. – Return home, shower, post-workout meal
7:15 a.m.– 8:00 a.m. – Travel to work
8:00 a.m. – 12:00 p.m. – Work
12:00 p.m. – 12:30 p.m. – Lunch
12:30 p.m. – 4:30 p.m. – Work
4:30 p.m. – 5:15 p.m. – Travel to home
5:15 p.m. – 10:00 p.m. – Hobby/social/personal time (depending on the day)
10:00 p.m. – 5:15 a.m. – Sleep

That 5:15–10:00 p.m. slot has varied, but it has included improv comedy classes, singing lessons, karate classes, parkour classes, rock climbing, shopping, dates, parties, cooking, Dungeons and Dragons games, early bedtimes, and more. You don't have to do the same things I do, but whatever you choose, budget the time for it. Apathy and laziness are black holes that will always try to pull you in, and if you don't plan to resist, you won't.

Chapter Summary

• List things you love, things you'd like to improve at, and things you suck at. Do some of each.

• Sucking is a sign that you're getting out of your comfort zone. Embrace it.

• Use the Internet to find clubs and activities to join.

• Minimize obligations and responsibilities. Devote at least one evening a week to rest.

Exercises

Exercise 15.1 – Immediate – Make Your Lists
Make the lists mentioned at the top of the chapter. What do you want to get better at? What haven't you done that you'd like to do? What do you suck at? Choose one item from each list and make these items your new hobbies. If you can, make at least one of them a social hobby.

Exercise 15.2 – Immediate – Research Your New Hobbies
Start looking for resources for each of the three hobbies chosen in Exercise 15.1. Seek out local clubs and classes you can join. Look on *Amazon.com* for informational books, or on YouTube for instructional videos. Write an entry in your journal describing how you will go about learning each of these new hobbies.

Exercise 15.3 – One Time – Clear Your Schedule
Write out your current daily routine. Label each item as an obligation, a responsibility, a social activity, or a personal activity. Brainstorm ways to cut down on how much time you're spending on your obligations and responsibilities. Of your current social and personal activities, what can you eliminate to make room for your new hobbies? Write an entry in your journal listing the specific steps you will take to make the changes you want. Schedule your first two weeks with your new hobbies. Remember, you don't need to adopt all three hobbies at once.

Exercise 15.4 – Ongoing – Implement the Plan
Begin taking the steps you outlined in Exercise 15.3. Document your progress in your journal. How successful have you been at cutting down on obligations and responsibilities? What techniques have you found effective? What hasn't worked? How was your first effort with your first new hobby?

Exercise 15.5 – One Time – Write about Sucking

After your first effort in a new hobby, write about how things went. What went well? What could be improved? How did it feel? Reread the "Love to Suck" section of this chapter and write an entry in your journal reminding yourself of why it's okay, and even good, to be struggling in your new hobby. Congratulate yourself for taking your first step.

Exercise 15.6 – Ongoing – Make New Friends
At each of your social hobbies, make it a point to chat with at least one person you meet. Learn names and practice the social skills discussed in part II. Ask for contact info and reach out to these people on social media.

Exercise 15.7 – One Time – Organize Your First Outing
After you've spent three to four weeks getting involved in your new hobbies, and with several new contacts, use social media, text messaging, and any other methods at your disposal to invite your new friends (and any old friends) out to do something fun. Go to an arcade, go bowling, sing karaoke, play laser tag. The activity should be as low cost and easy to get to as possible. Do not pay for your friends. Do not offer transportation unless they ask. If no one shows up, don't be discouraged. It's part of the growing process. Continue your hobbies and continue meeting new people. Try again in several weeks.

Part III: Physical Appearance

Chapter 16 – Exercise

If you want to be more physically attractive, exercise is the best way to achieve it. Fit bodies are sexy. Good health makes you better at sex, helps your self-esteem,[157] and makes you smarter.[158] Best of all, if you exercise you are being compassionate toward yourself, and this will create cognitive dissonance with any "I'm worthless" beliefs you've still got floating around.

To be successful at exercising, you'll want to make it a habit, and as we talked about in chapter 5, that habit will be easier to form if you focus on exercise's intrinsic rewards. No alarms go off to alert women that you just finished leg day, so if you're working out to impress women, your reward will be inconsistent, and you'll struggle. Treat working out as its own reward. Focus on the good feelings you get from doing it. You're improving yourself. The endorphins feel great. By lifting that pile of metal for an hour, you're helping your psyche, your health, and your strength. Give yourself kudos and let those good feelings be your motivator.

Setting the Plan

Your first step in starting your workouts is setting your implementation intention. Find a suitable spot in your routine where a one-hour workout can fit, and then create as specific a cue as possible. When I started lifting, my implementation intention was "If I wake up in my own bed, I will go to the gym." When I switched to rock climbing and parkour, it became "When I leave work, I will go to the gym." Find an action in your routine that you perform every day, connect your workouts to it, and let that routine become the new default.

When you have an implementation intention in mind, brainstorm what temptations might keep you from getting to the gym. For example, when I was working out in the morning, my biggest struggle was being too tired. Try to come up with a contingency plan. "When I'm tired, I'll have an energy drink." "When I'm tired, I'll listen to some music to pump me up." The longer you can keep up your routine, the more compelling your habit will be, and before long, lifting at that time every day will be part of who you are.

Record Your Progress

Lifting weights is hard work, and the benefits come slowly. At times, you'll feel as if you're rowing against the tide, you'll get discouraged, and your willpower will give out. One of the best ways to avoid this is to monitor the things that change every week—namely, the amount you're lifting and the number of reps. You might not notice the fraction of an inch of increased thickness in your bicep, but you will notice that you can do one more rep than you could last week. Bring a notebook and a pen with you to the gym to keep track of your weight level and reps per set. You can use a smartphone if you want, though I find them distracting. Make a grid on each page that shows what routine you're doing, the date, the exercises, and the weights and reps of each exercise. It should look like this:

Routine and Date
Exercise 1: Weight, # reps 1, # reps 2, # reps 3
Exercise 2: Weight, # reps 1, # reps 2, # reps 3
Exercise 3: Weight, # reps 1, # reps 2, # reps 3
Exercise 4: Weight, # reps 1, # reps 2, # reps 3
Exercise 5: Weight, # reps 1, # reps 2, # reps 3

Here's an example:
Day 1 (11/30)
Incline Bench Press: 190, 5, 5, 4
Flat Bench Press: 210, 5, 5, 5
Close Grip Bench Press: 190, 4, 4, 4
Military Press: 90, 5, 5, 5
Deadlift: 240, 6, 250, 4, 4
Pull-Ups: 20, 5, 5, 5
Chin-Ups: 20, 6, 5, 5

Even if it's only one more rep in each exercise, you should be seeing progress every time you go. The changes may be small, but they add up, and if you ever feel like nerding out and graphing them, a year of work can look pretty impressive. It helps you plan your commitment, keeps you motivated, and keeps you from having to think too much in the gym.

The Three Pillars of Building a Great Body

When you lift a weight, you're putting your muscles under stress, and that stress causes tiny injuries called "microtears" in your muscles. When your body heals those microtears, they heal bigger and stronger than they were before, which is how we develop strength. This process is called hypertrophy.[159] The goal of lifting is to stress our muscles enough to create lots of those little tears. If you're not lifting hard enough to do that, you're wasting your time. Second, if your body doesn't have the nutrients it needs to heal those tears, not only will your muscles not grow, they might get weaker, so you have to make sure you're eating enough to give your body what it needs. Finally, if you start tearing up your muscles before they've healed from your previous workout, that can screw things up too, so you want to give yourself plenty of rest. In short, building a strong, healthy, attractive body takes lifting right, eating well, and resting enough. Ignore any one of those three pillars and you're wasting your time.

Guidelines on How to Lift

Use Free Weights Instead of Machines

While machines are better than nothing, most of the scientific evidence indicates that exercising with free weights gets better results faster, even when compared to a Smith machine.[160] Free weights are more dangerous if you're not using proper form, so it's important to know what you're doing. Books such as *Starting Strength* by Mark Rippetoe are excellent resources to learn how to lift properly, but I recommend that you get some direct professional help on this one. Hire a trainer to teach you the basics. It should take only a few weeks and it won't break the bank. Ask the trainer to focus on free weights and form, especially with the exercises discussed in this chapter, and you should be good to go.

Favor Compound Exercises over Isolation Exercises

Compound exercises, such as the deadlift, are lifts that involve large groups of muscles acting in tandem. Isolation exercises, such as bicep curls, focus on a single muscle group. In research comparing compound-lift workouts to workouts with additional isolation exercises, the isolation exercises contributed nothing.[161] Compound lifts were responsible for all the progress. Isolation exercises have some uses, but the bench press, deadlift, squat, pull-up, and military press should be your bread and butter. If you have no idea what those are, check out the exercises at the end of this chapter; I've included links to instructional videos.

Lift Heavy If You're Advanced, Moderately If You're a Novice

Arguments over whether it's better to lift heavy weights with fewer reps and more sets or to lift lighter weights with more reps and fewer sets are among the fiercest in the sport. Traditional gym lore suggests that lifting in a weight range permitting eight to twelve repetitions per set is the optimal amount for hypertrophy. Others claim that a heavier range will build strength and muscle faster, while still others insist that a range permitting twenty to thirty reps is where it's at.

The truth is that I can't make one universal proclamation for all weightlifters. According to the American College of Sports Medicine, the right style of lifting can vary considerably depending on how experienced you are. Novice weightlifters tend to achieve the greatest hypertrophy by lifting moderate loads (70-85% of their one-rep-max) with eight to twelve repetitions per set for one to three sets per exercise. When working in this way, exercising two or three days per week with total body training is the best approach.[162]

For more experienced lifters, lifting heavier weights with fewer repetitions per set is unambiguously superior.[163] In this case, the American College of Sports Medicine recommends a weight range between seventy and one-hundred percent of your one-rep-max, with one to twelve repetitions per set and three to six sets per exercise. Personally, I work in the four to six rep range around eighty-five percent of my one-rep-max. Lifting with heavy weights also has the advantage of better increasing your metabolism when compared to lighter weights, which can help with fat loss.[164]

You will need to make your own judgment on which approach is right for you. If you've never worked out in your life, take the novice approach for at least a year. If you're experienced, switching to a heavier routine will earn you better results faster. If you have no idea what to do, consider hiring a personal trainer for a few sessions and ask for their professional opinion.

Rest Three to Four Minutes Between Sets If You're Advanced, Two to Three If You're a Novice

For heavy compound weightlifting, evidence indicates

that longer rest periods between sets achieve greater muscle growth than short rests due to an improved capacity for exertion. We can achieve the best results by resting no fewer than three and no more than four minutes between sets.[165] If you're lifting lighter, resting this much won't hurt you, but you'll be fine with two to three minutes.

Split Your Routine With Nine to Twelve Sets per Muscle Group If You're Advanced

An analysis of several weight-lifting studies conducted by Mathias Wernborn and his colleagues found that achieving a total volume of thirty to sixty repetitions per week per muscle group maximizes hypertrophy.[166] If you're a novice, splitting these repetitions into three total-body workouts per week with one to three sets per muscle group per workout should get you in that range. If you're an advanced lifter, you will need nine to twelve sets per muscle group per week to hit your numbers. This can be overwhelming as a total-body workout, and for this reason, the American College of Sports Medicine recommends splitting your workouts between muscle groups and performing four to six workouts per week.[167] You can perform all thirty to sixty repetitions in one workout, but dividing them between two separate days will lead to superior results.

Rest Your Muscles For Three Days If You're Advanced, Two Days If You're a Novice

One study of muscle recovery indicated that it can take anywhere from forty-eight to ninety-six hours for muscles to recover, depending on the nature of the workout and individual factors, including diet, sleep, hormones, and genetics.[168] When subjects engaged in more intense workouts, seventy percent were not fully recovered even after four days.[169] If you're following the suggestions in this chapter for advanced lifters, I thus suggest erring on the side of more recovery. Avoid working a muscle group any more frequently than once every three days, and make sure to have at least one full day of total rest per week. If you're a novice, feel free to do your full body work out every other day. If you need to take some extended time off, don't worry; your muscles won't atrophy. Humans can go at least five weeks without exercise without any measurable losses in muscle or strength.[170]

Progressive Overload

As we get stronger, we need to subject our muscles to increasing resistance in order to continue their development. This is called progressive overload.[171] The easiest way to achieve this is to add weight to your bars as you increase the number of reps you can perform. When you add five pounds to a dumbbell, ten pounds to a barbell, or twenty pounds to the leg press, it will usually cost you two reps on each set. If I start my bench press with 180 pounds on the bar and pull off six reps, I can raise it to 190 pounds and expect to do four on the next set.

Start the first set of each exercise with the weight you were able to lift in your last workout. Your goal is to do one more rep per set than you did last time. If, on your first set, you are able to do six reps if you're experienced, or ten reps if you're a novice, go up five pounds on your dumbbells, ten pounds on your barbell, or twenty pounds on the leg press. For your remaining sets, you're aiming for four reps or eight reps respectively. At your next workout, start with the same weight, but aim for one more rep than you did last time on your first lift. Following this approach, you should be increasing the weight every three to four weeks.

Lift Fast, Not Slowly

The more slowly you perform your reps, the more tension your muscles will endure and the fewer reps you'll be able to do. Some maintain that this sustained tension is a more effective way to build muscle, but the evidence suggests otherwise. The smaller number of reps appears to cost us more in muscle growth than the sustained tension gives us back.[172] As such, fast training with heavy weight leads to greater gains in strength than slow training.[173]

All this means is that you shouldn't intentionally slow down your lifting pace. The proper pace is quite natural. Aim for a tempo of "2-1-2." It should take two seconds to lower the bar to your chest, one second to pause, and then two seconds to lift it back up. Keep a similar pace with all of your compound lifts and you'll be in the right ballpark.

Do Not Stretch Before Lifting; Warm Up Dynamically

Stretching before exercise impairs performance,[174] doesn't prevent injury,[175] and may increase the odds of one occurring.[176] Static stretching is an excellent way to increase flexibility, but you shouldn't do it before lifting or other athletic activities. Stretch after your workout, or at a different time altogether.

Instead of stretching, do a dynamic warmup.[177] You want to increase blood flow to the muscles you'll be using and get them used to lifting the kind of weight you'll be subjecting them to. Do several sets of your primary compound exercise at 50 percent of the weight you will be lifting. When your heart's beating faster and you're feeling warm, you're ready to go.

Exercises

Chest

The bench press is by far the best exercise to work your chest.[178] The flat bench press works the entire chest; however, the upper part of the chest, the clavicular pectoralis, has muscle fibers moving in different directions from the pectoralis major, and growth can be stubborn. To emphasize the upper chest, do the incline bench press.[179] The flat bench press hits the lower chest just as well as the decline bench press, so doing the decline isn't necessary.[180]

• Incline bench press (barbell or dumbbell)

• Flat bench press (barbell or dumbbell)

Back

The deadlift is the lord of lifts. It works more muscles than any other exercise and happens to be the best exercise for the back.[181] It has a bad name because people who do it improperly frequently injure themselves. Make sure you learn proper form.

It usually makes sense to group our lats (the muscles along our rib cages under our armpits that stretch around your back) with your deadlift exercises. We work our lats best with pull-ups and lateral pull-downs.

• Barbell deadlift

• Barbell or Dumbbell row

• Pull-ups (weighted if possible)

• Lateral pull-downs

Shoulders

Our shoulder muscles are composed of three "heads": the posterior, anterior, and rear deltoids. The military press hits all of them, and we can do it seated, standing, with a barbell, or with dumbbells. I prefer seated barbell presses. Avoid any presses that place the bar behind the neck, as this can lead to injury. If you need additional work on your shoulders, they can benefit from isolating each head with shoulder raises.

• Barbell military press or dumbbell shoulder press (standing or seated)

• Dumbbell side lateral raises

• Dumbbell rear delt raises (seated or bent over)

• Dumbbell front raises

Legs

By "legs," I am referring to our quadriceps, hamstrings, and glutes (butt). We will work our calves separately. For these muscles, the squat is king. We can perform both front and back squats (named for where we position the bar), though I prefer back squats. In addition to the squat, we will use the Romanian deadlift, also known as the straight-leg deadlift, which emphasizes the hamstrings. We will also use the leg press.

• Barbell back squat

• Barbell front squat

• Leg press

• Romanian (straight leg) deadlift

Triceps

When doing bench presses, we can emphasize our triceps by moving our grips inward. The wider our arms are when doing our presses, the more we emphasize our chest and the less we emphasize our arms. To work triceps, do the reverse. The seated tricep press is also a solid choice.

• Close-grip bench press

• Seated tricep press

Biceps

Curling motions and chin-ups work our biceps best. You can curl with a barbell, E-Z bar, or dumbbells. I prefer dumbbell curls and chin-ups.

• Chin-ups (weighted if possible)

• Barbell curls

• E-Z bar curls

• Dumbbell curls

Calves

Some people have stubborn calves; others have naturally huge ones. How much you struggle with calves is genetic, and you're limited in how much you can do. The difference lies in the type of muscle fibers that make up the bulk of your calf muscles. Type I muscle fibers are designed for endurance and low force output, and tend to be smaller.

Type II fibers are built for high force but are easily fatigued, and tend to be larger. Men with a high concentration of type I fibers will always struggle to grow their calves. In either case, progressive overload and heavy lifting are still the way to make them grow fastest, and since they recover more quickly than other muscles, you can work them twice or even three times per week with few issues.

• Seated calf raises

• Calf press on the leg press

Abs

You'll often hear lifters say they never work abs because squats and deadlifts already work the core. Others work abs, but only through body-weight exercises such as crunches. Ab muscles follow the same rules as the muscles in the rest of your body. They require progressive overload to grow. While exercises such as the deadlift and the squat are excellent for working some of the core muscles,[182] they don't hit the rectus abdominus, the transverse abdominus, and the external obliques very well, and these are the muscles we associate with that sexy six-pack.[183] To engage these muscles, the best exercises are air bicycles and the "captain's chair" leg lifts,[184] the latter of which you can do weighted and thus progressively overload. Crunches are less effective, but still helpful, and we can use the cable crunch to progressively overload them.

• Captain's chair leg raises (weighted if possible)

• Hanging leg raises (weighted if possible)

• Cable crunches

• Air bicycles

• Decline crunches

Cardio

The focus of our discussion on cardiovascular exercise will be in regard to building muscle and burning fat as quickly as possible. If you have a different goal in mind, such as becoming a long-distance runner, this advice doesn't apply.

Training for endurance while trying to build muscle is difficult. Doing so sends mixed signals to our muscles, leading to lackluster results on both fronts.[185] The longer the cardio session, the more it interferes with strength development and hypertrophy.[186] We thus want to keep our cardio sessions as short and intense as possible. To this end, high intensity interval training (HIIT) is the way to go. When compared to steady-state cardio (jogging vs. sprinting), subjects doing HIIT burned more fat.[187] It increases our basal metabolic rate for a longer period following the workout (the "afterburn effect"),[188] and better suppresses our appetites.[189] For these reasons, it's the superior choice for our purposes.

There are many types of HIIT. Anything involving short bursts of intense exercise separated by short breaks can qualify. This can mean sprinting, rowing, jumping rope, pedaling, or whatever you like best. Exercises that resemble your lifting, such as rowing and pedaling, tend to work better.[190] Whatever you choose, try to do your HIIT separately from your lifting. If you have to do them together, do the HIIT after the lifting, so you're at full strength for your lifts. You should be able to recover fully from cardio within twenty-four to forty-eight hours, so feel free to do HIIT four to five times per week when you're burning fat. If you're just looking to maintain your level of fitness, twice is sufficient.

Chapter Summary

• Set implementation intentions to make working out a habit.

• Track your progress.

• Focus on heavy, compound lifts with free weights.

• Progressively overload your muscles.

• Design a workout routine appropriate for your level of experience.

• Do a dynamic warmup before you lift.

• Incorporate HIIT to burn additional calories.

Exercises

Exercise 16.1 – Immediate – Look Up the Exercises

Go to *Bodybuilding.com* and watch the videos for each of the exercises discussed in this chapter. Pay close attention to the models' form and their suggestions.

Incline Bench Press
Flat Bench Press
Incline Dumbbell Press
Flat Dumbbell Press
Close-Grip Bench Press
Seated Tricep Press
Barbell Curl
E-Z-Bar Curl
Dumbbell Curl
Chin-Up
Deadlift
Barbell Row
Pull-Ups
Lateral Pull-Downs
Barbell Military Press
Dumbbell Shoulder Press
Front Dumbbell Raises
Side Lateral Raises
Rear Delt Raises
Barbell Squat
Front Squat
Leg Press
Romanian Deadlift
Seated Calf Raises
Calf Press on Leg Press
Captain's Chair Leg Raises
Hanging Leg Raises
Cable Crunches

Decline Crunches
Air Bicycles

Exercise 16.2 – Immediate – Develop a Workout Routine

This chapter outlines everything you need to know to build a workout routine. If you would like sample workouts for novice and intermediate lifters that follow the suggestions here, an Excel spreadsheet is available at *thehotguyde.com/resources*. For additional workout resources, I recommend *Bigger Leaner Stronger* by Mike Matthews, *Starting Strength* by Mark Rippetoe, or *aworkoutroutine.com*, all of which feature excellent suggestions based on peer-reviewed material.

Exercise 16.3 – Ongoing – Start Working Out

Decide on an implementation intention and a specific time in your day when you'll start working out. Start monitoring your workout progress in your notebook.

Chapter 17 – Diet and Nutrition

The Basics of Nutrition

Good nutrition means making sure your body has everything it needs to do the stuff you want to do. If you're following the workouts discussed in chapter 16, that means lifting, plus whatever other physical activities you've taken on. If you're looking to burn fat, you'll need to cut down on your food intake a bit, but you'll still need to make sure you're getting the nutrition you need to develop muscle. For our purposes, we're primarily interested in the four macronutrients: protein, carbohydrates, dietary fat, and fiber. As long as you're eating a diverse diet, your micronutrients should be fine.

Protein

According to the Institute of Medicine, 10 to 35 percent of our daily calories should come from protein.[191] This is a big range, and as weightlifters, we'll need more protein than the average person to build our muscles. Research suggests between 1.3 and 1.8 grams of protein per kilogram of body weight is optimal for protein synthesis, with perhaps more for athletes.[192] Research concerned specifically with athletes dieting to lose fat found that 2.3 to 3.1 grams per kilogram of body weight was best for this end.[193] These are the numbers we'll be using for those purposes respectively.

Not all proteins are created equal. To determine what proteins are best for providing the amino acids (protein building blocks) you need to build muscle, we can refer to their Protein Digestibility Corrected Amino Acid (PDCAA) score. A score of 1.0 is perfect.

Food	PDCAA Score
Whey	1.0
Eggs	1.0
Soy	1.0
Beef	0.92
Peas	0.73
Oats	0.57
Peanuts	0.52
Wheat Gluten	0.25

Dairy products and meat are your best sources of protein, with nuts and some vegetables coming in second. Favor lean meats whenever possible, as fattier meats will make it harder for you to stay within your calorie limits. If you're a vegetarian, you're in for a tougher time, but don't worry. You have a few options we'll discuss shortly.

A quarter-pound hamburger contains 19 grams of protein. For an 180-pound man to hit his 1.3 grams per kilogram requirement for protein synthesis, he'd have to eat six burgers. That's a lot of food, and that's the minimum. If you're deliberate about your diet planning (eggs for breakfast, meat for lunch and dinner), it's possible to hit your numbers through food, but for many of us, it can help to add in some supplements.

The most popular protein supplements on the market today are whey, casein, egg, soy, rice and pea, and hemp. Whey rules the pack by a fair margin, and for good reason. Not only does it have a perfect PDCAA score, but your body absorbs it more quickly than any of its competitors.[194]

Protein	Grams Absorbed per Hour
Whey	8–10
Casein	6.1

Soy	3.9
Egg	1.3

Whey's rapid absorption makes it ideal as a post-workout supplement, as it immediately gives your body the protein it needs for muscle repair[195] and stimulates faster immediate protein synthesis than products that are absorbed more slowly.[196] It's also rich in leucine, one of the most vital amino acids for protein synthesis and muscle growth.[197] Some evidence suggests that slower-absorbing proteins (like casein) result in less protein breakdown and superior leucine absorption when compared to their faster competitors, and thus may make superior general supplements.[198] My suggestion is to use whey immediately after your workouts and to favor a slower-absorbing protein, like casein or egg, for any supplementation beyond that.

For those of you who are vegans, you might be looking at those PDCAA scores and figure soy is your best option. While soy is absorbed slowly and has a perfect PDCAA score, it has problems. Soy contains estrogen-like molecules called isoflavones that can alter men's hormone levels. One study showed a reduction in sperm count associated with soy and isoflavone consumption,[199] though other studies called those findings into question.[200] Soy's hormonal effects seem to depend on the presence or absence of certain intestinal bacteria living in thirty to fifty percent of humans that metabolize isoflavones into equol, an estrogen-like hormone.[201] Due to this possible health effect, I can't advise using soy protein.

If soy isn't an option, how about hemp? While hemp protein has none of the potential negative side-effects we see in soy, with a PDCAA score of 0.46,[202] it isn't a great option either. As a vegan, your best bet is rice and pea protein. While neither ingredient is impressive by itself, when combined they have a perfect PDCAA score and contain large amounts of leucine.[203] This mixture is often called "vegan's whey" for this reason, and is by far the best vegetarian supplement for our purposes.

Carbohydrates

There are lots of "diet gurus" out there who love to target carbs as the source of all obesity woes. Unfortunately for those who follow such crazes, they have no scientific merit. Studies showing the effectiveness of low-carb diets tend to replace carbohydrates with high levels of protein without replicating similar levels in control groups. Studies that have kept protein levels equal showed no superior results among low-carb diets.[204] In other words, it isn't the low-carb part of the diet that helps people lose weight; it's the high protein.

If that's the case, why not simply follow one of the low-carb diets that are high in protein? Eating sufficient carbs is necessary for our survival and valuable for weightlifting. Failing to eat sufficient carbs can inhibit the signals necessary for cellular growth, limiting muscle development.[205] They're also necessary to manufacture glycogen, an energy-storage compound our muscles tap into when we work out.[206] These factors are likely why research has found that low-carb dieters lose more strength; recover more slowly; and show lower rates of protein synthesis, higher rates of muscle breakdown, and overall less muscle growth than their competitors[207] — problems that all disappear when the subjects eat sufficient carbs.[208] Low-carb dieting also increases levels of the stress hormone cortisol while decreasing testosterone, both of which disrupt muscle development.[209]

Of course, not all carbs are equal. One way to evaluate our carbs is to see where they fall on the glycemic index, which ranks carbs according to how quickly they're absorbed by your body. Lower numbers mean they're absorbed slowly, while higher numbers indicate rapid absorption.

Food	Glycemic Index Rating

Glucose	100
Coca-Cola	63
Plain bagel	72
Graham crackers	74
Jelly beans	80
Strawberries	32
Whole milk	30
Red baked potato	93

If you can get the bulk of your carbohydrate calories from low-GI foods, you'll have more consistent energy levels across your day. Low-GI foods also tend to be denser in micronutrients. If you're about to work out, eating something sugary is fine and will give you a quick burst of energy,[210] and there's nothing inherently unhealthy about high-GI foods, but in general, if you can get most of your carbohydrate calories from oats, whole grains, quinoa, brown rice, and similar products, you'll be better off.

Dietary Fat

When "diet gurus" aren't demonizing carbs, they're attacking fats, and once again, following explicitly "low fat diets" can present a variety of hazards, especially for weightlifters. Low fat diets have been associated with lower levels of testosterone[211] and hindered athletic performance,[212] both of which are remedied with sufficient fat intake. Aim for between 20 and 40 percent of your daily calories to come from fat, more when you're bulking, less when you're cutting. This will keep your diet enjoyable and your hormone levels stable.

Both monounsaturated fats (from sources like olive oil and avocados) and polyunsaturated fats (from sources like walnuts, canola oil, and flax seeds) are quite healthy and can be eaten freely within the limits described above. There was a time when saturated fat showed signs of connection with heart disease; however, recent research shows no evidence of such a connection.[213] The American Heart Association suggests that saturated fat making up five to six percent of our daily caloric intake is fine.[214] Eat all three types of fat as part of your daily intake and you'll be in good shape.

There is another type of fat, called trans fat, which was invented for easier cross-country transport. It tends to be found in processed foods. Trans fats are associated with heart disease, insulin resistance, systemic inflammation, diabetes, and other problems.[215] The Institute of Medicine recommends consuming as few of them as possible.[216] If the nutrition label contains any at all, don't buy that item.

Fiber

Fiber is great. It reduces cancer risk,[217] heart disease risk, and LDL (bad) cholesterol levels.[218] It improves blood-sugar control, can increase weight loss, helps prevent weight gain, and decreases the risk of type 2 diabetes.[219] It's pretty simple: eat lots of fiber and you will live a longer, healthier life.[220]

The Institute of Medicine suggests that men should eat thirty-eight grams of fiber per day.[221] To do this, eat fruit instead of drinking fruit juice. Choose whole-grain cereals, pastas, and breads rather than white, processed versions. When you snack, eat vegetables instead of chips. Healthy food can be just as tasty as junk food; it just requires a little more creativity.

Water

According to the Institute of Medicine, men should consume 125 ounces (about a gallon) of water each day.[222] This includes the water in our food, which constitutes about one-fifth of the water in our diets, so we can cut this number down to 100 ounces (about twelve eight-ounce cups). Our needs are higher when exercising, so aim to drink a little more than that. Keep a full bottle of water near you at all times and drink from it regularly. When your urine's consistently running almost clear, you're getting enough water.

Micronutrients

It's best to get the bulk of your vitamins and minerals from nutrient-dense foods, and by eating a varied diet, you should be able to meet your micronutrient needs. Plenty of health gurus will recommend multivitamins, but there's little evidence of their benefits.[223] As Steven Salzberg, professor of medicine at Johns Hopkins University, puts it, "Supplementation with extra vitamins or micronutrients doesn't really benefit you if you don't have a deficiency."[224] Your doctor can determine nutritional deficiencies with a blood test (vitamin D is a common one), and if your doctor says you need a supplement, listen. Otherwise, don't waste your money.

Calculating Calories

The first step in planning your diet is to figure out how many calories you burn per day. To do this, you'll need to calculate your basal metabolic rate (BMR), which is the energy you burn every day by being alive.

Start by weighing yourself. Next, measure your body fat percentage, either by using a pair of calipers or with a bioelectrical impedance fat-loss monitor. Calculate your lean body mass (LBM) using the following equation: LBM = (1 − body-fat percentage expressed as a decimal) x total body weight. For example, if Jan weighs 180 pounds and has 20% body fat, his lean body mass is (1 − 0.2) x 180 = 144 lbs. Convert your LBM to kilograms by multiplying it by 0.454, and then calculate your BMR using the Katch-McArdle formula: BMR = 370 + (21.6 x LBM in kilograms). In Jan's case, it would be 370 + (21.6 x 65.38) = 1,412 calories per day.

With your BMR in hand, you can get an idea of how many total calories you burn per day. Your total daily energy expenditure (TDEE) is your BMR plus the energy you burn from your physical activity. You can estimate this pretty well

as follows:
- Light exercise (one to three hours per week): 1.2 x BMR
- Moderate exercise (four to six hours/week): 1.35 x BMR
- Heavy exercise (more than six hours/week): 1.5 x BMR

If Jan worked out five hours per day (moderate exercise), his TDEE would be 1,906. If Jan eats more than this number, he'll gain wait. If he eats less, he'll lose weight.

Calculating Macronutrients

Calculating your ideal macronutrient ratios depends on what you're trying to achieve. Generally speaking, you'll want around 20% of your calories to come from protein, 30% from fat, and 50% from carbs. When you're bulking, you'll want to be eating about 110 percent of your TDEE, with most of that increase coming from more carbs. When you're cutting, you'll want to be eating around 80 percent of your TDEE, with a heavier emphasis on protein and far smaller amounts of carbs and fats. Your personal numbers will vary, but to get a ballpark estimate, the chart below shows how many grams of each macronutrient you should eat per pound of body weight:

Maintenance		Build Muscle		Cut Fat	
Nutrient	Grams/ Pound	Nutrient	Grams/ Pound	Nutrient	Grams/ Pound
Protein	1	Protein	1	Protein	1.2
Carbs	1.6	Carbs	2	Carbs	1
Fat	0.35	Fat	0.4	Fat	0.2

The total calories calculated here may or may not match up with your TDEE calculation, so adjust your numbers proportionally. If you'd like help calculating these numbers, a link to an excellent macronutrient calculator is available at *thehotguyde.com/resources*. Keep in mind that both your TDEE and macronutrient ratio calculations are approximations, so as you track your progress, feel free to make adjustments to your diet as needed. If you're losing strength, eat more carbs. If you're hungry all the time, eat more protein. If you start experiencing strange emotional changes, eat more fat. If you're not making progress, eat more or less in general as needed.

Monitoring Progress

If you have less than 20 percent body fat and you're looking to lose weight, you can expect to lose between half a pound and a pound per week. Anything more rapid than that will tend to sacrifice muscle. If you have more fat than that to lose, you can expect as much as two or three pounds per week. If you're bulking, you can expect to gain half a pound to one pound of muscle per week, with one pound of fat to go with it. If you're new to lifting, you'll gain weight even faster as your muscles fill up with water and glycogen, but your rate will slow down over time. If you're eating a maintenance diet and still lifting, you can expect to gain around half a pound of muscle per month.

Your weight will fluctuate by several pounds every day. Don't let this bother you. To get consistent readings, weigh yourself under similar conditions every day. I recommend doing it immediately after waking up, naked, and after peeing. At the end of each week, take the average of the seven days. This will help control for things that vary each day, like water weight. When your weekly average rises or falls, that's how you'll know if you're making progress.

Meal Planning

I won't recommend any specific diets here. As long as you're favoring micronutrient-rich foods and hitting your numbers, you can eat whatever you want. For monitoring purposes, there are a few tools you can use to help you at *thehotguyde.com/resources*.

If you're dieting to lose weight, look for simple changes you can make that will carve extra calories out of your diet without making you feel much hungrier. Do you regularly drink soda or juice? Cut out all your "liquid calories." Used to whole milk products? Switch to low-fat versions. Eating lots of starchy food? How about cutting out the potatoes and eating a little more meat? If designing your meal plan seems too daunting, there are plenty of services out there to help you. Make a regular meal plan, hire someone to do it for you, or just eat what you want and monitor your intake. All of these methods work fine.

Chapter Summary

• Burn more calories than you eat and you will lose weight.

• Eat protein to develop muscle, and favor protein with high PDCAA scores and leucine.

• Carbohydrates provide your muscles with glycogen. Eat them, especially low-GI carbs.

• Eat a balance of monounsaturated, polyunsaturated, and saturated fat. Avoid trans fat.

• Eat plenty of fiber.

• Drink plenty of water—around one gallon per day.

• Plan your meals to hit your macronutrient goals. Monitor your caloric intake.

• Measure your weight every morning and take the weekly average to track progress.

Exercises

Exercise 17.1 – Immediate – Calculate Your TDEE and Macronutrient Breakdown

Use the information presented in this chapter to calculate your

TDEE and daily macronutrient needs to reach your goals.

Exercise 17.2 – Ongoing – Track Your Weight
Hang a weight log above your scale and start tracking your weight as described in this chapter, immediately after you wake, after peeing, and in the nude. A template is available at *thehotguyde.com/resources*.

Exercise 17.3 – Ongoing – Plan and Execute Your New Diet
Determine how you want to manage your caloric intake, either through a specific diet plan that meets your numbers or through monitoring your calories. Use one of the tracking services linked at *thehotguyde.com/resources*. Think about how you will prepare your meals every day, and how you will deal with temptations to stray. Refer to chapters 4 and 5 for help.

Chapter 18 – Hygiene and Grooming

Hygiene Is Necessary

If your hygiene is lacking, it's probably your biggest obstacle to dating success. Not smelling bad, and knowing how to groom yourself, are minimum requirements. If the contents of this chapter aren't already part of your daily routine, they should be your new first priority.

Oral Hygiene

Brushing Your Teeth

Brushing your teeth removes unsightly and potentially damaging food and plaque from your teeth. The American Dental Association recommends brushing at least twice per day.[225] Both manual and powered toothbrushes work fine. A fluoride toothpaste will protect your teeth from wear to the enamel,[226] but beyond that, toothpaste doesn't contribute much besides flavor.

Bacteria and fungus can grow on your tongue and cause bad breath, so when you're brushing your teeth, brush your tongue as well. Feel free to use a tongue scraper if you prefer. Nearly half of American adults suffer from periodontitis, which is inflammation of the gums.[227] Brushing your gums will reduce the problem, though it may cause them to bleed. The more consistently you brush, the less this will happen.

Flossing

The American Dental Association recommends flossing at least once per day.[228] Never use the same location on the floss twice, as this will transfer bacteria from between one pair of teeth to another spot. Shift along the strand of floss with each penetration.

Mouthwash

Mouthwash is optional, but beneficial. A good mouthwash will sanitize your mouth, help fight plaque, and help remove any bacteria or fungus that may be growing on your tongue. Swish it around for thirty seconds and rinse with water.

Whitening Products

For whitening teeth, 6 to 6.5 percent hydrogen peroxide strips are effective within seven to twenty-one days, and 80 percent of the effects have proven durable eighteen months after treatment. Strips can be used safely at home, with side effects including tooth sensitivity and gum irritation, both of which subside following the treatment. If you would like to whiten your teeth, strips are a good option.[229] For most guys, they're not necessary, but if your teeth are heavily stained from smoking or age, you may want to consider them.

Cleanliness

Showering

The outer layer of your skin (the stratum corneum) is composed of hardened, dead skin cells held together by lipids. When you shower with soap and hot water and you scrub heavily, you dissolve the lipids and undermine the integrity of this layer. The more frequently you shower, the more damage you cause and the less time your skin has to repair itself. This can lead to dry, irritated skin[230] and dermatitis.[231]

For this reason, wash no more than once per day. Use warm water instead of hot, and pat yourself dry with soft towels. Take your showers immediately after dirty or sweaty activities (such as your workouts). If you don't do anything especially dirty, it's okay to go a day without showering. If your skin is already damaged, moisturizing lotions can help.

Deodorant

Bacteria flourish on our skin by consuming the nutrients in our sweat, and body odor arises from that bacteria's digestive waste. Deodorants address this problem by limiting the growth of these bacteria and releasing perfume to hide the smell. Antiperspirants address the issue by creating gelatinous barriers over your sweat glands to reduce how much you sweat, cutting off the bacteria's food supply. Make sure to apply antiperspirant at night, rather than in the morning, so these barriers have time to form while you sleep.

Men's bodies vary considerably, and the best product for you will depend on your sweat. I prefer moisture-activated deodorants with built-in antiperspirant. You can use whatever you like as long as you're using something. If you have a female friend willing to give you an opinion about what deodorants go well with your natural scent, ask her to help.

Laundry

If you're having body-odor problems despite using deodorant and showering, it's likely a dirty-clothes issue rather than a body issue. Avoid wearing underwear or shirts for longer than twenty-four hours between washes.

Hair Care

The most popularly marketed hair-care products for men are all-in-one body wash/shampoo combos. These suck. Don't use them. Ordinary soap can damage your hair by breaking down its protective oils. If you do nothing more than buy separate soaps, shampoos, and conditioners, you'll be ahead of most men.

To purchase the right hair products, figure out what kind of hair you have.

• Dry: your hair tends to feel rough and dry

• Oily: your hair always looks and feels wet

• Thin: your hair is fine and sits limply on your head

• Thick: your hair is extremely deep and substantial

• Frizzy: your hair is unmanageable and inconsistent

• Normal: your hair does not fit into the above categories

You may have a combination of some of these characteristics. When you've identified your type of hair, look for a product to match it as follows:

• Dry: moisturizing shampoos and (more importantly) a moisturizing conditioner

• Oily: shampoos designed for oily hair

• Thin: shampoos and conditioners with "fortifying" and "thickening" agents

• Thick: normal shampoos and conditioners

• Frizzy: moisturizing conditioners specifically designed for frizzy hair

Shampoo your hair only as needed — probably every two to four days, but more often if your hair is oily. Limiting your shampoo use will prevent the soap from breaking down the oils in your hair follicles, helping it look healthier longer. While you should limit your shampoo use, use conditioner every time you shower. It will nourish your hair and make it easier to style.

Most gels, hairsprays, pomades, waxes, muds, clays, creams, mattes, and mousses will make your hair look sculpted and aren't pleasant for women to run their fingers through. Though most women want the men they date to look good, many don't like it when a guy seems to be trying too hard to look good, and an overdone hairstyle can put him in that category. If you're going for a specific look or stereotype that calls for a product, that's your prerogative, but make sure you know what you're doing. For most men, a good haircut combined with the appropriate shampoo and conditioner is all you need.

Hairstyle

Think of your hair as a fashion accessory, one you will always wear. Since it needs to match all of your outfits, it's usually better to keep it simple. You can use your hair to make a statement (an unusual haircut or color, for example), and it will catch people's eyes, but it'll be a liability in more-conservative settings, such as offices.

Even when you're staying in the realm of the ordinary, you have plenty of options. Buzz cuts, crew cuts, Caesar cuts, fades, the Harvard clip, the pompadour, and long, flowing locks can all look sexy. There aren't any firm rules here, but I recommend experimenting and trusting the trained eyes of professionals. Go to a salon (not a barbershop) and say you want a new look. Ask to experiment with whatever the stylist thinks would look best. Tip well. Take pictures of yourself from several angles immediately after the haircut and keep track of how many compliments you receive. Once your hair's grown out, repeat the process at a different salon. Test out three or four distinct haircuts in this way. When you have a favorite, bring your pictures to a cheaper barbershop and say that's how you'd like your hair cut from now on. You will look great and save money.

If you're balding, shave your hair off. Baldness is unattractive only if you're insecure about it. There are plenty of sex symbols who are bald, and the cultural opinion of baldness has shifted dramatically in the last half-century. Shaving your head shows that you're secure in your image, and it's hot.

Acne

Acne develops when dead skin cells cluster at the opening of a hair follicle, clogging the pore. The pore accumulates sebum (oil), bacteria, and keratin until it breaks, resulting in inflammation. The inflammation appears as small red bumps, and can also form whiteheads, blackheads, or inflamed nodules and cysts, usually on the face, back, neck, and chest.

Benzoyl peroxide is a safe and effective over-the-counter treatment for acne. It's an antimicrobial agent that's proven more effective than antibiotics and is unaffected by bacterial resistance.[232] It's also cost-effective compared to other treatments.[233] Salicylic acid is widely accepted as effective against mild acne, though there is a lack of evidence from randomized controlled trials. Don't scrub your acne-prone areas more regularly than you do the rest of your body, as this can damage your skin and create even more pockets for bacteria to flourish in. Use benzoyl peroxide combined with a non-acnegenic moisturizer on your pimples. If your acne is severe, and benzoyl peroxide treatments aren't enough, visit a dermatologist.

Shaving

The shaving industry in the U.S. has managed to convince the public that adding more blades to a razor improves the quality of the shave. It doesn't. It does, however, cost more money and cause more irritation. Throw out your five-bladed vibrating razors and stop wasting your money.

For your new shaving kit, you will need the following:

• A safety razor

• A brush (preferably of badger hair)

• A cake of shaving soap

• Pre-shave cream

• Non-acnegenic moisturizing lotion

• Blades for the safety razor

• A shaving bowl

There are additional materials you can use, such as antiseptic lotions or aftershave, but they're not necessary. You can use a classic straight razor as an alternative to the safety razor. If you do, you will need a strop and a hone as well. I will assume you're using a safety razor.

Coat your face in a thin layer of the pre-shave cream and add a few drops of water to your shaving bowl. Open your shaving soap and circle your brush around the edge to gather some soap; then agitate your brush in your shaving bowl until your brush is full of thick lather. Apply the lather to all of your facial hair and rub it in with your hands. This process makes your hair brittle and causes it to stand on end, making it easier to cut with the razor.

Pull your skin taut by either shifting your jaw or pulling on your skin with your hand. Always shave in the direction of the hair growth, which usually means downward. Shaving against the growth tugs on the hairs, irritating the skin and pulling the blade in, increasing the chance of cuts.

In smooth motions, run the razor along your face, cutting through the hairs. Some men prefer slow, long strokes while others prefer shorter, faster ones. Do whichever works for you. After your shave, rinse your face in warm water and inspect your work. Check for any stray hairs or patches. If you notice spots you missed, lather the necessary areas with your remaining shaving soap and go through them a second time. If you like, on your second run you can shave against the growth, though it's not necessary that you do. Shaving against the growth will get you a smoother shave, and since the hairs are shorter now, you've reduced the risk of cuts and irritation. If you cut yourself, apply pressure using a soft, dry cloth until the bleeding stops. If you cut yourself regularly, or you're experiencing a lot of irritation, replace your blade. It's probably too dull. After shaving, rinse your face and apply some non-acnegenic moisturizing lotion. This will prevent irritation, heal any damage to your skin caused by the shaving, and prevent the development of acne.

Masculine Hygiene

If you're an uncircumcised man, retract your foreskin and rinse your glans every time you shower. Dry semen and dead skin cells can accumulate under the foreskin, forming a gelatinous substance called smegma. It smells disgusting and women won't appreciate it if they put your dick in their mouths. If you have difficulty retracting your foreskin, it may be too small for your penis; this condition is called phimosis. Practice retracting the foreskin in the shower, as the steamy environment will make the skin supple. Over time it will stretch, and you should be able to retract it completely. If this is too painful, talk to your doctor. Alternative interventions may be necessary.

When urinating, you may have trouble with urine stuck in your urethra after you've finished. This urine can leak into your underwear, and your dick will smell and taste like piss. To fix this, sharply engage your Kegel muscles after you've finished peeing. This should shoot out the remaining urine. If this isn't enough, reach past the bottom of your scrotum to the soft skin below your anus and push up sharply. This should dislodge any liquid that remains. If you can dab the urine off the tip of your penis with a square of toilet paper, this will keep you cleaner too.

If odor in your nether regions is a regular problem, consider using some *Gold Bond* medicated powder. It will prevent sweat and other bodily fluids from accumulating. Also, make sure you are always wearing 100 percent cotton underwear, and change it when you get sweaty. Most cheaper, synthetic materials are waterproof and prevent your sweat from evaporating, which can encourage "jock crotch," a condition in which fungus starts to grow around your scrotum. It's itchy, it smells, and it looks like a sexually transmitted infection (STI). Wash regularly, change your undies, and make sure they're cotton, and this won't be a problem.

Pubic Hair

Keep your pubic hair trimmed close to the skin with a clipper or scissors. Completely shaving your pubic hair serves no practical purpose, but many women will appreciate it. It shows that you like looking clean and neat for your sexual partner, and some think it can make your penis look bigger.

Shaving your pubic hair has some hazards. Ingrown hairs and razor burn can look like the symptoms of an STI, and the skin around your pubic hair is so sensitive that it's hard to shave without causing some degree of irritation. Though it's painful, you may want to consider waxing instead of shaving, at least for your first time. When shaving, always start by trimming your hair as close to the skin as you can. Use your normal pre-shave cream and shaving soap with a new razor blade to avoid infecting the sensitive region with bacteria. Always shave with the growth (downward). Immediately after shaving, moisturize with a non-acnegenic moisturizer, and reapply the moisturizer at least daily. If you can find one with salicylic acid, all the better. Whenever you shower, wash the area with an exfoliating scrub.

Fingernails

What do you call a lesbian with long fingernails? Single. The same holds true for guys. If you have long fingernails when you're fingering your lover, you risk scratching her inside. Keeping your nails short ensures that doesn't happen. If you see any more than a small white trim along the edge of your nails, cut or file them as soon as possible. Your toenails are less important, since you're probably not using them for sex, but treat them with the same policy.

Lip Care

Soft lips are kissable lips. In the dry winter months, moisturizing is necessary. Avoid cheap oil-based balms and favor those with ingredients such as shea butter, glycerin, or coconut oil. Your lips should be moist and soft but not shiny. Apply your balm sparingly, but often.

Eyebrow Care

Eyebrow care is another place where most women want a guy to look good, but prefer it to look effortless. If you have a unibrow, pluck the innermost hairs. If some hairs are overgrown, those are worth plucking too. Beyond these two issues, don't worry about your eyebrows.

Chapter Summary

• Brush your teeth and tongue twice per day, floss once per day, and use a fluoride toothpaste.

• Shower when dirty in warm water, scrub lightly, and pat dry with a soft towel.

• Wear a deodorant that matches your natural scent. Wear antiperspirant if necessary.

• Wash your hair as needed with a shampoo appropriate for your hair, and condition regularly.

• Experiment with hairstyles at different professional salons until you find one that works.

• Use benzoyl peroxide as an effective over-the-counter treatment for acne.

• Shave with a safety razor, pre-shave cream, and shaving soap. Shave with the hair's growth.

• Rinse under your foreskin daily. Expel urine after peeing and dab your penis with toilet paper.

• Do your laundry regularly, don't wear a shirt for more than twenty-four hours, and wear cotton underwear.

• Keep your pubic hair neat. Take measures to prevent irritation if you shave there.

• Keep your fingernails and toenails short.

• In the dry winter months, apply high quality lip balm sparingly but frequently.

• Pluck unibrows and extra-long eyebrow hairs.

Exercises

Exercise 18.1 – Ongoing – Improve Your Hygiene

Take an inventory of all of the hygiene advice in this chapter you aren't following or have been approaching differently. Buy the necessary soaps, tools, deodorants, and the like, and incorporate their use into your routine.

Exercise 18.2 – Ongoing – Pick a Hairstyle

Follow the advice in this chapter to choose your new hairstyle. Look online for salons in your area and book an appointment. Make sure to take photos and keep track of any compliments you receive. After several experiments, decide what style you like best and wear your hair that way from now on.

Chapter 19 – Fashion

There's no quicker fix for your physical attractiveness than ramping up your style. For better or worse, the way you dress will always make a powerful first impression. In a 1990 analysis of studies on the social psychology of dress, 81 percent of the research indicated that people use clothing to evaluate competence, power, and intelligence, and 67 percent showed that people use it to judge character, sociability, and mood.[234] People are going to judge you by your clothes. You can be a victim of this or you can use it to your advantage.

When you walk into your first Painting 101 class, you learn about techniques developed by the greats in ages past. Someday, you're going to form your own style and create works that are unique and special, but only after you've mastered the styles that came before. Treat fashion as an art, and treat this chapter like a Fashion 101 class. I'm going to throw a lot of rules at you, and someday you're going to come up with your own style and break all of these rules, but you need to understand what the rules are before you break them. We want to show our personalities, but "showing your personality" doesn't give you carte blanche to wear your old college T-shirts and baggy jeans just as you always have. "Expressing the real you" and "Staying in your comfort zone" aren't the same thing. For most of your life, you've been pressured to blend in, and that's exactly how most men dress themselves. Confident guys dress to stand out. If you follow the rules in this chapter, you won't be at the pinnacle of fashion, but you will look good, you will stand out, and people will like how you look. Until you're so competent with your style that you find yourself commenting on celebrities' outfits and critiquing the mannequins at your local H&M,

stick to these rules and you'll stay out of trouble.

There's a fair amount of vocabulary in this chapter with which you might not be familiar. If you get confused, go to *thehotguyde.com/FashionVocab* for reference.

The Three Pillars of Dress

When choosing what to wear, we're concerned with the three Fs: fit, fabric, and fashion. How well do the clothes fit your body? How high is the quality of the material? How well does it convey your personality? All three are necessary, but of the three, fit is the most important. An outfit that fits well, even when cheap and in poor taste, can still work, but no amount of quality or expression can fix an outfit that doesn't fit.

Proper Fit

Shirts

The most important fit to check on a shirt is the shoulders. The stitching along the shirt's shoulders should end at the edge of your shoulder bones. If the stitching droops down your bicep, the shirt is too large. With dress shirts, the collar of your shirt should touch the back of your neck even when unbuttoned. When buttoned, it should touch all the way around, but without choking you. The collar's height should match the height of your neck: tall with long, short with short. The type of collar you should wear depends on the shape of your face. If you have a wide face, wear a spread collar; if you have a narrow face, wear a point collar. The sleeves of your shirt should come down just past the bones on your wrists, with about one-half inch of the cuff visible when you're wearing a jacket. The waist should fit closely to your body. There should be no billowing below the rib cage, and the fabric should mold to your chest. The bottom of the shirt should fall low enough that you can tuck it into your pants by a few inches, but no more.

T-shirts should be cotton, plain-colored, and molded closely to your body, bordering on tight. They're designed to show your body off, so if you're going to wear one, make sure you have the body to do so. If you don't, it's probably better to stick to button-downs and roll up the sleeves. The sleeves of your T-shirt should end on your biceps, not at your elbow, and the hemline should end just below your belt. Favor V-necks and Y-necks, as they'll show off your body better than crew necks, but make sure they don't show any chest hair. T-shirts are great tools for layering, so buy a whole slew of them in various colors, including colors too bright to wear on their own. Avoid printed tees unless you're going for a stereotype that features them (which we'll get into later).

Polos follow the same rules as T-shirts. Avoid polos with company logos, and never wear them with a blazer; it's too preppy. Don't tuck them in, and if you can wear them with khakis instead of jeans, it's a classic, winning look.

Sweaters serve two roles: as a middle layer between your shirt and jacket, or as an outer layer to keep you warm when a coat is too much. If you're wearing a sweater as a middle layer, choose a thin, lightweight sweater in a solid color. Cashmere and cotton knits work well. If you're using a sweater as an outer layer, choose a thicker knit with a colorful pattern. Sweaters should be a little longer than shirts, but aside from that, all the rules for shirts apply.

Pants

Dress pants fasten around your true waist, which is the thinnest point above the hips, near your belly button. The front of your pants should drape over your belly and fall straight down from there. Casual pants, especially jeans, rest lower, just above your hips or on your hipbones. If the pants sit any lower than this, don't buy them or you'll be featuring your ass crack. Always wear dress pants with suspenders. All other pants, including jeans, need belts. Never wear a belt and suspenders at the same time.

The center of your crotch seam should be snug against your body, giving you enough room to move, but no more. The pant legs should taper between the thigh and the knee to avoid excess cloth around the knees. They can be straight or tapered below the knee, but they should not flare out. The hem at the bottom of the pants should rest on the top of your shoe. Jeans can rest a little lower, on the laces.

When the bottoms of your pants' legs fold up, these are called cuffs. Cuffs shorten your pants and reveal the inside fabric. Designers like adding cuffs to their pants because it's a cheap way to make them fit more customers, but they don't help you. Unless you're specifically going for a dressed-down, cheap look, avoid cuffs.

Pleats add flexibility and stretch to the front of your pants. Unless you are a muscular or heavyset man who would benefit from the increased flexibility, avoid pleats.

When it comes to jeans, go with raw denim. Avoid anything torn or faded. The jeans should have a deep blue color and possess a metallic shimmer when held under light. If they're drab, they're low quality, so don't buy them. Jeans tend to come in four varieties: skinny, slim, straight, and relaxed. Most men will want slim-fit or straight jeans. Skinny is way too tight, and relaxed is too baggy. If you're used to wearing baggy clothes, proper-fitting jeans will feel uncomfortable, even feminine, but they will make you — especially your butt — look better. You should have a little trouble buttoning the top button of a good pair of well-fitting jeans, and using the pockets should be a little difficult. No extra fabric or diagonal folds should be around the crotch, and you should feel the fabric snug and flattening on your ass. Don't get jeans that flare out at the ankles unless you're trying to look like a hippie.

Something about the construction of jeans makes them a poor environment for bacterial growth, so you don't need to wash them as often as you wash your other pants. Denim enthusiasts maintain you can wash your jeans every three to six months and be fine, but I wash mine every five to ten wearings. If you can afford two pairs of jeans, alternate them, and hang them up in open air between wearings. This will further reduce their need for cleaning. If you want to make sure you're preserving them, have them dry cleaned.

Shorts are rarely flattering on men. If you wear them, make sure they end in the lower half of your thigh and are made from a lightweight material; don't choose denim, or cargo shorts. (It's probably best if you never wear shorts.)

Suits

For your first suit, you'll want a single-breasted black, navy blue, or dark gray suit with notch lapels. You can choose flap pockets, but jetted ones will look sharper. The collar of your suit jacket should touch your shirt collar all the way around your neck, but never cover it. If your jacket collar stands off from the shirt, it's too large, and if it bunches, it's too small. As with shirts, the seam of the jacket's shoulder should reach the edge of your shoulder bone and no further. The armscyes (the places where the sleeves meet your torso) should not dig into the armpit or sag. The lapels should not sag or bend away from your body, and if they do, the chest needs adjustment. Buckling the waist should be easy, and there should be no wrinkles or folds in the fabric when you do. The bottom of the suit jacket should end around the curve of your butt. The sleeves should stop at or above the bones in your wrist; they should be slightly shorter than your dress-shirt sleeves. If you get a blazer or sports jacket, its fit should follow the same rules as your suit jacket.

Neckties

The knot of your tie should correspond to the type of collar you have on your shirt. If you're wearing a point collar, trying to stuff a thick double Windsor inside will look ridiculous. Likewise, if you're using a wide collar, having a knot that's too small will make your tie look impotent. Make sure your knot fills the space allowed for it. The four-in-hand should be the only knot you'll ever need. If it isn't producing a thick-enough knot, you can use a double Windsor knot, but you'd be better off just purchasing a tie made of thicker material. The bottom of your tie should lie flat against your body. The tip should reach your belt. Never use a clip-on tie.

Underwear

Underwear protects you from your clothes and vice versa. It absorbs your sweat and is cheaper to replace than your nice shirts and pants.

Undershirts should be simple and made of cotton. The sleeves should go a little way down your biceps, covering your armpits. Undershirts should not be visible, so choose a style that accommodates your outerwear to make sure this happens. If you're going to be unbuttoning some of your dress shirt, wear a V-neck or scoop neck. You should avoid sleeveless undershirts with scooped necklines, since they won't protect your armpits, but if you're wearing a low-cut shirt, they're better than nothing.

Briefs are snug undergarments that cover the crotch. They're plain and functional, and will give your private parts support, but they're not attractive, especially when they're of the "tighty whities" variety. Boxers are looser undershorts. They're more socially accepted than briefs, but have a tendency to create lumps and wrinkles under your pants. Boxer briefs are the happy medium, and probably your best option. Make sure they're 100 percent cotton so they properly absorb sweat.

Color

Contrast

There's much ado about color in the fashion world, and most of it's more complicated than it needs to be. The single most important factor in choosing what colors work for you is finding the right contrast. The contrast between the colors in your outfits should correspond to the contrast between your complexion and your hair. Basically, if the tone of your skin is the same as the tone of your hair (fair skin and light hair, dark skin and dark hair), you have a low-contrast complexion, so you'll want to wear clothes with a similarly low level of contrast. If you have fair skin and dark hair, or dark skin and fair hair, you'll look better in clothes with high contrast. Consider red hair a medium/light hair color.

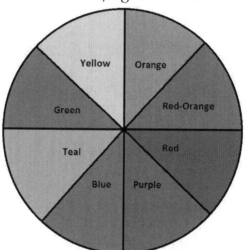

The color wheel is your key for identifying what colors contrast. Complementary colors, which are colors on opposite sides of the wheel, are high contrast, while analogous colors, the ones next to each other on the wheel, are low contrast. A low-contrast guy wearing a blue suit would want to wear a light-blue tie and a purple pocket square, while a high-contrast guy wearing the same suit could opt for a yellow tie and a red pocket square. Keep in mind that some conservative situations will call for your standard blacks, grays, blues, and whites, so if you're a high-contrast guy, you won't be able to dress in the colors that necessarily suit you best. In such situations, you'll need to express contrast through shades.

When it comes to shades (the lightness or darkness of colors), the same principle applies. High-contrast men benefit most from more-pronounced differences between light and dark (lighter pants with darker shirts, for example), while low-contrast men benefit from more-consistent shades throughout. Get your contrast right and you have 80 percent of the color game mastered.

Echo Your Body's Colors

Choosing colors that echo the colors in your eyes, lips, hair, and cheeks will help pull your ensemble together. If you're wearing a jacket that's similar in color to your hair, it makes a frame for your face, drawing attention to it. Your first suit should be a standard black or blue one, but if you're looking for a casual alternative, consider picking up another that matches the color of your hair, a tie that's the color of your eyes, and a pocket square that's the color of your lips. You may be shocked at how terrific a look that is.

Fairer-skinned men need to be pickier about their colors than darker-skinned men. If you have dark or olive-colored skin, you can wear pretty much any color you like. If you're fair-skinned, lighter tones—especially light pink—will tend to give you a "washed-out" look. Favor darker, bolder colors whenever possible.

Specific Color Suggestions

Match Your Leathers and Metals

Your belt buckle should match your jewelry. They don't have to be the exact same metal, but they should be in the same color family. Wear brass with gold, chrome with silver. Likewise, the leather of your belt should match your shoes. Wear brown belts with brown shoes and black belts with black shoes. Once again, they don't have to be the exact same shade—just in the same family.

Match Your Socks to Your Pants

The color of your socks should match your pants, with an exception of jeans, which can be worn with any dark-colored sock. If your socks don't match your pants, make it a deliberate statement. Use exceptionally bright socks (as a source of contrast) or pick a pair with an interesting pattern. If none of these is an option, match your socks to your shoes; that's better than nothing. Chances are, whichever one of these guidelines you follow, you'll be throwing out every white sock you own.

Neckties and Pocket Squares

Neckties and pocket squares can be in the same color family (dark green and light green, say), but they should never match exactly, no matter what your tuxedo rental place tells you. White pocket squares are formal; colorful ones are informal, and the brighter the color, the more casual the feel. Ties work the same way. Solid-colored ties in subdued colors (think blue) are the most formal. The brighter the color and the more elaborate the pattern, the less formal the tie.

Patterns

Solid-colored garments can be difficult to pull off, and they're usually successful only on high-contrast men wearing garments of different colors. Employing patterns can help you get some variety in your ensemble. The only rule for patterns is never to put two patterns of the same scale next to each other. Even if the patterns are different—for example, if you have small stripes and small dots—the outfit will look too busy. Thick, vertical stripes in one garment with small dots on the other would be fine. Vary the scale and you'll stay out of trouble.

Layering

Layering helps you deal with changing temperatures in colder months, and can also make your outfit more interesting. There are two basic rules to layering:

• Thinner garments go under thicker ones.
• Lighter colors go under darker ones.

When you're layering, your lower layers can be as loud as you want, as long as you don't expect to be stripping down to that bottom layer. You can have a "highlighter orange" T-shirt that serves no purpose except to be worn under a more subdued button-down or sweater. When picking out your middle layers (cotton sweaters and casual button-downs), keep the colors neutral so you can maximize flexibility in your outer layers. Pastels and soft tones such as grays and creams work best. Finally, make sure you layer looser items over fitted items to add some contrast in texture. A loose button-down work shirt worn over a fitted tee is a look you'll see all the time on models and celebrities.

Stereotypes

Since one of the main purposes of fashion is to manage other people's prejudices, it helps to be aware of what the most common stereotypes are in your culture. There's a handful of unattractive stereotypes you probably want to avoid. The first is the "average guy," whom you'll see everywhere. He wears a generic T-shirt, a pair of baggy shorts, white socks, and white sneakers. You won't meet many women who consider this look hot. Another common one is the "geek." This guy wears a short-sleeve button-down shirt with a busy pattern in colors that make him look washed out, and pairs it with loose-fitting slacks covering high-rising white socks. If either of these looks describes your wardrobe, you have some work to do.

On the other end of the spectrum, it's worth checking out some of the positive stereotypes popularly considered sexy in your culture. "Military guy," "surfer guy," and "rock star" come to mind. These styles will be polarizing. People who identify with the subculture your stereotype is associated with will have instant rapport with you, while those who dislike that subculture will be repelled. This is what you want. Your style will help you filter for compatibility. Don't aim for broad appeal; aim to make a statement. Any of the following is a potentially attractive stereotype:

- Goth guy
- Biker
- Skater boy
- Punk
- Rocker
- Male model
- Metrosexual
- Hipster
- Wall Street guy
- Surfer

Adopting a stereotype is an advanced method, and it's the sort of situation where you can throw out a lot of the rules in this chapter. A "rocker" stereotype would absolutely wear a printed T-shirt, even though we said not to. A hipster might wear jeans with cuffs, even though we said to avoid cuffs. Look up images of some of the sexiest men who fit into the stereotype you'd like to imitate, and look for clothes similar to what they're wearing. This will be the fastest way to adopt the stereotype and make sure you're looking good.

Using Stereotypes Ironically

By adopting certain stereotypes, you can undermine some negative prejudices people might have about you — for example, those due to race or build. If you're an Asian guy dealing with people assuming you're nerdy, adopting a contrasting stereotype, such as punk, will make people think twice. If you're a big, muscular guy who's pretty intimidating, wearing geek chic or hipster styles can be disarming and make people more comfortable.

As you improve your body language and physique, you can start to exploit usually unattractive stereotypes for an "ironic" look that's hotter than the sum of its parts. A muscular, confident guy wearing geek chic can look incredibly attractive, especially with rolled-up sleeves and stylish glasses. The irony of the style shows a staggering amount of social awareness that will be appealing to anyone who recognizes it. This is pretty advanced, so I don't recommend trying it until you have a firm grasp of the basics, but think about it for the future.

Assembling Your Starting Wardrobe

When you're putting together your wardrobe, think of it in two halves: one half full of basic, neutral-colored items that are your foundation, and another half of colorful statement pieces you'll wear less often but that will be the hallmarks of your style.

For the core pieces, pick up the following:

• A high-quality pair of dark, raw blue jeans
• At least one white dress shirt
• A pair of black Oxfords
• A pair of brown leather shoes with decorative designs, such as brogues or wingtips
• A navy blazer

- Gray wool pants
- A reversible black and brown leather belt (with metal that matches any jewelry you wear)
- Lots of black socks
- Undershirts and underwear

For the statement pieces, pick up:

- V-neck T-shirts in every color
- A gray or blue cotton or cashmere sweater
- A gray or navy blue peacoat
- A leather jacket
- A blue dress shirt
- A purple, teal, red, or other bright-color dress shirt for classy casual wear
- A dark or neutral button-down work shirt to layer with your brighter T-shirts

Among these items, you should be able to assemble dozens of impressive outfits. Some of the items (the shoes, leather jacket, and peacoat) can be expensive, and you may have to take your time saving money to get this all done. That's okay. Start with the essentials and work your way up. You don't have to throw out your current wardrobe all at once.

Copy the Best

Learning good fashion takes time, and if you're feeling a little overwhelmed, don't worry; it's normal. When you're starting out, to make things a little easier on yourself, and to avoid some costly trial and error, I recommend finding a role model. Most celebrities have style experts who either pick out their wardrobes or advise them about what to wear. You can benefit from their professional advice by imitating their looks. Look up someone who resembles you and hunt down photos of him in his everyday life, or check lists of the hundred sexiest men alive and note the clothes they're wearing in their photos. When you've found someone to imitate, browse in stores for clothes that resemble those outfits and buy them. This will expose you to some of the best style with minimal effort, and it'll get you looking good right away.

Laundry and Care

As we talked about in chapter 18, wash your clothes after every wearing; jeans and outerwear are the exceptions. Use cold water by default, and read the labels to find out how much heat each garment can handle in the dryer. A more mild heat will take longer, but will keep your cotton clothes from shrinking. Use a leather conditioner on your shoes every couple of months, and consider picking up some shoe trees for your shoes to help with odor, structure, and moisture. If you buy a leather jacket, it will probably be your most attractive but most expensive garment. Treat it with as much care as your shoes, and don't wear it in the rain.

Where and How Should I Shop?

You can find good clothes anywhere, even thrift stores. Internet shopping is cheaper, but unless you know exactly what you're buying, it can be hard to nail the fit without trying things on. If you're using the Internet, make sure the store you're buying from offers free returns.

Once you have your basics, the best way to expand your wardrobe is through adventurous window shopping. Go to stores you've never been to and try on clothes you never imagined yourself wearing. You might be surprised at what works. I also suggest bringing a female friend along for a second opinion, but be careful if you do so. Women tend to pick out clothes they like best on guys in general, not necessarily the best clothes for your build and complexion. Pick out clothes yourself and ask for her opinion once you've tried them on. Make sure to offer the same service for her, or offer to buy her lunch.

Chapter Summary

- Fit, fabric, and fashion are the most important considerations for your wardrobe.

- The contrast of your clothing's color should echo the contrast of your complexion.

- When layering, thinner, tighter, lighter-colored garments go under thicker, looser, darker ones.

- Exploit stereotypes to polarize people and undermine negative prejudices.

- Copy a role model when you're starting out.

- Wash your clothes regularly.

- Get out of your comfort zone and try on clothes you never thought to try.

Exercises

Exercise 19.1 – Immediate – Look at the Attire of Attractive Men

Google a list of the sexiest men alive. *People* magazine, *Glamour*, *Vogue*, MTV, and similar media publish such lists every year. Pay attention to the clothes the men are wearing. How do they fit? What outfits do you see most often? Typically, you'll see suits, shirtless pictures, and a smattering of casual attire. Pay special attention to the casual attire. What colors have these men chosen? How are they using layers? What stereotypes are they echoing? Write in your journal about any interesting finds.

Exercise 19.2 – Immediate – Pick a Role Model

Was there a man you noticed in Exercise 19.1 who resembled you? Is there another celebrity who resembles you, or one you admire? Search the Internet for candid photos of that celebrity and start a collection of photos of him in casual attire. Look on the websites of retailers near you for clothes resembling the sorts of clothes that celebrity wears. See if you can try on those clothes at those stores. If you can, and you like how they look on you, pick them up.

Exercise 19.3 – One Time – Go People-Watching and Window Shopping

Make a trip to the mall and find a place to sit and people-watch where lots of folks are walking by. Which guys' outfits stand out to you? What are the guys with attractive girlfriends wearing? What are the guys who seem like the leaders of their social groups wearing? What outfits look awful, and what is awful about them?

After you've been people-watching for half or three-quarters of an hour, take your newfound knowledge and go window shopping. Pick a store, find some outfits that resemble the ones you just associated with positive qualities, and try them on. Experiment with clothes that are wildly different from what you usually wear. Don't buy anything. If there's an outfit you like so much that you still want to buy it the next day, then go ahead.

Exercise 19.4 – Ongoing – Build Your Wardrobe

Purchase the essential core items listed in this chapter. When you have a functional wardrobe of good shoes, simple items, and some colorful garments, start expanding into more-elaborate designs. Choose a stereotype to imitate and pick up some relevant garments. Experiment with mixing stereotypes. Look into a loud pair of shoes or a few pieces of jewelry (such as a watch, ring, or earring), or follow the lead of your role model by adopting whatever statement pieces he uses. Keep track of what garments get the most compliments, especially from strangers, and write in your journal about these occurrences.

Part IV: Dating

Chapter 20 – Relating to Women

A lot of guys have confused ideas about what dating and relationships entail. Some put women on pedestals and think dating is all about impressing them with wealth or gestures. Others see it as a contest that requires domination, where we have to be more "alpha" than the other guys and push through women's "shit tests."

The first thing to understand about dating is simple. Women are people. They have feelings, they have goals, they fuck up, they get nervous, and they get confused—just as we do. They don't have a sixth sense about romance and they don't have infinite options. They like the emotional closeness of relationships and they like how it feels to fuck. A lot of the nerves and confusion guys feel comes from thinking that women are somehow different—probably because that's what men are told every day. Women, we're told, are a different species that operates under different rules, which is why we have to "say the right things" and "make the right moves" that lead to sex. That's not how it works.

Women are people. Imagine that some enormous, dumb woman with yellow teeth, bad breath, and a desperate demeanor comes over and starts touching you. What sequence of lines would she have to say to turn you on and make you want her more than anyone else? There isn't one. You simply aren't attracted to her. Women's sexuality isn't so different. Chemistry is a feeling. It develops when we like how a potential mate looks, smells, and sounds, and when that person says and does things that get you thinking about sex. Dating is basically just hanging out with people you like, and when you meet the ones you have chemistry with, you start thinking about fucking each other. What the seduction community calls "game" is basically just letting a woman know you're into her without turning her off.

There's no universal way to understand "women" because each woman is unique. Stacy grew up learning that sex is only for marriage, while Julia grew up seeing it as a delightful pastime. Do you expect Stacy and Julia to like the same guys, date the same way, and be turned on by the same things? Then why would you expect there to be one universally effective "pickup system" that appeals to all women? There are a few things most women have in common that result from biology and from living in a common culture, but it's not a long list, and even those things aren't universal. We'll talk about those common experiences and how they relate to dating, but for the most part, if you can focus on getting to know the person in front of you, you'll be miles ahead of anyone claiming to be some guru on the "creatures from Venus."

What Is "Creepy?"

Imagine you're in a world filled with men, but not the men you're used to. Every man in this world is a seven-foot-tall, 270-pound linebacker. Despite your smaller frame, your culture encourages you to dress in skin-tight, constricting clothing and walk in shoes that put you off balance. As you walk into a bar, all of these massive men turn their heads and stare at you. You know from experience that most of them want to sleep with you, and chances are you want to sleep with some of them too, but not all of them. You order a drink, and several of these guys come talk to you. Some of them stumble over their words and have shifty eyes. Some of them blurt out canned routines. Some of them insult you. When you reject them, some of them call you a bitch. You're also aware that under the right circumstances, even though such men are reviled, and even though there are laws to protect you, some of these men would rape you. This dynamic characterizes your entire life — at work, in coffee shops, on the street, and at school. How does this make you feel?

"Creepy" is an emotion women feel when they have even the slightest inkling that a man might be a rape threat. The best metaphor I've heard to explain it is how you would feel with a cop in an isolated location. Everything will probably be okay, but there's a non-zero chance that he's a bad one. He could beat you up, even shoot you, and he'll probably get away with it. Though it's unfair to all the decent cops out there, there will always be a little bit of anxiety in the back of your mind playing out that scenario, and you'll be a little slower to trust him than you are to trust other people. For many women, that's how they feel about men.

Different women find different things creepy, but since "creepiness" is inherently linked to rape, any and all expressions of unreciprocated sexual interest can be a little creepy. "This guy wants to have sex with me and I don't want to have sex with him. How will that work out?" Creepiness can be exacerbated by any of the following:

• Anxious body language from the guy (lack of eye contact, crossed arms, shuffling feet)

• Insecure sexual expression (hovering, trying to touch but not touching)

• Staring

• Unwelcome physical contact

• Rejections, implicit or explicit, that are ignored

• A dangerous environment (can't escape, no one else around)

You can't control how a woman feels toward you, but you can be sensitive to the things most likely to creep her out. Try to avoid aggressive or anxious behavior and body language, since both can suggest dangerous intentions. Avoid showing sexual interest when you are in environments she can't easily escape (on the bus, in the elevator, when she's working, when she's your subordinate). When you do show sexual interest, if her body language or words suggest discomfort, back off, say "No problem, have a good one," and leave. No matter how unthreatening you try to be, there will always be some women you'll creep out because of your looks, your race, her own past experiences — or just because you're a stranger and a man. You can try to ask her what's wrong and show her that you're not a threat, but most of the time there won't be anything you can do. You just have to chalk her up as not compatible with you and move on. Make your intentions clear, honest, and direct, respect her boundaries, follow the guidelines here, and you'll stay out of trouble most of the time.

Attractiveness and Shame

In many cultures, especially in conservative ones, women are told that their physical attractiveness is the most important thing about them: "Be young, be pretty, find a good husband, produce many children." When the elderly couple next door tells three-year-old Vanessa she's beautiful, it's a nice compliment, but one that indicates that her looks are important. When the bullies at school mock her for her acne, she learns that physical flaws will bring her pain. When every magazine and billboard she walks by features Photoshopped models more beautiful than she will ever be, she learns to feel inadequate. Many of the obsessions with makeup, fashion, diet fads, and other trends marketed to women exacerbate and exploit this social pressure for profit. Some women learn to focus pathologically on their flaws, leading to body-image issues and crippled self-esteem — even, and sometimes especially, among the most attractive women.

When women succeed at beauty, to the degree that that's possible, they still have problems. They'll enjoy all the privileges associated with being beautiful, but attract a lot of unwanted attention. Jealous women will try to slander and humiliate them. Men will approach them more often—usually not the men they want. Most men willing to approach strangers are either arrogant or socially oblivious. When such women reject them, they're the most likely to persist and the most likely to become belligerent. Like prison guards who live their lives exposed to the worst of society, women who undergo these experiences often acquire a jaded, bitter perception of men, leading to some defensive and even cruel habits. You'll find that when women aren't interested in you, instead of rejecting you directly, they'll vanish, never to be heard from again, or they'll send you mixed signals, never quite rejecting you but never saying "Yes" either. They know it's not great, but they feel as if they have to do things that way. They don't know how you're going to react to rejection, and some guys react badly, even violently, so women take the least threatening path they can.

Madonnas and Whores

There's a pervasive myth out there that women want sex less than men do. It's completely false. Women's desire for sex is just as great as men's, if not greater. What's different is the intensity of the inhibitions on that desire. Sex, for women, is more hazardous. Their accelerators don't have any less gas, but women are traveling on a twisty road, so they're forced to ride their brakes.

Just as they do with beauty, women face a "double bind" when it comes to sex. For their entire lives they are taught that a "perfect woman" is a sexually skilled and insatiable virgin. High-status men in centuries past preferred virgins because it guaranteed that the children in their direct genetic line inherited their wealth. Remaining a virgin became a woman's best—and often only—way to raise her social status. The reason "slut" is such a vile insult is that it robs a woman of her potential social mobility. In a world where chastity is the source of your value, having sex makes you worthless, and other promiscuous women are threats. They make your chastity less valuable and tempt your monogamous mates to cheat. Slut-shaming is a tool to control other women, both to dominate them in the social hierarchy and to disarm them as threats to your relationship. It persists mostly because our social taboos haven't caught up with the invention of birth control.

Because of this social pressure, women, and to a lesser degree men, pressure women to avoid (or at least pretend to avoid) casual sex. However, that social pressure doesn't make sex feel any less wonderful. Women are capable of multiple orgasms, and sometimes the sex is so excellent that they're left convulsing, half passed-out on the bed. Rest assured, they want it.

There's a case to be made that though women want sex just as badly as men do, they're pickier about whom they'll have sex with. Since it can be more difficult for women to climax than for men, they want to make sure they're going home with guys who'll satisfy them. Imagine if you went out and every night you were surrounded by women who wanted to fuck you, but more than half the time "fucking" meant a weak-gripped hand job that stopped before you came. You probably wouldn't be keen on having that experience over and over again, but the minute you met a woman who could get you off every time, you'd want to fuck her constantly. If you're someone who can give your lover those kinds of nights, you'll find out just how mythical the "low female sex drive" truly is.

Since women are pressured to be virgins, but passionately long to have sex, they tend to develop one of three strategies. Some women buy into the sex-negative culture 100 percent, slut-shame other women, and limit their own sexuality. Others reject the culture, adopt a "sex is fun and casual" perspective, and do their best to ignore the harassment that lifestyle brings. Most fall somewhere in the middle. They have as much sex as they can, but they keep it secret. For these women, deciding whether to sleep with you depends as much on how well they can hide it as it does on how much they like you.

Now that you know a bit about women's sexual politics, what can you do to help? For starters, you can adopt a radically sex-positive attitude. As far as you're concerned, the words "slut" and "whore" don't exist. Sex is awesome. People who think it's dirty, or who criticize women for having it, are weirdos. You will never judge anyone for whom they sleep with or how they like to fuck. At the same time, you appreciate that other people will judge your lover, and since you don't want her to have to deal with bullshit, you shut up about it. Don't brag about sex, don't talk about past lovers, don't criticize anyone's sexuality, and most of all, don't talk about having sex with her. If you can show her that she doesn't have to worry about sex-negative stuff around you, you'll minimize one of the biggest hangups she has about sex, and not only will she be more comfortable sleeping with you, she'll enjoy it more — and she'll make sure you do too.

Pregnancy

Imagine if every time you had sex you could be infected with a parasite. This parasite will eat your food but still cause you to gain weight, make you feel sick all the time, and induce mood swings you can't control. When you remove the parasite, it's more painful than being shot, you have to be conscious during the procedure, and to top it off, you're now an unwilling parent. How would this make you feel?

Having children can be wonderful, but if that's not what you want, sex is a potentially life-changing danger. In

Relating to Women

order to sleep with you, not only does a woman need to overcome her fear of you as a physical threat, as well as all the slut-shaming social bullshit, she has to deal with the threat of carrying an unwanted fetus in her womb for nine months. Make this an easy choice for her. Always carry a condom, be willing to wear it, and if it tears, be willing to split the bill for the morning-after pill.

Career vs. Family

Career and family are more incompatible for women than they are for men. Pregnancy, childbirth, and raising kids will mean months, and can mean years, of reduced professional productivity. They can't go to classes, attend meetings, make deals, or take on any major professional responsibilities when parenting consumes half or more of their time. Though more and more men are taking on the "stay at home dad" role, the biological ability to nurse a baby, and the cultural expectations in most societies, still pressure women to be mothers first and professionals second. Because of this, most women have to make a choice pretty early in life; they're either going to prioritize their careers and have little intent to start a family, or they'll prioritize their relationships and families and work only as necessary. Since the middle ground is untenable, you won't meet many who ride the line.

The best way to address this problem is to focus on women with values compatible with yours. Don't date the CEO if you want to start a family, and don't insist on splitting the bill if you want to be a breadwinner. In this case, rejection is your friend. If the woman you're dating has fundamentally different values from what you want, you're not compatible and you shouldn't be together. I've found that when it comes to casual sex, professional women are more open to "fuck buddy" arrangements, since they're not looking for commitment and family. You'll break fewer hearts meeting

250

women at the entrepreneurship conference than in the church parking lot, so keep that in mind when choosing your venues to socialize.

How to Learn More

There are three activities I've found that helped me learn how to relate to women:

• Talking with women

• Following media popular with women

• Reading feminist literature

Read some feminist literature, such as works by Gloria Steinem, or *The Vagina Monologues* by Eve Ensler. You don't have to agree with everything (and in the case of the radical stuff, I hope you don't), but it's helpful to know the sorts of things that have upset women enough to organize a multigenerational activist movement to change. Read *Cosmopolitan*, fashion magazines, and romance novels. Watch romantic comedies. Most of all, talk to lots of women. Make friends with them. Hang out with them. Enjoy their company for its own sake. As I've said from the start, women are people, and cool people are worth spending time with whether you're sleeping together or not. If there's chemistry, great; you can hook up. If there isn't, it's also great. Spending time with interesting people is its own reward.

Chapter Summary

• Women are unique individuals. Be slow to generalize.

• "Creepiness" is an icky feeling associated with the fear of rape. Shifty behavior exacerbates it.

• Women are pressured to be physically beautiful, but have problems when they succeed.

• Women enjoy sex, but are shamed for engaging in it.

• Pregnancy is a big deal.

• Women often have to choose to focus either on their careers or on building families.

• To learn more, study feminism and popular female-oriented media, and get to know women.

Exercises

Exercise 20.1 – Immediate – Follow Some Women's Media
Pick up some material marketed to women and watch/read/listen to it. What's its appeal? What desires does it fulfill? If it's feminist literature, what issues does it raise? If it's advice, what big problems is it trying to help with? Write in your journal about your discoveries.

Chapter 21 – Meeting Women

Women are everywhere. Every time you step out your door you have countless chances to meet someone. Often we think of the handful of women we already know as our "dating pool," which tends to make us desperate and clingy. They aren't your options. Every woman on earth is an option. The only limit is your comfort zone.

You don't have time to date every woman on earth, so you have to set standards. A lot of women are too old or too young for you. You can give it a shot, but if they're at a completely different stage of life, there'll be problems. Many of them aren't single. Some of them aren't interested in men. Some won't like to have sex the way you do, and many won't share your values. Without even considering whether you're attracted to each other, you can rule out more than 90 percent of women, which is what you want to do. By having standards and not jumping at every woman who shows you affection, you show them you're not desperate, which has nothing but good implications. It suggests that you have dating experience and that other women are probably interested in you. Even more important, it indicates to a woman that if she says "No" to you, you're less likely to react badly.

In my experience, you can expect around 5 percent of the women you meet to be compatible enough for a one-night stand, 1 percent for a two- to three-month relationship, and one in a thousand for a long-term relationship. It's a pretty small ratio, which is why you'll want to be meeting lots, and why rejection is your friend. Rejection isn't a signal that you're not good enough; it's a filter for mediocre experiences. Every time you're rejected, and every time you reject someone else, it frees you to find someone who's truly right for you. The single life can be lonely, but it's still better than an unhappy relationship. When you get that text message saying she's washing her hair for the next hundred years, remind yourself that it could be worse. You could be married to her. When you start meeting women whom you click with, you'll be grateful for every rejection you've ever had.

Where to Meet Women

Becoming attractive presents a sort of paradox, in that trying to do it is itself an unattractive thing to do. Meeting women is similar. If you're going to a club to "pick up chicks," you'll find your mindset works against you. Thinking in terms of "How can I get her to come home with me?" makes you outcome-dependent. You'll be focusing on manipulating her, and you've given her power over how much fun you're having. If, instead, you go out thinking "How can I have the most fun?" and keep that question fresh in your mind, you'll be operating from a much stronger position. When you meet someone you find attractive, if instead of "How can I manipulate her into sleeping with me?" you're thinking "What's she like? Am I compatible with her?" you'll be bringing much more energy and curiosity to the interaction, and your fun will be infectious. If you were that woman, and you were choosing between the manipulative guy and the fun guy, who would you go home with? This is why we never go out *to* meet women; we go out *and* meet women.

Even when meeting women is on your mind, you don't want to meet just any women; you want to meet compatible women. The best way to do that is to focus on stuff you'd do for its own sake with women around. Opt for the social hobbies you were interested in from chapter 15, or join clubs connected with your individual hobbies. Walk up to women, as we talked about in chapter 8, chat with them, and if you're attracted to one, ask her out. Sometimes the woman will like you; sometimes she won't. Either outcome is fine. Think of romance and sex as the whipped cream on the sundae, not the sundae itself. You're going to enjoy things whether romance is there or not, and when it is, things are even better.

Types of Venues

If you're looking for places that will make it easy for you to introduce yourself to women, look for warm venues. A warm venue is any place that encourages or requires strangers to interact with one another. You won't get nervous about approaching people because the decision to approach isn't yours. These are the best places for beginners, and ideal even when you're experienced. Cold venues are places that discourage social interaction and require you to violate social norms. They require courage in the best of times and invite scorn in the worst. Moderate venues are unstructured social atmospheres. It's up to you to approach, but in those venues, unlike in cold ones, people will usually be happy that you did.

Warm	Moderate	Cold
Meetup events	Bars	The street
Speed dating	Conventions	The train
Social sports teams	School/college	Bus stops
Parties	Nightclubs	Grocery stores
Dance classes	Rock concerts	Malls
Acting classes	Online dating	Museums
Clubs/societies	Karaoke	Parks

I won't discourage you outright from approaching people in cold venues, but I will encourage you to make it unnecessary. I know guys who've met friends and lovers that way, and it's entirely possible to get good at it, but in my opinion, its rewards are too few and too inconsistent for the risks involved. A woman you approach on the street is much less likely to be compatible with you than a woman you meet through your hobbies. You're going to have to approach a lot, and every time, that approach will have a price. As we talked about in chapters 8 and 20, women tend to feel threatened by strange men approaching them, and the sorts of guys who do it tend to be either guys who've trained themselves to disregard other people's feelings or guys too socially unaware to realize they're upsetting people. They often make the women they approach uncomfortable, earning themselves a bad reputation and salting the earth for everyone else. I never had trouble meeting more attractive and compatible women than I had time to date through warm and moderate venues alone. I've made plenty of approaches in moderate venues, but I've made fewer than five cold-venue approaches in my life. Some guys have had success with it; good for them, but it seems to be the sort of thing you'd do only if you're not already meeting lots of women. It's as if you're a business owner — sure, you can sell products by making cold calls out of the phone book, but wouldn't you rather meet customers through referrals? When you're living an interesting life, and you're meeting dozens of women through your hobbies, I don't see the appeal of approaching in cold venues.

Top 10 Places to Meet Women

#1 Friends' Parties

Parties are great. Introductions are natural, everyone's out to have fun, and the single people are usually open to hooking up. Since you have friends in common with the other guests, you'll also tend to be more compatible. There are no downsides to parties.
Rating: 5/5

#2 Social Dance Classes

Salsa, swing, tango, blues — any kind of social dance classes will introduce you to dozens of women a night, no matter how shy you are. You'll be touching and smelling each other, which will accelerate chemistry. You can flirt in relative privacy while in the lesson, and the transition to intimate dancing after the lesson is seamless. The only downsides of dance classes are the frequent interruptions during partner changes and the loud music, which can make talking difficult. If you can find lessons with a quiet bar area in which to chat, that's gold.

Rating: 5/5

#3 *Meetup.com* and Similar Social Website Events
Meetup offers limitless opportunities catered to your interests. Everyone's looking to be social, so introductions are easy. Most folks who use Meetup are pretty shy, so since you're actually working on your social skills, you'll probably be one of the most outgoing people there. Avoid events geared toward singles, as they tend to attract the most eccentric personalities. Join groups oriented toward hobbies — book clubs, social sports, cooking groups — and you'll do far better.

Rating: 4/5

#4 Online Dating
Everyone on an online dating site is looking to hook up, find love, or both, so your advances will be relatively welcome. Most sites let you know when someone "likes" you, which removes some of the guesswork. With sites that ask you survey questions, you can filter for compatibility, at least in values and hobbies if not in chemistry. On the downside, some users will have misleading pictures and biographies, and you'll have some disappointing first dates. The profiles and messages can also rob some of the excitement from your first interaction. As with the Meetup groups, you'll encounter a disproportionate number of eccentric personalities, so be careful. Since women tend to receive dozens if not hundreds of messages a week, it can also be hard to be heard over the noise. We'll talk about these issues in greater depth in chapter 23.

Rating: 3/5

#5 Social Sports Teams

People who play sports tend to be fit and attractive, and if they're playing in a sport you like, they're more likely to be compatible with you. Being on the same team builds natural rapport, and if you're on opposite teams you can have playful competitiveness. Most such groups throw parties afterward, and you should favor groups that do. If there's no postgame socializing, this is a 3/5.

Rating: 5/5

#6 Yoga Classes

Yoga's great for your health and flexibility. You will be one of few men in class, and the women will tend to be attractive. It's a moderate venue, not a warm one, and the guy who does yoga to get laid is a cliché. Only do yoga if it truly interests you, but if it does, you'll meet more attractive women than you'll have time to date.

Rating: 4/5

#7 Solo Dance Classes (Jazz, Tap, etc.)

You will likely be the only (straight) man there. The women are usually physically attractive, ambitious, and intelligent. It is also the single best way to improve your posture and bodily awareness. If you're willing to tolerate people criticizing you for doing a "feminine" activity, you'll have an endless stream of attractive women entering your life.

Rating: 5+/5

#8 Acting and Improv Classes

These are a great social workout, and the women you meet will be more physically attractive and funnier than average. Duet scenes and physical contact exercises are excellent for sparking chemistry. Actors and comedians tend to live melodramatic lives, so be wary of that. Otherwise, these are gold.

Rating: 5/5

#9 Nightclubs and High-Class Bars

Sweaty, sexual dancing offers infinite opportunities for chemistry and intimacy. Almost everyone there will be open to a one-night stand. Club-goers tend to be physically attractive, as the unattractive are discouraged from coming. On the downside, clubs are moderate venues with cold tendencies, as people can be cruel and judgmental. The loud music prevents conversation, so interactions have to be shallow. Your attractiveness will depend heavily on your looks and dancing skills (though that's a plus if those are strengths for you). Cover costs and overpriced drinks make clubs a pricier option. If you can find an offbeat club, such as a Goth club, or a club with a theme, such as one hosting an eighties night, it will tend to be friendlier.
Rating: 3/5

#10 Travel Group

Everyone wants to have sex on vacation. If you're part of a travel group that includes women, you're likely to sleep with at least one of them. You'll be spending lots of time together and you'll get to know each other well. There is a guaranteed end point, so the stakes are low. Opportunities for sex arise naturally in such environments. The only downside is that the relationship must be short-term. Transferring a vacation relationship to real life tends to be messy. As long as you're okay with cutting things off at the end of the trip, travel hookups are a blast.
Rating: 5/5

How to Approach Women

In Warm Venues

Warm venues encourage friendliness and closeness. You're not in a rush. Relax, be social, be friendly, and don't try to hit on everyone. You're not there to collect phone numbers, and you don't need to play the odds. Everyone's looking to be friendly and make connections, and you've got the whole night to do it. When you find someone you like, spend most of your time with her. Don't get upset if she chats with other people and don't be shy about doing the same, but keep coming back to her and striking up new conversations. Think of her as your "girlfriend for the night." If you run around the venue hitting on everyone, people will start to assume you're a player and no one will want to invest in you. Start with some friendly banter with everyone, pick one woman you're attracted to, get to know her, dance, flirt, and chat. Sometimes it won't work out, but if you're hopping between people like a starving mosquito, it definitely won't.

In Moderate Venues

Here's the mentality you want in a moderate venue: "I'm a social guy looking to have fun. I don't know if I will like any of the women here, but I damn well want to find out." You're not looking to get laid; you're looking to make friends, and if you happen to be sexually attracted to one of your new friends, you can make it obvious. Chapter 8 covers all the social skills you need for moderate venues. Walk up to groups, compliment them, and ask to join. Learn people's names, get to know them, banter, joke, listen, and flirt if it seems appropriate. If you click with someone, ask for her number — or take her home. You don't have to be quite as "one-night monogamous" as in a warm venue, but if you're really connecting with someone, you might want to tone it down with anyone else.

If you approach an individual woman, keep it simple. Your only goal is to walk up, deliver your compliment and ask permission to join her, and then listen. "Hey, I noticed you chilling here and thought I'd keep you company. You mind if I join you?" You're not looking to take her home, you don't have to charm her, you don't have to do anything; you're being social and friendly, and you're bringing the fun. If she doesn't want your company, no problem. The stakes are nonexistent. Once you've tried it once, you'll be surprised just how easy it can be. A lot of women go out at least open to the possibility of meeting a guy, and if you're following the advice in this book, trust me: you're the guy she wants to meet.

In Cold Venues

In cold venues, you are interrupting someone to get her attention. If you're going to approach, the rule of thumb is to open with why you are interrupting her. If the only reason you can give is that you think she's good-looking, open with that and ask her on an instant date. "Hey, you're so cute, I'd be kicking myself all day if I didn't come flirt with you. You wanna grab some tea and hang out at the café down the street?" With this approach, you will often get rejected and you will still creep some women out, but it's by far your best option. You're not deceiving her, there's no incongruity between your words and your body language, and you've made it easy for her to reject you and get away if she needs to. It's also confident as hell, and the idea that you're so attracted to her that you "had to come flirt with her" can itself be a turn-on. Anything other than this approach will set off her warning signals. "He's clearly interested in me; why is he being deceptive about it?" If she turns you down, just say "No problem; thanks," and leave. If she's interested, follow through on your invitation and start to banter.

There's one alternative to the direct approach, but it comes into play only if you aren't already attracted to her. Maybe she's cute, but you have higher standards than just "cute," and you're curious whether she meets them, and that curiosity is what's inspired you to approach. If that is genuinely the case, approach her with whatever about her piqued your interest. "Hey, I've gotta say, your fashion sense is impressive." "Your dog is fucking adorable. What's his name?" Banter with her for a bit, and if she seems cool, say so. "You seem pretty cool; you wanna grab a drink down the street?" "You seem pretty cool, you wanna trade numbers and go out sometime?" As long as you're being direct and respecting her boundaries, you should be okay.

How to Flirt

Flirting is telling someone you're thinking about sex with them without saying so — and sometimes with saying so. It's primarily communicated by your tone of voice, in your body language, and through innuendo. Here are the basics of flirting:

• Hold eye contact with her longer than you would with someone you weren't into.

• When you shake hands, keep holding hers even after you've stopped the handshake.

• Touch her. See chapter 24.

• Smile with teeth when she compliments you or tells a joke.

• Deepen your voice.

• Use innuendo—especially words with suggestive double meanings.

Flirting is subtle. Often the only difference between it and ordinary banter is increased eye contact. At some point, though, you want to make your interest explicit. "This is my favorite conversation I've had in a long time. You want to go out this weekend?" "I'm having so much fun with you. You wanna go do this thing with me tomorrow night?" Imagine if someone you were attracted to said that to you. You'd be excited, right? That's how she'll feel when you tell her. Directness shows confidence and sexual intent. It shows that you're not in the least afraid of rejection, that you act on your feelings, and that you're excited by her. She'll probably say

"Yes," and if she doesn't, it'll usually be in a tone of regret. "I'd really like to, but I have a boyfriend, I'm sorry!" That's all there is to flirting. It's banter plus touching and eye contact, eventually leading to a direct expression of your interest. Look her in the eyes, touch her, and let her know you're into her. She won't always say yes, but when you're expressing your interest so clearly, she'll definitely think about it.

How to Ask a Woman Out

Things Not to Do

"Confess"

Imagine the following: James Bond has spent the last hour of a film with his female co-star. In a private duet scene, he says "I need to tell you something. I have a crush on you. I know that you might not have feelings for me, and that this is awkward, but I've really, really liked you for a long time, and I want to confess those feelings to you now." You'd laugh out loud. The lines would be completely out of character, and that writer would be fired.

One of the questions I get most frequently from guys is how they should "confess their feelings" to a woman they like. The answer is: Don't. Act on them. Ask her on a date. You can let her know "I think you're crazy cute," but you need follow it up with "You wanna go out tomorrow night?" Simply "confessing" without following it up with an invitation suggests that you're expecting rejection. Don't make that choice for her. Ask her out and give her the chance to say "Yes."

Number Collecting

I see this all the time in bars. Guys walk up to women and talk to them just long enough to get a phone number; then they move on to the next one. What the hell are they doing? Do they think those numbers are going to go anywhere? No. All those guys are doing is looking for validation. "These women gave me their numbers. They're so into me!" Actually calling those numbers would risk destroying that illusion, so for most of these guys, it never happens. When you ask a woman for her number, do it for a good reason. You're meeting up on Saturday, and you need her number so you can find each other when you get there. Phone numbers are means, not ends.

Postponing the Question

You're chatting with a woman, but you're hesitating to ask her out because once she rejects you, you know things will get awkward. I have news for you. If she doesn't want you to ask her out, it's already awkward. As soon as you know you want to see more of her, ask the question. Don't stall, don't wait until the "right moment"; ask immediately. Yes, this is scary, and you're facing rejection, but remember, that's what you want. If she rejects you early on, you won't be waiting around for days wondering if she'll text you back, and you'll be free to meet another woman that night. If you can keep your ego out of it, you'll realize the rejection leaves you better off. Find another woman, chat for a bit, decide you like her, make plans, ask for her number, and then keep hanging out with her. Setting up a date doesn't mean your night has to end there. She may yet go home with you, and whether she does or not, you have plans for later.

What to Do Instead

While you're chatting, look for things you have in common that will make for a natural first date—common interests, hobbies, and the like. "Just climbed my first 5.8 this week." "No shit, you climb? I'm going climbing Thursday; you wanna come?" "Sure. I can do Thursday." "Cool. What's your number?" As soon as she gives you her number, send her a text message with your name and the logistics. You can add a short flirty message if you want. "Jason's number, he's cute and he climbs. Rock Spot, Thursday 7:00."

If you don't find any obvious first dates in your chat, invite her to one of the dates listed in the next chapter. "Hey, the Fluff Festival's happening Sunday and I was thinking of going. Wanna come?" "Yeah, sure." "Cool, let's trade numbers." If you're overbooked, or can't think of a date, that's okay. Let her know that you're into her and that you want to ask her out, but can't yet. "Hey, so I think you're cool and I wanna ask you out, but I'm booked for the next week. You wanna trade numbers and connect next weekend?" "Sure." "Okay, what's your number?" This isn't ideal, especially at a bar, since there's a good chance she'll forget who you are in a week, but it's better than nothing.

Handling Lukewarm Interest

When you ask a woman out, sometimes she responds ambiguously. "I can't." "I have plans." She isn't saying she's not interested, but she isn't saying "yes" either. There are all sorts of reasons a woman might do this. Most likely it's just that she's not into you but she's afraid of how you'll take a direct rejection, so she's waffling and avoiding the question. Alternatively, her interest might be lukewarm, and she's looking for something to tip the balance one way or another. It's also possible that she actually has plans but she's not assertive enough to propose another date.

Whatever reasons she has, you want to get a clear "Yes" or "No" from her, which means encouraging her to be assertive. "Okay, you want to try for another time, or you want me to stop asking?" Give her permission to reject you. Remember—when you're being vulnerable and direct, you're demonstrating that you're not interested in bullshit, that you're not afraid of rejection, and that you're sensitive to her wishes. This has nothing but positive connotations. If she comes back with "Yeah, I wanna get together, I'm just not free Saturday," offer a different date. If she winds up saying "No," you've avoided wasting your time and energy on something that was never going to happen anyway.

Same-Night Hookups

Sometimes you'll meet someone and hit it off so well that you'll both want to hook up that night. For these situations, think of some simple date ideas within walking distance of your place that you can bounce to: ice cream shops, bars, video game arcades. You want it to be a short time commitment that's easy to leave, ideally with a quiet and private spot where you can make out and chat. Invite her to head there: "Wanna go grab some ice cream?" "I know a cool place to grab a drink. Wanna come?" Most women will assume this is an invitation to come over and have sex (unless they're very naïve), and will respond accordingly. Don't assume it's a "yes" to sex, but it's a strong sign of interest.

The next venue is your opportunity to connect emotionally. There's no rush. If you haven't kissed her yet, you should be going for it there. When you finish your drinks or ice cream, if you still want to hook up, be direct. "I live down the street. Wanna come over?" If she says "No," it doesn't necessarily mean "No, never." She could want to get to know you better. She could have a rule against sex on the first date. She might think sleeping with you that night would jeopardize her chances of making you her boyfriend. Who knows? She has her reasons. Whatever they are, she's spent this much time with you and clearly likes you. Ask her out for another date in the next couple of days. If she rejects you or doesn't reply, that sucks, but it happens. You'll just have to move on.

Chapter Summary

• Focus on meeting women in warm and moderate venues.

• Parties, dance classes, Meetup events, social sports, yoga, acting and improv classes, online dating, nightclubs, bars, and traveling are your best bets.

• When in warm venues, focus on connecting with just one woman.

• When in moderate venues, be social first and flirty second.

• When making a cold approach, be direct if you're attracted and friendly if you're unsure.

• To flirt, hold eye contact, hold your handshake longer, touch her, smile, deepen your voice, use sexual innuendo, and express your interest directly.

• When you approach an individual woman, say your introduction and just listen. You don't need gimmicks.

• Don't "confess" your feelings, collect phone numbers, or procrastinate in asking her out.

• Look for common interests that make a natural first date, and invite her to join you.

• When you ask for her number, make sure it's serving a purpose.

• If she's waffling, give her a chance to reject you or let you know she likes you.

• If chemistry is strong, invite her to a venue close to your place to hang out one on one; then invite her over.

Exercises

Exercise 21.1 – Immediate – Brainstorm Venues

Write out a list of ten warm and ten moderate venues in your area. Use the Internet, *meetup.com*, and any other resources you can think of. Highlight the venues that interest you most.

Exercise 21.2 – Ongoing – Start Attending One Warm Venue Regularly

Choose one of the warm venues from Exercise 21.1 that you can start attending regularly: a class, Meetup event, dance lesson, or something similar. If it overlaps with one of your choices for Exercise 15.1, all the better. For the first couple of weeks, all you have to do is go. If you make new friends or find opportunities to flirt, great, but that's not required.

Exercise 21.3 – Ongoing/Responsive – Approach a Woman in a Moderate Venue and Ask Her Out

Go to one of the moderate venues on your list and practice approaching groups of people. "You guys seem fun; whatcha celebrating tonight?" Try to go to at least two moderate venues per month—more if possible. As you make friends, get their numbers and invite them to future outings. On one of these outings, ask out one of the women you meet. "Hey, I'm looking at doing XYZ this Saturday. Wanna come?" If this is scary for you, make sure to include it on your exposure list. Write in your journal about your experiences.

Exercise 21.4 – One Time/Partner – Play the "Cold Approach" Game in a Moderate Venue

At a moderate venue, such as a bar, go out with a buddy and play a game involving cold approaches. Have a list of cheesy pickup lines to try out. Give your buddy $100 and ask him to give you $10 after every approach you make. You don't have to go home with anyone; this is purely an exercise to get over your nerves. Feel free to add this into your exposure hierarchy.

Chapter 22 – Planning Dates

In 2002, *Star Wars Episode II: Attack of the Clones* hit theaters. It was the story of how Anakin Skywalker, the Jedi Knight who was to become Darth Vader, fell in love with Padmé Amidala, the future mother of the main characters in the classic trilogy. The actors were attractive. They wore exotic and sexy clothing. Their dates were in the most mind-blowingly beautiful and clichéd romantic settings, including sunny fields, moonlit balconies, and a room lit by firelight. They laughed, smiled, and exchanged sweet nothings. Despite all of this, it was widely hailed as the worst romance in the history of cinema.[235]

I bring this film up to demonstrate a simple lesson: you can't manufacture chemistry. You can plan a romantic moonlit walk on the beach or sip champagne on New Year's Eve, but chemistry doesn't come from the venue; it comes from the two of you. We develop attraction to each other through subconscious signals picked up by our five senses. How do we like this person's face? Does she look healthy? Does he smell as if his immune system is different from mine, so our babies will be strong?[236] Is his voice masculine?[237] We look for behaviors suggesting confidence and agreeableness. Our subconscious minds evaluate our dates for mating potential, and we experience these evaluations as emotions. Sometimes we get horny. Sometimes it "doesn't feel right." When you're planning your dates, there's no formula for manufacturing love, but you can at least arrange things to maximize your opportunities for discovering chemistry and minimize the common pitfalls. At the end of the day, though, if you're not right for each other, you're just not right for each other.

Things Not to Do for First Dates

The Dinner Date

When most people imagine a romantic date, they think of two people eating at a fancy restaurant. It's the bread and butter of dating, and it sucks. While such dates are not the worst option, it's difficult to conceive of a kind of date more perfectly designed to hinder chemistry.

Dinner dates are interviews. You exchange biographies and watch each other chew. You never see the other person at an emotional extreme. What is she like when she's excited, thrilled, or happy? How does he handle a challenge? You don't know. Since it feels like an interview, both of you try to "put your best foot forward." Neither of you is being genuine. There's no touching, smelling, kissing, cuddling, or anything resembling what humans do to bond biologically. You're limited to eye contact and verbal flirting. To put a cherry on the shit sundae, restaurants usually sit couples across from each other: the single most confrontational arrangement possible.[238] Everything about a dinner date conspires to limit chemistry, and even encourage hostility.

If you must go on a dinner date, choose a circular table and sit at a right angle to your date, rather than across from her. If you're at a booth, sit next to her, or sit at the bar. If you have to sit at a table across from her, maintain eye contact as much as possible. With luck, the two of you will be compatible enough to overcome the hazards of the shitty situation.

The Movie Date

I have a theory that the classic "dinner and a movie" date was invented by conservative parents to be so awful that it guaranteed their kids would never have sex. As bad as dinner dates are, movie dates are worse; they might be the worst dates you can possibly have.

The point of a first date is to get to know each

other and uncover chemistry. A movie date achieves neither. You don't talk to each other, you don't look at each other, and you're probably not comfortable touching each other. You leave with the same questions you arrived with. Don't go on movie dates until late in the relationship.

The Bar Date

A bar date is any date where drinking beverages is the main event. While they're not great, bar dates are better than the other two listed above. They're more casual, alcohol can be a social lubricant, and you're both less likely to put on a façade to impress the other person.

The problem with the bar date is that, even though talking is the only thing you can do, it's not easy to talk. Bars are loud, crowded, and anything but intimate. To get the sort of atmosphere you want, you'll have to hunt down a dive bar, but inviting a woman to a dive bar screams of alcoholism or questionable intentions. If you ever find yourself in the unfortunate situation of meeting a woman at a bar, look up other activities nearby. Have a drink and then bounce to that next activity as soon as possible.

How to Plan a Romantic Date

We want our dates to be fun, cheap or free, memorable, brag-worthy, open to spontaneity, conducive to conversation and chemistry, and easily escapable if things go south. A good date entertains you, puts you at ease, and lets you be yourselves. You're never struggling to make conversation and you always have a plan for the next activity. Ideally, those plans are flexible, so if she says "Hey…you wanna go to my place?" you don't reply, "That would be nice, but I already bought tickets to the butter sculptures." Keeping your activities free and flexible also lets you take advantage of serendipity. You had planned to go to the mall, but that R-rated hypnotist show you walked by sounds more fun. Since you weren't committed to the mall, you can swap it out.

A good date moves around. When you're moving from venue to venue, it feels more like an adventure, and your memories will record it better than if everything you did happened in one place. If you become a couple, you'll have a great first-date story. If it doesn't work out, at least it failed spectacularly. You're doing it right when even the women who reject you thank you for such a great night.

Three Activities

A simple way to achieve the above goals is to plan three distinct activities, each taking about an hour. The first activity should be the focus. It's the crux of the date, the thing you invited her to do the night you met her. It should be the most exciting and most physical activity, but not necessarily the most romantic. If you're going to spend money on the date, this is where you should do it.

The second activity should be low-key. You just burned a lot of energy in the first part, so this is your opportunity to settle down and talk. Though dinner shouldn't be the centerpiece of your date, stopping for food fills this role well.

The third activity is the most flexible. At this point, you've been together for two hours, and you should have a good idea of how much you like each other. If the date's not going well, you want to be able to cancel your third activity without losing anything, so never spend money ahead of time. If the date's still on, though, this is where you ramp up the romance. The third activity should be the most private and intimate. If you haven't done so already, it's the event during which you kiss her. If it can be close to your place or hers for an easy bounce to a hookup afterward, all the better.

Suggestions for Each Part

Part 1

- Drag show (best date on this list)
- Flying a kite
- Fashion window shopping (pick out and model outfits for each other)
- Rock climbing
- Partner-dance lesson
- Kayaking
- Ice skating
- Hiking
- Cooking class
- Chocolate factory/brewery tour
- Read books to each other at the library/bookstore
- Mini golf
- Drive-in movie (exception to movie rule because you can talk and cuddle)
- Shooting range
- Karaoke
- Bowling
- Arcade
- Go-carts
- Thrift store outfit shopping
- Playing with animals
- Botanical gardens
- The beach
- Pottery-making
- Toy store
- Minor-league sports
- Carnival/theme park
- Laser tag

- Water park
- Paintball
- Ingredients and cooking—she picks ingredients, you cook (this takes skill)
- Geocaching
- Researching each other's birthdays in old newspapers at the library
- The zoo
- Planetarium
- Off-roading
- Fruit or flower picking
- R-rated hypnotist show
- Concert

Part 2

- Ice cream
- Quick dinner/lunch
- Coffee/tea
- Grab drinks
- Walk in the park
- Feed the birds
- People-watching
- Picnic
- Watch the sun set
- Stand-up comedy (preferably amateur so you can go in and come out to talk)
- Improv show (preferably interactive)
- Museum
- Art gallery
- Outdoor symphony
- Buy <$5 gifts for each other in under ten minutes at a department store/dollar store

- Watch the city lights turn on at night from a distance
- Bar with board games

Part 3

- Frisbee golf
- Grab drinks
- Billiards
- Ice cream
- Stargazing
- Painting
- Wine, cheese, and romantic music
- Outdoor movie night (laptop and speakers in the back yard, or projector on house if you have one)
- Watch planes take off near the airport
- Act out plays together
- Fondue
- Go dancing
- Playgrounds
- Build a fort at your place
- Pick up food and cook together
- College observatory
- Bake/make ice cream
- Play Hide and Seek
- Movie at your place
- Legos
- Board games (with sexy rules, like "Strip Sorry," or Truth or Dare Jenga)
- The beach at night
- Video games
- Origami
- Moonlight swim

- Fireplace marshmallow roasting
- Build a snowman
- Walk the dog
- Watch the sunset
- Poetry reading
- Hot-tub rental

Ideas for Dates after the First

Some things make great dates, but poor first ones. They cost too much money or they're not conducive to conversation or chemistry. When you know her well, and after you've had sex, consider these dates too.

- Private-room karaoke
- Whale watching
- Sunrise picnic
- Hot-air balloon ride
- Meteor-shower watching
- Live dance performance
- Symphony
- Live theater/musical
- Children's museum
- Escape rooms
- Movie date
- Dinner date
- Couples' massage
- Boating
- Watching cartoons
- Volunteering together
- Uncharacteristic venue (go to a Goth club, a fetish club, etc.)
- Paint each other's bodies
- Do each other's makeup

• Glassblowing class

• Short-range road trip

Sample Dates

The Mall Date
• Fashion window shopping

• Eat in food court

• Watch the sunset

Beach Date
• Fly a kite at the beach in the evening

• Walk down the beach as the sun sets

• Grab drinks at the beach bar

Drag Show
• Go to a drag show

• Grab drinks at another bar

• Play sexy board games at your place

Latin Night
• Have a salsa lesson together

• Dance in the club

• Wine and cheese with Spanish guitar at your place

Nerdy Date
• Museum or planetarium

• Café or bar with board games

• Read plays together at your place

1930s Date
• Thrift-store shopping for 1930s-style outfits

• Drive-in movie

• Swing dancing

Comedy Date
• Go to a comedy show

• Grab some drinks

• Watch a terrible movie at your place and make fun of it

Middle-School Date
• Mini golf

• Ice cream

• After-hours playground

Water Date
• Aquarium

• Moonlight swimming (some cities have skyscraper rooftop pools)

• Drinks

Music Date
• Concert

• Drinks

• Karaoke

Pacing

No two dates are alike, but generally, less than one hour into the date you should both be comfortable with some physical contact (holding hands), and within three hours, you should have kissed. It's not a race and there isn't a time limit; it's just how things normally progress if there's good chemistry. If you've finished your second activity and you're not comfortable holding hands, consider ending the date. If you're finishing up your second date and still haven't kissed, you probably shouldn't go out again. The pace can be slower if you're in a more conservative culture, but if you stall for too long, your date will start to think you're either not confident enough to make a move or you're not interested.

Dealing with Cancellations

A woman is sometimes going to cancel your date, which is why you want to avoid spending money ahead of time. Sometimes she's not into you. Sometimes she's just bad at following through on plans. Maybe she met another guy, or wasn't single to begin with. Cancellations will be a part of the process, especially early on, and especially with online dating. Don't take them personally and don't let your self-esteem get involved. Congratulate yourself for putting yourself out there and asking her out.

As you get more experience and start to raise your standards, things will improve. Always try to get a clear "Yes" or "No" when you ask a woman out, and if her answer's ambiguous, assume it's a "No." This will cut down on cancellations a lot. Make sure the day, time, and location are clear and that she has them in writing (with a text message). This will cut down on the "Shit, I forgot" cancellations. If you're in doubt about whether your date will show up, send her a text an hour before you are scheduled to meet. "Hey, still good for 7?" Don't leave your house until she responds. If she cancels on you at this point, or she doesn't respond at all, never talk to her again. She is both unreliable and inconsiderate. If she cancels, apologizes, and offers to reschedule immediately, forgive her once. This shows enough consideration to earn the benefit of the doubt.

How to End a Date

If You're Both Not Interested

If you weren't feeling any chemistry, it's likely she wasn't either. She should be fine with ending things pretty simply. Say "Thanks for coming out; it was good to meet you," and leave. That's all you need to do.

You Aren't Interested, But She Is

A lot of people try to "let their dates down easily" when the attraction's one-sided. Perhaps you've experienced this from the "rejected" side. Does it help? Nope. It still sucks. The truly sensitive route is to make your rejection direct and unambiguous. "I don't think I'm interested in getting together anymore, but thanks for meeting up." If she asks you for any reasons or suggestions (which will never happen), you're not obligated to give them, but it's helpful if you can. Just explain in a couple of sentences what turned you off.

You Are Interested

If things have gone well, and you're interested in hooking up, invite her over. "Hey, you wanna come over to my place?" If she says "Yes," don't assume that means she's definitely up for sex, but it's a pretty solid indication that she is. If she says "No," no problem. Some women will be offended that you asked, but in my opinion, asking is the best policy, since the only alternative is dishonesty.

If you have a second date in mind, invite her to it, either in lieu of or in addition to inviting her back to your place. "You up for getting together again? There's a drag show Friday I was thinking would be fun." If you don't have a date in mind, ask her what her feelings are in general. "That's cool; you wanna get together again?" Remember that giving her every opportunity to reject you is the most confident route. If she's not interested, she'll say "I don't think so" or something similar. Otherwise, she'll say "Sure." "Okay, let's touch base tomorrow and make plans." Make sure to follow through. Sometimes her "Yes" will be a lie, since many women feel uncomfortable rejecting a guy in person, so don't get too excited. She might ghost or change her mind. If that happens, you just have to move on.

Date Multiple Women

A lot of our conversation here has addressed dealing

with rejection, flaking, dishonesty, ghosting, and the like. These are all hazards you'll frequently face in dating, especially early on. You should assume that every woman you're meeting is seeing other men, and until you start seeing each other regularly during the high-value real estate times such as Friday and Saturday nights, you should be seeing other women as well, and you shouldn't get too attached. You won't be able to help investing a little bit, and you should, but if you "fall in love" with every promising connection, you're going to get hurt over and over again. Remember that rejections, even rude rejections, are part of the experience. They aren't a reflection of your worth as a person. All they mean is that you and she weren't compatible. There are compatible women awaiting you in your future. Stay excited for them.

Chapter Summary

• You can't manufacture chemistry, but you can maximize the chances that it will develop.

• Avoid dinner dates, movie dates, and bar dates. Eating and drinking should never be main events.

• Dates should be cheap, fun, memorable, brag-worthy, open to spontaneity, conducive to conversation, triggers for chemistry, and easily escapable if things go badly.

• Plan three one-hour activities for your dates: a high-energy activity, a low-key, chatty activity, and one intimate activity that allows for kissing and cuddling.

• Around an hour into the date, you should be holding hands. At the three-hour mark, you should have kissed.

• Be direct in your rejections. Give reasons only if she asks. Take rejection in stride.

• Date multiple women until you're sure you're both serious.

Exercises

Exercise 22.1 – Ongoing – Scope Out Date Venues

Have a look at the ideas for dates in this chapter, along with any others you can come up with. What venues are nearby that would make good first-date locations? Visit them. Walk around their neighborhoods to find second and third activities to bounce to. Carry a notebook and write down your ideas. Practice walking from venue to venue so you don't need to refer to a GPS or map to get around. Over the next two weeks, try to come up with five fun three-part date ideas.

Exercise 22.2 – One Time – Find "Hookup" Date Locations Near Your Home

Take an evening to visit potential date locations within half a mile of your home. What bars, ice cream shops, and similar venues are available for bouncing to on the way to your place to hook up? Visit these venues and determine which ones are the most fun, private, and romantic.

Exercise 22.3 – Ongoing – Start Inviting Women to Your Planned Dates, and Go on Them

When asking out the women you meet in Exercise 21.3, start incorporating your date ideas from Exercise 22.1.

Exercise 22.4 – One Time – Try a "Challenge Date"

There will come a time when you'll be meeting a woman in an unfamiliar area but you'll still be responsible for planning the date. This exercise will prepare you for that situation. Pick a bar in a part of town you're not familiar with. You have one hour to explore the area surrounding that bar and plan the three activities in your date. Write any places worth bouncing to in a notebook and memorize how to get to each one. You are not allowed to use the Internet. When you have the full date planned out, walk once through the route. If this proves to be difficult, consider trying this exercise more than once.

Chapter 23 – Online Dating

In this chapter, we'll talk about the wonderful and precarious world of online dating. It's something I recommend you try, but that I hope you ultimately don't find necessary. Online dating is simultaneously the easiest and the most frustrating way to meet women. On one hand, the barrier to entry is nonexistent. You'll have less social anxiety sending a message than you'll have walking up to a woman in a bar. You can send twenty messages in the time it takes to talk to one woman; if the messages are good, almost all of them will get replies, and half of those will turn into dates. On most sites, you're also able to filter results to find women with interests and values compatible with your own. I have met plenty of people who've found spouses and hookups alike through online dating, and I had plenty of success myself. It does, however, have problems.

Though the low barrier to entry makes things easier, it's also online dating's biggest liability. Anyone and everyone with an Internet connection, from the eccentric to psychopaths to the mentally ill, can make profiles. A lot of users aren't looking for relationships, or even sex; they're seeking validation. Online dating is a variation on social media, and as with most such apps, these sites are designed with addiction and instant gratification in mind. No matter how attractive the users are, they'll be greeted with a deluge of romantic options, encouraging them to adopt an irrationally vast "abundance mentality." Users start to see their romantic options as disposable, and you'll find that you, and the women you date, will tend to be more shallow, crueler, and flakier than people you meet in person.

Online dating is a great way to get out of your comfort

zone, and if you follow the advice in this book, you'll almost definitely enjoy several hookups and perhaps even a relationship. Along the way, you'll have to deal with several strange personalities and a lot of flakes. You'll find that if you're not crazy for each other within the first ten minutes of a date, many women will dismiss you for the next guy on the menu, and if you're not careful you'll find yourself doing the same thing. It's a great way to get started, but bear this in mind, and be wary of this tendency.

How to Have Success with Online Dating

The Picture

The single most important element of your dating profile is your picture. The shallower the program is (think Tinder), the more important your picture will be. If your pictures aren't good, your profile won't get clicked, and nothing you write will matter.

Your primary picture should be high resolution and of excellent quality. Whether it's a portrait or a picture of you playing a sport, your face should be visible and free of shadows. Even if you're not particularly handsome, a high-quality picture is better than a blurry or gravelly one. Don't compromise on this.

Your secondary pictures are there to illustrate your personality. Pictures that show you engaging in activities (sports, dance, and the like) are better than portraits. Pictures with cute animals are gold. Babies and kids are questionable and better avoided, especially on Tinder, and especially if you're older, unless you're a dad and want to let people know. Group photos with other guys can make you more attractive,[239] but make sure it's clear which one you are, and never use a group shot as your primary picture. Photos with women are a mixed bag. They show that there are women in your life, but they raise questions such as "Is he a player?" and "Why aren't they dating him?" I've found it's better to leave them out.

Shirtless pictures are okay, with a few caveats. If you have a body to show off, your shirtless pictures will be your best performers. If you don't have a body to show off, don't. Even if you're an Adonis, don't use a mirror selfie. Mirror selfies suggest that you don't do anything that makes use of your body (such as beach volleyball), and you don't have a friend willing to take a photo of you. Keep your shirtless photos in context—at the beach, playing a sport, or in a photo shoot.

If you're any good with Photoshop, consider modifying your photos to make jokes. Photoshop your picture onto a cover of a magazine that says "Most-Eligible Bachelor" or "Sexiest Man Alive." Photoshop the dating site's logo onto your picture with a message saying "Your Soul Mate" or "This Week's Sexiest Match." Anything of this sort will be out of the ordinary and attract some attention, especially on picture-focused apps such as Tinder.

If you can afford it, hire a professional photographer to take some photos. Browse through his or her portfolio to see the sort of work the photographer is capable of, and try to find one who has experience advising models about how to pose. Favor a female photographer, especially one you find attractive, as it will be easier to "flirt with the camera" while she's shooting. Wear your best clothes for the shoot, and bring four or five outfits. Avoid suits unless you're over forty. Take some smiling photos and some serious ones. Take inspiration from the photos in your "Sexiest Men Alive" research from Exercise 19.1. With a decent professional cover photo, you'll outperform most guys on the site.

Username

If the site allows you to select a username, pick something clever. Avoid using your first name plus a series of numbers, as that's what most people do. Favor adjectives and verbs. What's a quality you like about yourself, or a quality you want to have? What's something you like to do? When I started on OKCupid, I was a shy guy trying to become more outgoing, so I decided on the username "Social." It's not really important, but something clever is better than something boring.

The Bio

The second most important element of your profile is the first sentence. It absolutely must be funny. I opened my profile with "I was born at a very young age and have been growing older ever since. I'm very outgoing at first, but once you get to know me I'm real shy." Keep the jokes as universal as possible, or at least related to online dating. Wordplay is your best bet.

Any time you can turn your passions, goals, job, or stories into puns or quips, you'll earn points. You want your readers to be laughing as they read about you. Follow the same rules in your profile that we talked about in our storytelling in chapter 8. If you can't make something funny, make it emotional. Talk about your passions or how something makes you feel. Use imagery. If you mention work, talk about what you do; don't just share a title.

Version 1:

"I'm a biomechanical scientist. I like to ride bikes and read fantasy novels. I have a cat named Mittens. I grew up in the Midwest but moved to the city last spring."

Version 2:

"Every morning I wake up and stare at stats about old men lifting heavy stuff and putting it back down. Apparently it's good for them. If you're a fitness nerd who likes to read studies on exercise, you might've read one of my papers.

"On Saturdays I take my bike on the trails around Chempachuan Hill. If you go early enough you can see deer. I don't have pics to show you. You'll have to come with me to see.

"Last spring I moved here from a small Midwestern town. When your high school class is ten people and eight of them are guys, you don't get to do a lot of dating, so I'm new to this whole thing. And yes, prom queen rivalry there was vicious.

"I have a five-year-old triple-pawed cat named Mittens who allows me to live in her apartment. Don't believe her bullshit. The belly rubs are a trap."

There's so much there that women can message him about—the cat, the biking, the prom queen story, working out, and more. There's even a built-in first date for any fellow bikers who would be up for joining him.

This is what you want to aim for—funny, emotional, conversational topics and date ideas. Keep this in mind with every section of your profile. Make it a joy to read and women will want to meet the guy who wrote it.

Writing Messages

Here are some of the most-common messages women receive on dating sites:

- "hi"

- "ur hot"

- A canned pickup line

- A lengthy biography of the sender

- A detailed description of the way the sender wishes to fulfill his fetishes with her

All five of these are off-limits. If you send any of the above, you'd better be gorgeous or you're not going to get a reply. When you're writing your messages, keep them short and focus on three parts:

- A compliment explaining what motivated you to message her

- A joke or a flirtatious line

- A question

Reading her profile before messaging makes hitting those three points a lot easier, so do it. Try to find things besides her looks to comment on (though looks aren't off-limits). These steps alone will put you ahead of most of the guys messaging her. The flirty line adds a sexual tone to the chat, and the question gives her something obvious to respond to.

"First time I've ever been attracted to a flamingo. That costume alone makes me want to ask you out. You've gotta be a hell of a Halloween companion.

"So you're a baking master, you say. I dabble in it. You have a specialty?

"P.S. My name's Zach."

When she replies, treat it like a conversation, just as we talked about in chapter 8. Look for any "free information" and focus on the most-emotional content. Any time you can make a joke, do so, and never stop showing your interest in her. If she flirts with you, show her that you liked it by commenting and flirting back. As soon as you know you want to meet her, ask her on a date. Unless the messages are extremely short, this shouldn't take more than three or four exchanges. If it's taking too long, say so. "Hey, so you seem cool, and I'm not into the online pen-pals thing. You wanna meet? I'm free tomorrow night." Offer the date idea and give her your number. "How's mini golf sound? My number's 555-555-5555."

If she says "Yes," ask her to text you, or ask for her number too. You'll want to call her when you reach the venue so you're not both wandering aimlessly. Online dating is notorious for cancellations, so you might want to check in an hour beforehand to make sure you're still on. Don't be surprised if she cancels, but if you made a good connection in your messages, it shouldn't happen often. The funnier and more emotional your conversation, and the clearer you are with your interest and logistics, the less often you'll deal with cancellations.

The Hazards of Online Dating

Catfishing and Webcam Ads
There are a lot of fake personas on dating sites. Some people create them for shits and giggles; others are fronts for webcam porn sites or are trying to steal user identities. Never share your personal information on a dating site except your phone number, and even then only when you're confident she's a human and ready to meet up. If you're skeptical, try running a reverse photo search with *tineye.com*. A lot of scammers steal photos from models or attractive Facebook users to make these profiles, and this service is a good way to find out. Always meet your dates in public places, even if you're anticipating a one-night stand. You can go back to your place once you're sure she's not catfishing.

Misleading Photos and Descriptions
Some users will use outdated, Photoshopped, or outright stolen photos on their profiles, and may lie in their profile text. I never had to deal with this much, but it happens once in a while. Meet up for the date, do the first activity, then let her know you're not interested. That's all you can do.

Chapter Summary

- Your primary photo should be high quality (professional if possible) and feature your face.

• The best secondary photos illustrate your life and hobbies. Sports and hobby photos or pictures with animals are best. Group photos are acceptable only if you stand out.

• Shirtless pictures are okay if you have the body and it's in context. Never use mirror selfies.

• Photoshop your photos to make them funny if possible.

• Funny profiles are the best profiles. If you can't make it funny, focus on emotions.

• Write messages with a compliment, a flirty joke, and a question.

• There are weirdos on the Web. Be careful.

Exercises

Exercise 23.1 – Ongoing – Create an Online Dating Profile

Take an hour to go through your photos and write up a charming online dating profile on OKCupid, Plentyoffish, or whatever website you'd like to try. Follow the suggestions in this chapter.

Exercise 23.2 – Ongoing – Write to Five New Women Online per Day

For two weeks, send messages to five different women per day. These messages must be to women you have not messaged before, so if you get responses and choose to write back, that's great, but those responses don't count toward your five-message requirement. The goal of this exercise is to practice writing messages, not to set up dates, though if you're following the advice in this chapter you're almost definitely going to be scheduling dates. Pay attention to what sorts of messages get the strongest responses, and write in your journal about your experiences.

Chapter 24 – Getting Physical

Physical touch is how people express intimacy. You will never connect with someone as deeply as you will when you're touching. But how do you do it—and when?

My general answer for "When?" is "Within the first hour." The first chance to break the touch barrier is when you meet, through shaking hands, hugging, or high-fiving. If that goes well, future touching will be easier. A woman who likes you will usually be comfortable touching hands within one or two hours after meeting, in the form of dancing, holding hands, or walking arm in arm. If she doesn't like you, she'll avoid touching you at all. Unfortunately, in a dating context, a lot of women tend to be passive, so they'll acquiesce to touching even when they're uncomfortable with it. A romantic relationship has to be physical at some point, so you need to make a move, but we don't want to violate the women who don't want to be touched. How can we respect everyone's wishes?

The obvious route would be to ask for permission. "May I touch you?" If that were the solution (and I wish it were), this would be a short chapter. While some women will adore you for this, many won't. Some will interpret your question as indicating a lack of confidence. Some will be unwilling to say "Yes" because of internalized slut-shaming. Some will say "Yes" because they're afraid of how you might react to a "No." As weird as it might sound, verbalizing the question can make it more likely that a woman will feel violated than if you'd simply made a move.

The best solution I've found is to touch her in a way that's obvious, gives her every opportunity to reject you, and focuses on the least-invasive areas of her body. This approach reduces the stress on women who are hesitant to verbalize their objections (but would be okay with, say, turning their heads away from a kiss), and it comes across as more confident. If she exhibits any defensive or anxious gestures, or she asks you to stop, back off and ask her what's up.

Breaking the Touch Barrier

Different parts of our bodies imply different levels of intimacy. Shaking hands is less personal than a hug, and hugs are less personal than stroking her hair. In order of intimacy, our body parts are as follows:

• Hands/arms

• Torso

• Legs

• Head/face/neck

• Sexual areas (breasts, inner thigh, ass, vagina)

To break the touch barrier in the least invasive way possible, always start with the hands. Shaking hands and giving high fives are both things we do with perfect strangers, and neither should make anyone feel violated. The longer you hold the touch, the more intimate it will be. Holding hands is more intimate than a high five, and a long hug is more intimate than a short one.

Within the first hour of the date, preferably once you've started to connect in conversation, reach out to hold her hand. Don't hover, don't surprise her, don't hesitate, and don't pull it back if she doesn't grab it right away. Make eye contact and smile. You're establishing trust. You're showing that you want to bond with her and you're going to respect her boundaries. You watch and listen for her "No," and you respect it if it comes. When she touches you, you're warm and friendly. You're connecting with her; you're not some pervert rushing to fondle her breasts. Once you've reached one level of intimacy, you can move on to the next. If you're holding hands, you can interlock your fingers, rest your hand on hers on the table, thumb wrestle, arm wrestle, or walk arm-in-arm down the street.

If she's been comfortable holding hands for a little while, she will probably be comfortable with touching of the legs and torso. If you're sitting next to each other, you can try resting your leg against hers. If she's uncomfortable with this, she'll withdraw by leaning away from you or find an excuse to move her legs. If that's what she does, stay calm and back off a bit. If she likes your touch, she'll press her legs into yours. Another option is for her to rest her hand on your thigh. If you've been flirting a lot, you can try resting your hand on her thigh, though that's a bolder move. Keep in mind that the inner thigh is more sexual than the upper thigh, so letting your hand drift down may switch things from "comfortable" to "violating." Hugs, from the front or from behind, and dancing are the simplest ways to breach the torso barrier. If you hug from behind, make sure it's obvious that that's what you're doing. If she's comfortable with holding hands, touching legs, and extended hugs, she's probably up for a kiss.

Kissing

Like your first reach for her hand, your move to kiss should be slow, deliberate, and obvious. Give her every opportunity to reject you, not only to show your respect for her boundaries but because the closer you are to rejection, the more confidence you're conveying.

The Basic Kiss

Kisses are simple; you press your lips together. Bad kisses usually come from trying to do too much, not too little. Keep your lips relaxed. Don't pucker or smile. Don't use any tongue. As you move toward her, rotate your head slightly to your right so your noses don't collide. Interlock your lips so that either your upper or lower lip parts hers, and let her lips breach yours. Hold the kiss for a few seconds, then break.

Get Your Body Involved

Kisses are foreplay. They don't always lead to sex, but they should always have a sexual connotation. You and she have entire bodies that can get involved. As you make out, wrap your arms around her back and pull her into you. Thrust your hips forward and let her feel your dick against her. Hold her at her waist. Claw at her back. Let your hands slide up the back of her shirt and run your hands along her bare skin. Grab her ass. If you're standing, position one of your legs between hers so your thigh rubs against her vulva. Grab a clump of her hair close to her scalp and pull it as you kiss her (she shouldn't feel pain, but she should feel you grabbing her hair). If she wasn't thinking about fucking you before, she will be now.

Many women fantasize about being dominated by their mates. Fulfill that fantasy. Pin her against a wall or other object as you kiss her. If she'd rather pin you, let her. Use the environment to your advantage. Sit her on a desk as you kiss her and thrust your hips between her legs. Sit on a chair and invite her to straddle you. Get creative. Different women will like different things, so always be receptive to her reactions, but in general, anything that shows sexual desire and intent will turn her on.

Tongue

Using your tongue while you kiss increases the kiss's intensity. Think of your kisses like a piece of music. The song starts off soft and measured, but as the emotional intensity blossoms, it changes into something more intense and upbeat. Using tongue is like that transition. If you're loud and fast for the whole song, the switch doesn't have any impact, but if you're slow and quiet for most of the song, and then suddenly burst into intensity, the song gets much more exciting.

Shoving your tongue in her mouth the whole time is obnoxious, but used sparingly, tongue kissing can be incredibly hot. Keep it to around 10 to 20 percent of your kisses and you'll be in good shape.

When you tongue-kiss her, part her lips with your tongue and push it directly into her mouth. Massage or "wrestle" her tongue with yours for a few seconds, and then return to kissing with your lips. Make sure your tongue stays active. Don't push it in and then leave it limp in her mouth, and don't dart it in and out either. Push in, massage, pull out. When your lips are interlocked in a regular kiss, you can also use your tongue to massage her lip while it's between yours. Don't do this often, but it's another good intensifier at your disposal.

Teeth

Used properly, teeth are a powerful kissing tool. As you're kissing, slip her lower lip between your teeth and lightly pull it into your mouth. This creates a mixture of danger, trust, and eroticism that most women find exhilarating. Be careful not to bite; we're not trying to draw blood here, but do let her feel it. Hold her lip between your teeth strongly enough to allow you to caress it with your tongue, then allow her lip to pop out.

Erogenous Zones

There are certain spots on the human body that are pleasure centers. When you touch and kiss them, endorphins, which make your lover feel good, are released. While all of these zones exist on all women, different women will prefer different ones. You will need to explore your date's body to discover what she likes most. Squirming, moaning, screaming, clawing, pulling your hair, and otherwise expressing pleasure are all signs you've discovered something she likes. Pushing, saying "No," or otherwise asking you to stop means you should stop.

Nape of the Neck

This is the spot where her neck meets her shoulder, and it's an area seemingly universally enjoyed by both men and women. Make it the first erogenous zone you try. Licking, sucking, and lightly biting anywhere along the side of her neck, especially the nape, will feel fantastic to her. Be careful about sucking or biting too hard, as you can burst blood vessels, causing a bruise called a hickey. Some women love this, but most won't appreciate it.

Back of the Neck

The back of the neck isn't a spot you'll usually want to kiss or bite, since it's protected by hair. Massaging it with your hand, however, will flood her with relaxing endorphins. Stroke it while giving her a massage, while sitting next to her watching a movie, or while kissing her.

Front of the Neck

The sheer vulnerability and trust of the gesture when you lick the front of a woman's neck may turn her on. But this is the least important part of the neck.

Ears

Another highly popular erogenous zone is the ears. Licking and playing with the ears are nearly guaranteed to turn most women on, and some can even reach orgasm when you do so. Some women prefer earlobe sucking; others prefer feeling your tongue run along the ears' ridges. Massaging the outer rim with your fingers or tongue is worth trying as well. Immediately below the ear, on her neck, is another hypersensitive spot almost as pleasurable as the nape of the neck. Stimulate it with kisses or by licking it.

Wrists

Wrists are hit or miss. Some women love them; most couldn't care less. It's best to stimulate them with a series of kisses or with the tips of your fingers. If she's responding well, double down with sucking and kisses. If she's indifferent, dismiss the wrists and move on.

The Sides of Her Belly

This one requires her to be unclothed from the waist up, but with the right woman, it's an extreme turn-on. Kiss all over her sides, grab them, lick them, and suck on them. If she likes it, suck hard. Some women are ticklish and don't like this region being stimulated at all, so if she expresses that feeling, back off.

Feet

Feet are a surprisingly intimate area of the body. A foot massage carries a lot of sexual connotations and feels fantastic. I recommend against kissing and licking feet for hygienic reasons, but if you're willing, there are some women who'll love it.

Thighs

The thighs are erogenous in proportion to the proximity to her vagina. The closer you are, the more exciting the touch. Massaging, kissing, and grinding against her inner thighs will turn her on tremendously. It's also a fantastic tease. If you kiss her inner thighs for several minutes, she'll be begging for you to go down on her.

Breasts

Breasts are second only to the vulva as an erogenous zone. Whether she's clothed or naked, massage the breasts firmly but gently with your entire hand. Her nipples will be the most sensitive spots on her breasts, so be extra gentle when working with them. Run your tongue around the areola (the colored skin surrounding the nipple) and lick and suck the nipples themselves. It will be incredibly stimulating and erotic, and some women can even reach orgasm this way. Though individual women's preferences will vary, poking, squeezing, and nipple-twisting tend to be uncomfortable. Don't do them.

Cuddling

Spooning

Spooning involves cuddling while facing the same direction, with one person's front against the other's back, like a pair of spoons in a drawer. The person in back is the "big spoon," and though it's usually the physically larger person, it doesn't have to be. It's popular, and it's many couples' favorite way to cuddle.

Spooning presents a few problems: the arm problem and the hair problem. If the little spoon has long hair, the big spoon will usually have to inhale it, tickling the nose. The little spoon should tuck the hair under to keep it away from the big spoon's face.

The arm problem is that, while in the spoon position, both cuddlers have all of their body weight on the arms under their bodies, which can be painful. One solution is for the big spoon to slip a forearm into the notch between the little spoon's shoulder and neck, preferably under a pillow. With some adjustment, this can leave the big spoon comfortable all night, and the cuddles need not ever be broken.

Face to Face

In this position, the two people lie on their sides facing each other. It's intimate and allows for kissing, talking, and eye contact; however, it involves two trapped arms, and there's no good solution for that. This is a short-term cuddling position that's good for kissing and foreplay.

Chest Cuddles

Men have a spot between their pectoral muscles and their shoulders that is incredibly comfortable for their partners to sleep on. While the man lies on his back, the woman can rest her head on this spot and be comfortable for hours. This is an excellent long-term cuddling position, and she's probably going to fall asleep in it, especially after sex. If you don't plan on sleeping, keep a glass of water and source of entertainment (such as the TV remote) nearby to prevent boredom and dehydration. If you're a man with a large torso, the elevation of your chest may cause neck pain for your cuddle partner after a while, so consider elevating her body. Stuff a pillow under her to make a ramp leading to your chest, or pull her further up onto your torso.

Upright Seated Cuddles

The person in the back sits with legs spread, and the smaller person sits between them. The larger person's arms are wrapped around the smaller person. This is an excellent position for watching TV and can be sustained for hours.

Lap Cuddles

The head of one person rests on the lap of the other. The lap provider should stroke the cuddle partner's hair.

General Advice

Whatever way you choose to cuddle, try to keep a fair number of pillows handy to stuff into uncomfortable gaps. Cuddles can get pretty warm and sweaty, so keep your room cool. If you want, stuff a sheet between your bodies to absorb some of the sweat and disperse the heat. In general, good cuddles maintain as much body contact as possible, so as long as you're doing that, you're probably fine.

Hugging

Hugs are to lovers what handshakes are to strangers. They break the touch barrier and they set the tone of the relationship. A good hug can be the start of a great physical relationship. You may never recover from a bad one.

How Not to Hug

Turning Your Shoulder In

You'll notice that people who are uncomfortable hugging tend to hug at an angle. They shift a shoulder toward the other person to minimize body contact, limiting the intimacy. Don't be one of these people. Perform your hug facing forward with your entire body. The more body contact you make, the more loving your hug will be.

Tapping Out

Patting a person's back while hugging serves the same purpose as tapping out while wrestling. It signals that you want it to end. If you tap a person's back when you hug, it will reduce the level of intimacy; don't do it.

Jutting Your Butt Out

Another way people make as little physical contact as possible is to lean forward at the hips when entering a hug. This prevents any contact below the waist. You'll see this most often between family members, homophobic men, and people who want to make their lack of sexual interest clear. If you're going to hug someone, stay upright. You don't have to press your pelvis against the other person (though this is a great way to flirt), but don't go out of your way to minimize contact.

How to Hug

Don't underestimate the power of a good hug. Hugs release oxytocin, making us feel snuggly and happy. They improve our health[240] and bind us together.[241] A good hug should be like a good handshake: firm, loving, and sustained for several moments.

Wrap your arms around your hug recipient and hold her close to you, making as much body contact with your chest, belly, and arms as possible. If you're taller, wrap your arms around the tops of her arms, allowing hers to slip under your armpits. Relax your upper-body muscles and let your body mold to hers. Hold the hug for between five and twenty seconds. If she squirms or signals discomfort, loosen and release.

With a lover, it's appropriate to hug closer and longer

than with other people. Hold your hugs for at least twenty seconds, as this is the threshold for maximum oxytocin release. Encourage her to rest her head on your chest or shoulder. In addition to making as much body contact as possible, you can rub her back, scratch the back of her neck, or hold her head. Whatever else you do, stay still and enjoy the moment.

Chapter Summary

• Remember that physical touching is fundamental to human intimacy.

• Make all motions to touch obvious and deliberate. Don't be sneaky. Don't hover.

• In order of intimacy, our bodily regions are: hands—torso—legs—face/head/neck—sexual areas. When she and you are comfortable with sustained touching at one level, you can move to the next.

• Kiss with soft, interlocked lips. Use your tongue sparingly.

• Remember, her neck, ears, thighs, feet, wrists, breasts, and the sides of her belly are erogenous zones. Kiss, lick, and caress them.

• Cuddling is the best way to bond. Use whatever position lets you do it longest and closest.

• When hugging, don't turn your shoulder in, "tap out," or bend at the waist.

• Hug closely and firmly for five to twenty seconds.

Exercises

Exercise 24.1 – Immediate – Watch a Good Kiss
Look for examples of good kisses in Hollywood films. In my personal opinion, the single best kiss in film history is in *The Hole (2001)* between Thora Birch and Desmond Harrington. You can watch it here: *https://youtu.be/yB3MSmW6-v4*. Notice how they kiss, how they use their hands, and their intensity.

Exercise 24.2 – Partner – Practice Hugging

Pair up with a partner and practice hugging each other for twenty seconds. If you're in a large group, make sure everyone gets to hug everyone else. Notice any urges you have to tap out or increase the distance between your bodies. Try to resist these urges as you deliver your hugs.

Exercise 24.3 – Ongoing – Go People-Watching and Watch Other People's Physical Contact
Return to the venues you visited in Exercises 9.2 and 10.3. Look for people making physical contact with each other — lovers, people flirting, friends hugging, strangers shaking hands. Watch the reactions of those involved. What signs show that they're enjoying the physical contact? What signs show they aren't? Do this exercise at least three times and write in your journal about what you notice.

Chapter 25 – Sex

Most of the literature you'll find on sex either will feature detailed descriptions of anatomy, technique, and sexual positions, or will focus on emotional intimacy and sex therapy. If I were to choose which of these is more important, I would choose the latter, but both are indispensable. You can have the best fingering technique in the world, but if she's not in the mood, she's not going to enjoy it. Likewise, she could be hornier than a Minotaur convention, but if you don't know where to lick, you're not going to give good head.

The first and most important thing to understand about sex is that women are sexually unique. The things that turn one woman on will be different from those that do it for the next. Their favorite positions won't match. Some will want you to talk dirty; some will find it a turnoff. Some love giving blow jobs; some find them degrading—and some like giving them because they find them degrading. The "masterful" technique your ex-girlfriend loved might not do it for your new fuck buddy. The most valuable trait you can have as a lover is a persistent and powerful yearning to learn about your partner and explore her unique sexual pleasures.

Most of a woman's sexual pleasure has more to do with her than it does with you. How she perceives her body, what she believes about sex, how often she pleasures herself, her emotional state on a given day, and countless other personal factors have more effect on how much she likes fucking you than your technique or your dick. Being a man with whom she feels comfortable is the most important characteristic you can have. If you don't trigger her insecurities, judge her, or practice any "sex negative" beliefs, you'll be ahead of the curve. If you're someone she's consistently found she can trust, she'll enjoy sex with you more than with anyone else. The combination of curiosity and sensitivity will make the difference between a mediocre lay and the best sex of her life.

Psychological vs. Physiological Arousal

The classical perception of sexual arousal is a physical one. When men want to have sex, they get hard; when women want to have sex, they get wet. The reality isn't that simple. Research has suggested that our physiological sexual responses do not always correlate with our psychological sexual desires. In one meta-analysis, men's physiological and psychological arousals correlated an average of sixty percent of the time, while women's correlated only twenty-six percent.[242] To have good sex, it's important to make sure both systems in both people are running on all cylinders. If her body's into it but her mind isn't, you'll be raping her, and that's all kinds of bad. If her mind's into it but her body isn't, she'll want it, but it'll be painful and unenjoyable. Being a great lover isn't just having the right dick or knowing the right techniques; it's about making the sex amazing for her body and her mind.

Turning Her Mind On

In the 1990s, Erick Janssen and John Bancroft developed the dual-control model of sexual response. Basically, you can think of getting aroused as like driving a car. Some things push the accelerators; other things hit the brakes.[243] When your fuck buddy pushes you into the wall and kisses you hard, your brain hits the gas on your arousal and you feel an urge to fuck. When your grandma walks in the room when you're going to pound town, your brain hits the brakes and you feel an urge to stop. If you're having trouble revving up to 100 percent, it could be because nothing's hitting your gas pedal, or it could be that something's slamming on your brakes. Turning each other on is all about pressing each other's accelerators while you're releasing each other's brakes.

Common Accelerators

According to research by Katie McCall and Cindy Meston, most of women's accelerators fall into four categories:

• Love/emotional bonding cues (security, feeling loved, commitment, emotional closeness, protection, support, and being given "special attention")

• Erotic cues (sexy movies, erotic stories, watching or hearing other people having sex, thinking about sex, their partner's desire for them, noticing their own or their partner's arousal)

• Visual cues (attractive and well-dressed potential partners, attractive bodies, confidence, intelligence, class)

• Romantic cues (dancing closely, sharing a hot tub, massages, watching a sunset, laughing or whispering, sexy smells)[244]

Basically, anything that's related to sex, love, hot guys, or romance will turn most women on and get them thinking about knocking boots. Pick up a popular romance novel and you'll see these features in spades. There's not as much emphasis on the sex act itself as on the circumstances surrounding it. The writing focuses on buildup, sensations, and descriptions. In my opinion, the best way to understand how women's psychological arousal works is to read a couple of successful romance novels.

Everyone you meet will have her own mix of accelerators, and your best bet for discovering them is to ask her what they are and explore them. Some women will want you to handcuff and choke them. Others will want you to whisper words of love. You'll need to handle things case by case, but for most women, you'll be in good shape if you can focus on the following:

- Develop a secure feeling of trust and connection
- Show your desire for her
- Share erotic imagery (dirty talk, porn, sexting)
- Look good
- Create a romantic environment (light candles, play music, eat aphrodisiac foods)
- Touch her (cuddling, kissing)

If you'll permit me to step away from the science and share my experience, I can't put enough emphasis on those first two bullet points. The single most common reason women have told me they enjoyed sleeping with me was how much they felt they could trust me. They knew I wasn't going to violate them and they knew I cared about their pleasure. They were able to relax and just enjoy the sex. The more you can show that you'll respect her boundaries and that you care about how she feels, the more free she'll feel to come. With the trust in place, show her how badly you want to fuck her (with an emphasis on *her,* specifically), and she'll have no trouble getting in the mood.

Common Women's Brakes

In a series of focus groups, researchers Cynthia Graham, Stephanie Sanders, Robin Milhausen, and Kimberly McBride studied what women said turned them on and off.[245] Many of the most common brakes didn't concern men at all. Stress, body-image problems, and concerns about reputation were heavy hitters. Issues that did involve guys included worries about pregnancy, feeling "used," judgmental partners, a lack of reciprocity, and a lack of freedom to be sexual.

If you've been following my suggestions from previous chapters, most of these should make sense. Don't criticize her body, don't brag about your sex life, be willing to use contraception, and don't shame her for the way she likes to have sex. As long as you're following that advice, you won't trigger any of those brakes. The rest of the brakes amount to being a trustworthy and sensitive lover. There are a lot of guys out there who see women as means to ends. They want to get their rocks off. They want the validation that fucking women represents. If you don't see her as a means to an end, but rather as a human being who's doing a fun and intimate activity with you, you won't be the kind of guy who turns women off in those ways. Do you give a shit about how she's feeling? Are you interested in pleasuring her? Answer these questions "Yes" and you'll stay out of trouble.

There's one more brake the survey brought up that's a little touchier to address. Many of the women were extremely turned off by men who "asked for sex" or were "too polite." Here are some quotes from the research:

"If somebody asked me to do something, I hate that. Like, 'Will you go down on me?' and stuff and like blatantly ask me. It will eventually get there, they don't have to ask me, but like, the asking is the biggest turn-off ever."

"My husband, as long as we've met…he's just a very polite young man and he just would, you know, while we are in the throes of sexual passion, he would just say 'May I have sex?' or something like that, and I wish [he] wouldn't ask. That's a turn-off." "It's like, just do it." "Even now, he'll say something like, 'Well, tonight can we have sex?' or something like that, and I'm like, 'Why don't you just come and you know, kiss me and like that.' 'Don't make me say okay.'"[246]

Some might look at that and think, "Ha, look at that, feminists! Women don't want us to ask for consent. They want us to move in and fuck them." It's easy to jump to that conclusion, but in the context of everything else these women were bringing up, that's not what they were saying.

Think of it this way—you come home from work, exhausted, and your wife comes over to you and says, "Will you get around to having sex with me now?" How does that make you feel? I'd be willing to bet not super turned on. In fact, you might even find yourself resenting having sex with her at all. On the other hand, if she came up to you, wrapped her arms around you, rested her hand on your chest, nuzzled your neck, and started nibbling on your ear, you'd probably start thinking about fucking her. If then, she whispered, "You want to fuck me, hun?" you'd probably be a lot more eager.

The difference is the interest she's taking in your pleasure. She's putting in the effort to turn you on before asking if you want to fuck. It's not that women don't want you to care about their consent; it's that they don't want you to think of sex as something women give you. Sex is something you do together, not a service she provides. There's a big difference between "Can I have sex?" and "You wanna fuck?" The latter shows an interest in her wishes. It shows that you're not looking to consume; you're looking to participate. You're also giving her total freedom to say "No." Inviting her to fuck is the assertive approach. "Asking for sex" is passive aggressive. As long as you genuinely care about her feelings, want her to have a good time, and respect her boundaries, you should be fine inviting her verbally or nonverbally to have sex. If she starts showing any resistance, stop, back off, and ask her what's on her mind.

In short, if you want to avoid the common brakes most women have, do the following:

• Always be willing to use protection, and always have condoms available.

• Don't brag about your sex life to other people.

• Take pleasure in foreplay and exploring your lover's body.

• Avoid any critical or negative comments, especially ones that relate to her sexuality or her body.

• Care about her pleasure and her consent.

• Don't think of sex as something she provides. Turn her on and share it with her.

Female Sexual Anatomy

A big part of being a good lay is knowing your way around your lover's sexy parts. Here's some vocabulary you'll need to know:

• **Vulva:** the external genital organs of a woman, including the labia majora, labia minora, clitoral glans, and the entrance to the vagina.

• **Vagina:** the muscular tube leading from the external genitals to the cervix. Vaginas tend to be three to four inches deep, but can double or even triple in depth when she's aroused.

• **Clitoris:** a large, mostly internal structure surrounding the vagina, built for sexual sensation. It is composed of three chambers, a pair of legs called the crura, and the glans, which is a visible bulb above the labia on the vulva. The glans is the female analogue to the "mushroom head" of the penis, and is even more sensitive.

• **Cervix:** the narrow opening in the back of the vagina leading to the uterus. When she's aroused, the cervix goes deeper and higher into the woman's body.

• **Labia majora:** the outer "lips" of the labia.

• **Labia minora:** the inner "lips" of the labia.

• **Hymen:** a membrane along the lower edge of the vaginal opening. An "intact hymen" is not an indication of virginity, as is widely believed.

• **Urethra:** The tube connecting the bladder to the vulva through which urine flows. It is separate from the vagina.

• **Bartholin's glands:** Glands on the inside of the vagina that release fluid during sexual arousal to create lubrication and odor.

• **Skene's glands:** The homologue to the male prostate, the Skene's glands swell during sexual activity to cut off the urethra and prevent urination during intercourse. In some women, during orgasm, the intense contraction of vaginal muscles can squeeze the Skene's glands, expelling the fluid, resulting in ejaculation (squirting). It's widely claimed that this fluid is urine, but it's actually a clear alkaline fluid closer in composition to male prostatic fluid.

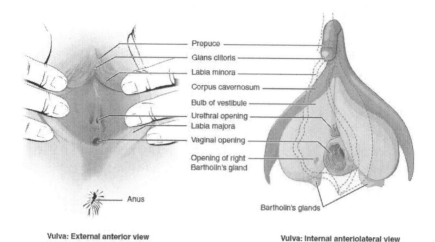

Vulva: External anterior view

Vulva: Internal anteriolateral view

Image created by OpenStax College, licensed under Creative Commons[247]

Female Orgasms

Popular sex literature maintains that there are several types of orgasms: clitoral orgasms (caused by stimulating the clitoral glans), G-spot orgasms (caused by stimulating the upper wall of the vagina), blended orgasms (both of these at once), cervical orgasms (caused by stimulating the back of the vagina), and more. There is some truth to these distinctions, but their labels are misleading. G-spot orgasms are actually a variation of clitoral orgasm, as they're caused through stimulation of the internal sections of the clitoris. What people call "cervical orgasms" result from stimulating a spot unrelated to the clitoris, but it's not the cervix. Some women can experience other types of orgasms as well, through stimulation of the anus, the breasts, the ears, and even through sheer force of will, though these are all less common. There's some debate about whether different orgasms are truly different, but brain scans suggest that they are.[248]

For most women, directly stimulating the clitoral glans, usually with fingers, tongue, or a vibrator, is the fastest and easiest way to come. Stimulating the G-spot is the second most reliable method, and tends to be more powerful. At the deepest point of the top wall of the vagina, right above the cervix, where the vagina starts to curve upward, is the anterior fornix erogenous zone, popularly known as the "deep spot," and this is the source of cervical orgasms. It's unclear what exactly this spot is, but evidence suggests these orgasms are the most powerful of all.[249]

Sexual Technique

When moving from making out to sex, it helps to start with some oral sex or fingering to help fully arouse your partner's body. If you're in any doubt, I recommend following a "one orgasm rule." Make sure she comes at least once through fingering or cunnilingus before you penetrate her to make sure she is completely aroused and ready. Her arousal is not so physically necessary as your erection, but that doesn't mean it's any less vital for her pleasure.

Massaging the Vulva

A good way to start your foreplay is by massaging the different areas of her vulva. Make sure your hand is well lubricated with artificial lube, saliva, or her vaginal fluids. The following four techniques are ranked in order of how stimulating they feel. Start at level 1 and work your way up to level 4.

1. Slowly and lightly massage her labia with your fingers.

2. Peek your fingers less than a centimeter into the entrance of her vagina and massage the entrance in slow, circular motions.

3. Rest your middle finger on the underside of her clitoral glans and move your hand in circles.

4. Move your fingers up and down, or sideways across, the clitoral glans as if it's a little "speed bump," gradually increasing your speed.

Different women have different levels of sensitivity,

and some may find some of these techniques too stimulating, especially level 4. If she's able to handle level 4, she'll probably come quickly and repeatedly. If it's too much for her, don't go past level 3. If level 3 is too intense, use the same technique, but instead of stimulating the underside of the clitoris, drag your finger down from the top of her glans and use her clitoral hood as a barrier. The clitoral hood is the female equivalent of the male foreskin, and just as stimulating your "mushroom top" through a foreskin isn't so intense, so it is with her. If she's so sensitive that she can't handle even this variation of level 3, you might want to skip manually massaging her vulva and stick to cunnilingus.

Manual Penetration

Manual penetration, or "fingering," is when you use one or several fingers to massage the anterior wall of her vagina, stimulating her clitoral cluster, popularly referred to as the G-spot. With your lover lying on her back and with your palm facing up, penetrate her with your middle finger. Curve your finger up and back toward you, as if you're making a "come hither" motion. You should feel some ridges along the top. Just beyond those ridges, about three to four inches inside the vagina, you should feel something spongy. That is the clitoral cluster. Massage this area in smooth, consistent strokes with your "come hither" motion. I like to think of it as trying to "tickle her belly-button from the inside." If she's squirming, moaning, or clutching the bed, you're doing it right.

As she gets more aroused, start to stroke her cluster a little harder and a little faster. If it can fit, add a second finger (either your index or ring finger — it doesn't matter). Match your strokes to the pace of her breaths. As she gets closer and closer to orgasm, she may start holding her breath, or screaming. At this point, start stroking her cluster as fast as you can. Move your entire arm up and down if you have to. You won't hurt her; remember, that thing's built to push out a baby. Continue until she stops you. If you want to make things even more intense, rest one hand on her pelvis and apply light pressure downward. This will sandwich her clitoral cluster between your hand and your fingers.

Cunnilingus

Cunnilingus is stimulation of her vulva, especially her clitoral glans, with your tongue. For most women, it's the easiest way to come (without a sex toy).

The secret to giving great head is simple: enthusiasm. You have to love it. Eating her clit isn't about pleasuring her. It's about you. You love the taste. You're ravenous for her. When you're down there, you're creating art. If you can adopt this mindset in how you give head, you'll be the best she's ever had.

Cup your whole mouth over the area around her clitoral glans and lightly lick it. Start with slow strokes and gradually speed up as she gets more aroused. Most of your licks should be oriented vertically. Horizontal licks back and forth across the glans are good, as are circular motions, but both should be secondary.

In addition to licking, feel free to use some light suction occasionally. Cup your mouth around the glans and lightly suck it into your mouth. Softly humming with your tongue against it can provide a faint vibration effect, which she'll enjoy. This is especially effective if you have a low voice.

When you're eating her out, you want to stay down there as long as possible—basically until she stops you. Consistency is key, so try not to take breaks. Two issues make this a challenge: neck pain and a numb mouth. Neck pain can be addressed with proper positioning before you begin. Keep your neck straight and your face facing down as much as possible. Move her to the edge of your bed, or angle her upward, so that you can eat her clit without tilting your neck. As for the numb mouth, there's no good solution I'm aware of.

It's stamina. You'll improve with practice. If you absolutely must take a break, fill the void by fingering her. If you don't continue stimulating her in some way, she'll lose the momentum you've been building, and it will be more difficult for her to climax.

How to Receive a Blow Job

There are four basic rules for receiving a blow job.

1. Do not thrust. Your dick will be in a warm, wet place. You'll feel an urge to thrust. Resist it. You'll be in danger of gagging her, making her vomit, or generally upsetting the lady kind enough to suck your dick. Let her control how much she takes inside her mouth, and let her do her art.

2. Show her you're enjoying it. You know how fun it is when she's screaming and coming thanks to you? She likes that feedback too. Grab her hair, grip the blankets, moan, say "oh my fucking God," and express your enjoyment of her blow job. It's a lot more fun to give head when your partner makes you feel you're a champ at it.

3. Be wary of how you come. If she doesn't want you to come in her mouth, give her a tap on the shoulder when you're close. If you pull out, be careful not to come in her eye. (It stings like hell.) Don't ejaculate in her hair, as it's difficult to wash out.

4. Consider your diet. The food you eat affects the flavor of your semen. I don't have any studies on this, but I'm told drinking pineapple juice helps a lot.

Intercourse

Before you penetrate her, check to see how aroused she is. When women are aroused, they pant, their voices get shaky, and their faces become flushed. Her vagina should be dripping wet. Ideally, she's already had at least one orgasm from your foreplay. If this is all true, she's ready to fuck.

There are hundreds of sexual positions and techniques. You can explore those on your own. Here are a few rules of thumb that make the most difference.

Angle up. The internal parts of the clitoris, the clitoral cluster, and the "deep spot" all run along the anterior wall of her vagina. Anything you can do to stimulate that wall will pleasure her better than touching another place. No matter what position you're in, try to get your dick rubbing against the top wall, as if you're aiming for her belly button. If you're in missionary position, stuffing pillows under her butt or raising her legs up to your shoulders will work great.

Read her signals and maintain a consistent rhythm. Our sexy bits like simple, repetitive motions. They don't like variation. Try to keep a consistent rhythm with your thrusts. In particular, a woman will give you hints about the rhythms that will make her come; observe how she's moving her hips, and her rate of breathing. Try to match your thrusts to these rhythms. Generally, a moderate rhythm will be better than a fast one, and too slow is better than too fast. You can have moments of fast, hard fucking (especially immediately leading up to an orgasm), but for most women, slow and steady will win her race.

Listen to her. If there's something she says she likes, do more of it. If there's something she says she doesn't like, stop doing it.

Don't neglect the rest of her body. Just because your dick's in her doesn't mean her erogenous zones turn off. Biting and licking her neck or ears, kissing her, pulling her hair, clawing her back, licking and massaging her breasts, and everything else we've discussed will still arouse her. Keep on doing them while you fuck.

When she's close to orgasm, don't stop and don't slow down. When she's coming, you'll feel her vagina start to grip your dick. She may start screaming, moaning, arching her back, and tensing all of her muscles. Nothing's wrong. Keep going. Thrust harder. Push through her tightening vagina and maintain your pace. The better you can do this, the more mind-blowing her orgasm will be.

Improving Performance

You can have sex with a partially flaccid penis, but it tends to be better for everyone involved if you're rock hard. Don't be shy about asking for what you need. When you've been pleasuring her for a bit, feel free to put her hand on your dick to show you'd like a foreplay hand job, or move to titty-fuck her. When you're starting out, feel free to focus on a rhythm and on angles that are the most stimulating for you before you focus on pleasuring her. We want to be generous lovers, but you're looking to enjoy this too. Be a little selfish sometimes, especially when it comes to getting yourself aroused.

If you find that you often come too early, or go soft, it's probably a problem with the way you masturbate. Many guys are in the habit of cranking hard on their dicks while they watch porn. No matter how incredible a woman's vagina is, it will never have the tightness or dexterity of your hand. Practice with a looser grip and slower strokes. Try to last as long as you can without orgasm. If condoms are the problem, practice masturbating with a condom on. If distraction is a problem, practice bringing your mind back to sex the same way you bring it back to your breath when you meditate. Consider putting a moratorium on porn and masturbate only to fantasies of women you know in real life. If you can limit your masturbation to a few times per week, that may improve your performance too.

Kegel Exercises

Kegel exercises strengthen the muscles of your pelvic floor. This will give you more-pronounced erections, give you more control over your orgasms, and allow you to launch your semen farther. You can feel your Kegel muscles by imagining you're trying to stop yourself from peeing.

The nice thing about Kegel exercises is that you can do

them anytime. Practice three sets of twenty reps of held Kegel tension for five seconds whenever you'll be sitting somewhere for a while, such as at work or when you're watching a film. You should notice improvements within days. If you like, try flexing your Kegels while inside her vagina. I'm not sure what women feel when you do this, but they seem to like it.

After-Sex Care

If you're having sex without condoms, have some tissues, paper towels, or a cloth ready so she can clean herself up if she wants to. If you're using a condom, throw it in the trash, and keep some more nearby in case you want to go again. Sex is sweaty, so it's prone to dehydrate both of you. Prepare some glasses of water ahead of time if you can. If she's cold, wrap her up in some blankets and hold her. Above all, cuddle. This is the single strongest opportunity for you to bond as a couple. Take advantage of it. The prolactin from your orgasm will be making you drowsy, but try not to fall asleep immediately. If you do, fall asleep cuddling her.

What to Do If You're Too Small

You're at a disadvantage with a small dick, but as long as you're making them come somehow, and as long as you're sensitive to their sexual desires, most women won't care about your size. Get ridiculously good at cunnilingus. Favor the deep-penetrating positions, such as legs-on-shoulders. If you precede intercourse with fingering, consider starting with your smallest finger. Vaginas tighten around whatever is inside them, so if the first thing you penetrate her with is smaller than your dick, your dick will feel bigger when it enters.

What to Do If You're Too Big

You need to move more slowly than other men, and you need to devote extra time to foreplay to make sure she's well lubricated. For you, the one-orgasm rule isn't a courtesy;

it's a requirement. If you rush to penetration too quickly, you'll tear up her vagina and she'll be in pain for days. Avoid the deep-penetrating positions such as legs-on-shoulders or you'll plow into her cervix, which hurts like hell. Over time, she'll get used to your size, but be extra gentle with first-timers. Look for properly sized condoms; normal ones will be prone to tearing.

Chapter Summary

• Be curious about what pleases your partner.

• Sexual arousal involves turning her body and her mind on.

• Sex, love, attractive men, and romance tend to trigger psychological arousal in women.

• Stress, body-image problems, reputation concerns, judgmental partners, pregnancy fears, and a partner's lack of interest in her pleasure turn a woman off.

• Women reach orgasm through stimulation of the clitoris, the G spot, and the deep spot, among other, less common ways.

• Massaging her vulva, fingering her, and cunnilingus are pleasurable sex acts on their own, and make great foreplay before penetration.

• When penetrating, angle your penis upward so it rubs the anterior wall of her vagina.

• Maintain a consistent rhythm and pay attention to her signals.

• Practice masturbating in a way that resembles intercourse, and do your Kegel exercises.

Exercises

Exercise 25.1 – Immediate – Check out the Instructional Sections of Porn Websites

Many free online porn websites have "instructional" sections that teach viewers how to finger, give cunnilingus, and the like. Browse through these sections and see what you can learn. Links are available at *thehotguyde.com/sexlessons*.

Exercise 25.2 – Ongoing – Read Three Sexually Explicit Books Marketed to Women

Look up the most popular sexually explicit romance novels, such as *Fifty Shades of Grey*, *Bared to You*, *Gabriel's Inferno*, and *On Dublin Street*. I also recommend reading *My Secret Garden* by Nancy Friday, and the updated version, *Forbidden Flowers*, both of which are compilations of women's sexual fantasies. While reading all these materials, keep in mind that they are fantasies. Just because Anastasia likes Christian Grey's stalking doesn't mean women want that in real life, and just because rape fantasies are so common doesn't mean women want to be raped. They are arousing only because they're fantasies, and the women are safe and in control.

Exercise 25.3 – Ongoing – Practice Kegel Exercises

For two weeks, work some daily Kegel exercises into your routine. If you need additional information on how to do them, visit the relevant link featured at *thehotguyde.com/resources*.

Exercise 25.4 – Ongoing – Practice Masturbation

Practice masturbating in a way that prepares you for sex. If you're unaccustomed to wearing a condom, practice masturbating with a condom on. If you're not familiar with condoms, use this as an opportunity to try on different-sized condoms, and experiment with which ones feel best to you. Try masturbating with a loose grip. Try to delay your orgasm for as long as you can. Try to stay hard as long as possible. If you want a special challenge, practice staying or becoming aroused immediately after ejaculating.

Exercise 25.5 – One Time – Investigate Sexual Positions

Pick up a copy of the *Kama Sutra* or one of the many other books on sexual positions. If you have a smartphone or tablet, download an app on sexual positions and browse through them. Pick ten or so that seem most intriguing to you and visualize yourself doing each of them. If you have the chance, try them out.

Exercise 25.6 – One Time – Prepare a Romantic Atmosphere
Think for a moment about how you can turn your place into a welcoming, comfortable, sexual space the next time you invite a woman home. Pick up some candles and a lighter. Browse YouTube or whatever music service you prefer for romantic music. (I recommend Spanish guitar.) Find some classy alcoholic beverages to keep on hand, such as nice bottles of wine. Have some aphrodisiac food ready: exotic cheeses, strawberries, or anything chocolate.

Chapter 26 – Nonmonogamy

One-Night Stands

One-night stands don't have to last only one night, and when they do, it's usually because the sex sucked. Many men (and some women) are notorious for seeing one-night stands as disposable sex romps. If that's how you think of them, you'll probably be right.

When you invite a woman over, whether you intend for it to be a one-night stand or you're hoping to start a new fuck-buddy arrangement, it's in your interest to make your best effort. The more curious and giving you are in the bedroom, the more likely your partner is to reciprocate and the more fun you'll both have. Take pride in being a great fuck, and since you guys have shared one of the most intimate things in the world, treat her with some courtesy. Offer her a ride home. Offer her breakfast the next morning. Even if it doesn't go any further, you'll be glad and proud that you show your lovers a good time.

No matter how good a lay you are, I'm sorry to say, some women will ghost. Some will sneak out in the middle of the night. Some will get up to leave as soon as you're done. There are countless possible reasons and it's not worth your time to figure them out. Don't expect the women you take home to want anything more than one night of good fucking or you're going to get emotionally burned. If a woman keeps coming back, and you're looking for something more, that's when you can feel free to bring it up.

Always wear a condom. Yeah, I know they suck, but it's the right call. You don't know if she's on birth control and you don't know if she has any STIs. A night of pleasure isn't worth catching HIV. Also, if you're not interested in a relationship, and she'll sleep with you only if you say you are, let her go. That move might not feel great at the time, but it's in your best interest. If you don't, then in exchange for your night of sex you'll be inviting drama into your life. In my experience, emotionally stable women don't demand a relationship the night they meet you to fuck; only the manipulative, unstable ones do that. If she's going home with you, she's probably already decided to sleep with you. Issuing those sorts of irrational demands in the bedroom is the reddest of flags. You don't want to sleep with this one, and rejection is your friend. If you're not looking for a relationship, and your one-night stand is demanding one, the only right answers are "Nope, not looking for anything serious" or "I don't know you well enough."

Friends with Benefits

A "friends with benefits" arrangement involves having recurring casual, nonmonogamous sex. It has several advantages. You're having sex, which is healthy and fun. Neither of you is emotionally invested, preventing heartbreak and jealousy. You are both able to date and sleep with other people, allowing for sexual variety and adventure. In many ways, it has all the benefits of a single life and a relationship.

The disadvantages can vary from nearly nonexistent to serious depending on how the arrangement changes. Humans are pretty bad at staying unemotional about the people they sleep with. We tend to get attached and jealous. Sooner or later, one party eventually wants something more. You can avoid this by having rules against the things most likely to lead to pair bonding, such as cuddling, but it will still probably happen. For this reason, fuck-buddy arrangements are usually short-term. They either develop into relationships or fall apart.

A lot of guys have asked me how to bring up the "fuck buddy" conversation. Every fuck-buddy arrangement I've ever had started with an excellent night of sex. We didn't negotiate it; we weren't friends who decided to start fucking; we just fucked, and it was good. Once you have that first good night of sex, becoming fuck buddies is just a matter of keeping on doing it. If you ask people to be friends with benefits before you've even had sex for the first time, how can they know what they're getting themselves into? They don't, so of course they'll say "No." Platonic friendships can turn into fuck-buddy arrangements, but even in those cases, you fuck first and talk about it later.

Polyamory

Polyamory means "many loves." It refers to any of a variety of romantic relationships with more than two people involved. Sometimes this means several people are all committed exclusively to one another. Sometimes it means a couple is emotionally committed to each other, but without sexual exclusivity. I won't get into all of the variations here; suffice it to say, it's a style of relationships where sexual and emotional commitment to someone doesn't necessarily preclude sex or romance with other people. It carries a different mixed bag of advantages and disadvantages than do monogamy, friends with benefits, or the single life. Polyamory at its best can provide the same emotional intimacy and support that monogamy does, perhaps in an even more satisfying way, since you're getting your intimacy and support from several people. It can also provide the sexual variety you'll get from a "friends with benefits" arrangement without sacrificing emotional intimacy.

The challenge of polyamory is the complexity. With one lover, you have just one relationship to take care of. With two lovers, you have three: one for each pair of people. Even if two of these people aren't sleeping together, their feelings toward each other still matter. The larger the polyamorous arrangement, the more complicated the system, the more support you need to give, and the more sensitive you need to be. The challenge increases exponentially, and it takes only one broken relationship for everyone to get hurt.

All of the relationship skills we'll discuss in chapter 27 apply to polyamory. My personal inclinations are monogamous, so I haven't ventured into the polyamorous subculture and thus can't speak about it with authority, but it might be right for you. If you're going to go that route, make sure it's clear from the outset. Once you're in a monogamous relationship, if you feel yourself attracted to someone else and you say to your girlfriend "You know, I think I might be polyamorous," she will be upset. Polyamory is possible only with openness and honesty from the beginning. If you're hiding your interests, or changing the rules after years of commitment, you're not polyamorous, you're cheating. Sometimes this conversation can go well, but chances are, you're going to be better off breaking up. If you'd like to learn how to approach polyamory ethically and effectively, pick up a copy of *Opening Up: A Guide to Creating and Sustaining Open Relationships* by Tristan Taormino or *More Than Two: A Practical Guide to Ethical Polyamory* by Franklin Veaux and Eve Rickert.

Chapter Summary

- Put your best effort into your one-night stands.
- "Friends with benefits" arrangements evolve naturally from your first night of great sex.
- Polyamory allows for emotional attachment with several lovers. It may be right for you.

Chapter 27 – Monogamy

The Purpose of Relationships

People crave emotional connection. It's the third level of Abraham Maslow's hierarchy of needs, right after "safety." When we're children, we seek this connection with our parents, and as much as we try to hide our needs as adults, they never go away. In 1994, research conducted by Cindy Hazan and Phillip Shaver showed that relationships between spouses strongly resemble those between parents and children.[250] Just as we need our mothers and fathers to hold us and care about us, we need that closeness with our lovers. We need them to respond when we're upset and show us that they care. In couples-therapy circles, this is called "connection," and it's the heart of healthy relationships. If a couple is having problems, it's usually because that connection is lacking.

Loving connections with others help us cope with stress[251] and pain.[252] They make us more capable of honesty and courage.[253] People in loving relationships live longer,[254] are more open to learning new ideas, are more comfortable with ambiguity,[255] understand themselves better,[256] and are better at managing negative emotions.[257] Since I met my girlfriend, I've been happier than ever before in my life, and that includes when I was having regular casual sex with several women. There is, however, a dark side. When relationships are unhappy, not only do these benefits vanish; everything gets worse. Permanently single people live almost as long as happily married couples. The worst performers are the divorcees.[258] Men and women whose spouses did not show them love have a greater likelihood of heart problems and high blood pressure, and have more stress hormones in their blood.[259] Injuries suffered by members of unhappy couples heal more slowly,[260] their immune systems don't work so well,[261] and they're ten times more likely to be depressed.[262] Happy relationships are amazing, but if you're in an unhappy one, it's worse than none at all.

Why Have a Relationship?

You're giving up a lot when you ask a woman to be your girlfriend. You'll enjoy less sexual variety, you'll have to reject people you'd otherwise sleep with, you'll have to devote time and energy to bonding, you'll have to deal with fights, and you'll have to spend time with her friends and family. If things go badly you'll get hurt, and it'll take weeks or months to recover. If you get married and things go badly, legal and financial problems can torment you for decades, especially if you have kids. There's no shortage of people who take this decision lightly, and often they get burned.

If you're a guy who's had little to no dating success in your life, chances are you'll feel inclined to jump into a relationship with the first woman who shows you affection. It's a bad idea. You'll likely be hesitant to assert yourself with her for fear of losing the relationship, and you won't be prepared for the challenges monogamy brings. Before you commit to someone, I encourage you to ask yourself the following:

• Am I desperate for women's attention or validation?

• Have I dated enough women to know what I want in a relationship? Do I have a clear idea of my needs, or am I willing to "take anything I can get"?

• When I date other women, do I find myself wishing I were spending time with her instead?

• How do I feel about having sex only with her for a long time—potentially forever?

• How do people who have my best interests at heart feel about this woman?

• Am I aware of her flaws? If she had these flaws forever, would I still want to be with her?

If you can provide an answer to every one of these questions, and you still come out wanting to be monogamous with this woman, then cool. Give it a shot. If any of these standards is giving you cause to hesitate, you probably shouldn't commit.

What Makes Relationships Fail?

Go to any relationship advice forum and you'll be inundated with opinions on why relationships fail. Many will insist humans simply aren't built for monogamy, and that one partner will inevitably be drawn to cheat. In research conducted by Lynn Gigy and Joan Kelly at the Divorce Mediation project, the vast majority of divorced couples indicated their marriage ended because of a lost sense of closeness or because they did not feel loved and appreciated. Few cited an extramarital affair as even partially to blame.[263] A desire to cheat doesn't cause a loss of connection; a loss of connection leads to cheating.

According to a study by Ted Huston, the presence or lack of emotional responsiveness is the single best predictor of the quality of a marriage five years later. "The results provide little support for the idea that emergence of distress (e.g., increasing negativity) early in marriage leads to marital failure but instead show that disillusionment—as reflected in an abatement of love, a decline in overt affection, a lessening of the conviction that one's spouse is responsive, and an increase in ambivalence—distinguishes couples headed for divorce from those who establish a stable marital bond."[264] If your girlfriend needs your emotional support and you don't provide it, those are the moments that kill your connection: "I can't trust him to be there when I need him. I need to find someone else."

John Gottman's research on how couples handle conflict provides insight on the issue as well. When couples start fights with a negative tone — what Gottman calls a "harsh startup," such as "Why do you always leave the dishes in the sink?!" — it strongly predicts problems. Certain types of negativity are especially toxic. When one partner attacks the character of the other ("You're so forgetful") as opposed to focusing on behavior ("I didn't like how you forgot our plans"), it's toxic for the connection. Contempt, in which one partner feels disgust toward the other and uses mockery, cynicism, or sarcasm to criticize him or her, is even worse. When the partner on the receiving end of these attacks gets defensive, the connection is torn even more, and after extended periods of fighting this way, the defensive partner (who is, 85 percent of the time, the man) will often start to stonewall (ignore) the partner. When researchers observed all four of these behaviors in couples' fights, they could predict that couple's divorce with 82 percent accuracy.

Another strong indicator of the likelihood of divorce is when members of a couple fail to acknowledge each other's repair attempts. A repair attempt is any time you try to de-escalate the tension during a fight. It can be an apology, a smile, a hug, an expression of emotion, or even a demand such as "Stop shouting." If you can recognize your partner's repair attempts, your relationship stands a much better chance of lasting. Failing to acknowledge repair attempts raised Gottman's divorce prediction accuracy to 91 percent.

Did you ever talk to a friend after a breakup who has nothing but hateful things to say about his or her ex? That's not just a case of sour grapes. Couples in the late stages of this spiral become so bitter and hostile, and love becomes so scarce, that every moment they spend together feels uncomfortable and cold. Not only do they start to feel awful toward each other, but their harsh feelings infect their memories. Instead of remembering the joy and flirtatious vibe of their first date, or the ecstasy of their honeymoon, they find themselves recalling only the bitter, spiteful events, sometimes even making up nasty things that never happened. When couples have reached this point, a relationship is extremely difficult to salvage.[265]

How to Be a Good Boyfriend

The most insidious thing about the habits that destroy your connection is that they're normal. When you get home from a long day's work, it's understandable how you could miss your wife's distressed feelings, especially if she doesn't think she has a right to share them. She'll tell herself, "He's tired; I shouldn't bother him with this," or "I'm an adult; I should deal with this myself." Missing the cues doesn't make you a bad person, but from your wife's perspective, you still weren't there, and her feelings of abandonment don't disappear. She'll feel the same way a child feels when her mother doesn't respond to her cries, and so will you, with the positions reversed. These accidental moments chip away at your connection and the damage accumulates over time. You find yourselves losing sexual interest in each other and fighting over small, stupid things. Neither of you can pinpoint when your relationship started to suffer, but suffer it does.

Fortunately, this same principle works in reverse. Just as small events of abandonment will destroy your relationship, small acts of connection and love will strengthen it. Relationships aren't built on grand gestures; they're built on little ones. Every time you hug your girlfriend when you see her, when you send an email to let her know you're thinking of her, when you surprise her with dinner, or when you buy her a little gift because it reminds you of her, it helps. Research suggests that in stable relationships, positive interactions outnumber negative ones at least five-to-one.[266] For some reason, these habits come more naturally to us early in a relationship than later on. The trick is never to abandon them.

Get to Know Your Partner

We don't always have a clear perception of our partner's world. What's stressing her out right now? What's she aspiring to? Whom is she spending time with? What are her hobbies? What's her favorite movie? If these are questions you're struggling to answer, this is a weak point in your relationship. Make it a point to ask her these sorts of questions. Ask her how she's doing and what she's been up to; listen to her talk about what she's been dealing with. Asking shows that you care about her, and knowing the answers can help you plan small acts of love.

Using What You Learn

It always helps to carry a notebook or use your journal to keep track of how your girlfriend answers those questions, and of other little things she mentions. Did she say she's looking forward to a movie? Write it down as a date idea. Did you see her admiring a piece of clothing in a store? Write a note with the store's name and a description of the garment. Is her headset broken? Pick one up on your way home. Does she like spicy food? Look up spicy recipes and surprise her. If you keep track of these things, you'll never lack for ways to show affection.

When you're planning little gifts, I recommend against spending much money. You might genuinely mean to give with no strings attached, but some folks still feel pressured to reciprocate. The best gifts are ones that are low in monetary value but high in sentimental value. Look for gifts that have special meaning to her. Make her something. Make an MP3 compilation of songs that remind you of her. Record yourself reading her favorite childhood book for her to fall asleep to. Buy supplies for one of her hobbies or a token gift that has meaning in your relationship. There's nothing wrong with jewelry and flowers, but they'll never have as much meaning as the Beanie Baby kitty that you got because she mentioned it was her favorite. If you do insist on flowers and jewelry, or some other expensive gift, try to make it unique to her in some way. Use her favorite gemstone, favorite flower, or favorite color. Finally, make sure your gifts truly are without strings. If you're giving gifts hoping for sex, or you're trying to patch over a fight, you're trading short-term comfort for long-term pain. The foundation of your relationship must be your connection. When you start making transactions, you're doing business, not creating love. Give gifts because you want to give gifts, go out because you want to go out, and have sex because you want to have sex.

Admire Her

Admiration is the opposite of contempt. If you can spend every day looking for little things you appreciate about your girlfriend, you'll never have a problem with criticism. "Thanks for helping me with the dishes." "Thanks for helping me pick out that outfit. I got a lot of compliments." Let her know the things you admire about her, and also remind yourself of them once in a while too. Make a list of fifty things you love about her, and the next time you have a fight, remember it. You can reprogram your cognitive biases to favor connection just as you can reprogram them away from "I'm worthless" beliefs. Keep practicing admiration and you'll avoid the pitfalls most couples suffer.

Turn Toward Her

Ben and Julia are sitting on the beach, staring at the seagulls. "How high do you think a seagull can fly?" asks Ben. "I don't know," says Julia," I've never seen them go that high." "Maybe it's 'cause they're hunting when we see them," says Ben. Another couple, Travis and Becky, are talking about the same thing—except things aren't going so well. "How high do you think a seagull can fly?" asks Travis. Becky shrugs dismissively. These conversations might seem pointless, and they kind of are, but there's a subtext to them that means everything.

Partners in relationships make bids for each other's attention. When your girlfriend calls you to ask if she should pick up milk, the milk doesn't really matter; what matters is that she's including you in her small life decisions. She's looking for your attention. Whenever she makes these bids, you can turn toward her and say, "Yeah, I think we need milk," or "I'm not sure, but grab some to be safe," or you can turn away by staying silent or saying "I don't care." Gottman's research showed that those who were happily together six years after his study turned toward each other an average of 86 percent of the time, while those who divorced turned toward each other only 33 percent of the time.[267] If you can practice turning toward your lover, you stand a much better chance of staying together.

These days, one of the most common ways people turn away is with electronics. Instead of paying attention to your lover, you're on social media or playing mobile games. This drains your connection. The more you can cut such distractions out of your life, the more your relationship will benefit. If you're unwilling to take that step, specify times when your electronics are off-limits: during dinner, when out on a date, when out with friends. It's not so good as eliminating them completely, but it helps.

Soften Your Startups

Earlier we talked about how harsh startups are poison to your connection. To fix that, you need to soften them up. The easiest way to soften a startup is to take some responsibility for the problem when you bring it up. "I know I play a role in this too, and I'd like to talk about our electricity bill." Let your partner know how you feel about the situation and what you need from her. "It's making me anxious. I don't think we can afford this. Can we find some ways to cut down on how much we use?" Remember that the situation, not your lover, is the problem. Instead of saying, "You're leaving the lights on too much," ask her for suggestions of ways you can both cut down. You're not enemies. You're a team looking to solve a problem.

Make and Accept Repair Attempts

No matter how compatible and socially skilled the two of you are, you're going to have fights. Sometimes you'll be stressed out and irritable. Sometimes you'll just disagree. You or your girlfriend might use a harsh startup or criticism. She'll do it not because she wants to hurt you, but because she's hurting. When you're in a fight, you're going to feel the urge to shift blame and defend yourself. If, instead, you can find a way to answer her attacks with a repair attempt, such as "What's really wrong?" "You might be right," or "Hey, I'm here, I'm on your side; let's talk about this," you'll find that your fights lose their edge and become productive. Likewise, there will be moments when you are the belligerent one and she is the one making repair attempts. If she says "I'm sorry" or "I didn't mean to hurt you like that," accept her efforts. If you can prioritize your connection over "being right," you'll maximize your chances as a couple.

Use "I" Statements

We talked about "I" statements in chapter 13, and they're every bit as important here. Whenever you have an issue to bring up, speak in terms of your feelings, not in terms of your partner's crimes. "You don't care about me anymore" is an attack. "I'm feeling left behind" is a fact. The latter way's less likely to make her defensive. Speaking in terms of facts and feelings will help you avoid the worst pitfalls, and starting your sentences with "I" will make sure you do.

Let Her Influence You

In Gottman's research, there was an 81 percent chance of marriage destruction when men were unwilling to let their wives share power.[268] I haven't been a big fan of dominance throughout this book, and this is a big reason why. Even if dominance is sexually attractive, which is questionable, it's absolutely antithetical to healthy romantic relationships. Listen to your girlfriend. Compromise with her. Come to decisions through consensus, not force. This doesn't mean acquiescing to everything; those relationships are toxic too. You still need to be assertive, but assertive people compromise, and your voice can't be the only one that matters.

Create Rituals That Celebrate Your Love

Remember how our habits create cognitive dissonance with our self-defeating thoughts? If you regularly engage in routines that build your connection, they'll do wonders to help fight off the stuff breaking it down. They can involve a weekly date night, an anniversary celebration, or a daily cuddle session. Brainstorm ideas with your girlfriend and find what works for you.

What to Do When Your Friends or Family Members Don't Like Your Lover

When you first start seeing someone seriously, your brain will be flooded with euphoric chemicals. In these early days, you're not an objective judge of your lover's qualities. If your friends or family members don't like your girlfriend, hear them out; there's a fair chance they're right.

After those first few months have passed, and once

you've heard out the critics, if you're still sure you want to be with your girlfriend you must always unconditionally side with her. It doesn't matter if it's your family or your best friend. It doesn't matter if she's wrong. If someone challenges your wife, you side with your wife. If you don't, it will be an abandonment experience for her, and your relationship might never recover. Right or wrong, you must have her back. If she's wrong, you can talk about it in private, but when it matters, when you're in front of the people threatening her, you have to be there for her, even and especially against the people who can sway you most. You are a husband first and everything else (except father) second. Have her back when she needs you or you won't have a relationship.

Chapter Summary

• The core of any successful relationship is a loving connection.

• Relationships are worthwhile only when they're good. Practice high standards.

• A lack of emotional responsiveness, harsh startups, criticism, contempt, defensiveness, stonewalling, and a failure to accept repair attempts kill connections.

• Practice getting to know your partner. Admire her. Make countless small gestures of love.

• Always turn toward her, soften your startups, make repair attempts, and receive them gracefully.

• Use "I" statements, practice loving rituals, and let her influence you.

• In any conflict between your lover and other people, side with your lover.

Exercises

Exercise 27.1 – Immediate – Take an Inventory of Your Monogamy Readiness
Earlier in this chapter I suggested several questions to ask

yourself before delving into a relationship. Whether you're actively dating someone now or not, ask yourself those questions. How desperate are you for attention from women? How clear a picture of your ideal mate do you have? Answer them in as much detail as possible in your journal.

Exercise 27.2 – Immediate – Brainstorm Loving Gestures You Could Make Toward Your Lover
Take twenty minutes to brainstorm loving gestures you could make toward your girlfriend. What special dates could you plan? What clever gifts are you capable of making? What little surprises can you invent? In addition, think of a few grand gestures. What vacations could you plan? What fancy date could you arrange? Keep these notes in your journal or in another place you won't lose them.

Exercise 27.3 – Partner – Learn and Practice Positive Relationship Exercises
I wrote this chapter to give you the most important guidelines for when you get into a monogamous relationship. It will help you, but it will not stand in for a counselor, or even a book on couples therapy. If you're in a relationship, pick up copies of *Hold Me Tight: Seven Conversations for a Lifetime of Love* by Sue Johnson and *The Seven Principles for Making Marriage Work* by John Gottman and Nan Silver. Both books have numerous exercises the two of you can practice to get through any struggles you are facing.

Chapter 28 – A Sample Approach to Self-Improvement

Congratulations. You've made it to the end of *The Hot Guyde*. You now know everything you'll need in order to become one of the sexiest men you'll ever meet. It's time to start putting that knowledge into practice.

The Hot Guyde covers a wide array of skills and exercises, only some of which will be useful for your specific situation. I don't know you, so I can't tell you what to concentrate on, but I can give you an example of how to set up your plan.

Chuck is a 23-year-old recent college grad. He's shy, passive, and obsessed with people approving of him. He's had two relationships, both of which ended with him being dumped, and both of which lasted less than a month. He isn't a virgin, but you can count on one hand the number of times he's had sex. Chuck has just finished reading *The Hot Guyde*, and to get the changes he wants, I've planned out his goals for the next forty-five weeks.

Some of Chuck's activities will be repeated week after week, and to differentiate new activities from the repeats, I've bolded the new activities. Activities that are meant to be repeated indefinitely are not listed every week, but rather stated as such in the first week of that activity in bolded text. Keep in mind that in addition to the things listed in a given week, the previously listed "forever" activities are happening too. These will be things such as journaling, meditation, and working out. When an activity refers to a specific exercise from *The Hot Guyde*, I've included the exercise number in parentheses.

In hopes of keeping him from being overwhelmed, I've

staggered all of Chuck's hobbies and new habits. He's never doing more than three hobbies and two new habits at a time. Though he's busy, I've made sure to give him plenty of free time to rest, go on dates, and take advantage of invitations from friends.

All of Chuck's goals are 100 percent within his control. Chuck can't control whether women want to go out with him, so "go on four dates per week" would be a bad goal. Instead, he has goals such as "Send twenty messages on OKCupid."

All of the activities listed can be thought of as mandatory minimums for the week. "Go on a date" doesn't appear on the schedule because it involves elements outside of his control (the woman's consent), and thus can't be mandatory, but that doesn't mean Chuck isn't doing it. As Chuck meets women and makes friends, he should absolutely devote some of his free time to dates and socializing.

When you're designing your plan, I encourage you to keep all of these points in mind. Remember to:

• Not demand that you practice more than three active hobbies at the same time.

• Avoid learning more than two new habits at a time.

• Avoid goals that depend on the choices of others, i.e. "Go out on two dates."

• Give yourself plenty of free, flexible time to schedule dates, accept invitations, and rest.

As you progress, it's a near guarantee that things aren't going to go as planned. You might need more time to deal with your toxic automatic thoughts, or you might not move up your exposure ladder as quickly as you'd hoped. Keep your plan flexible and don't think of setbacks as failures. Hold yourself accountable, but stay realistic and acknowledge that you don't know how hard — or easy — everything is going to be before you try it. Make changes to your goals as you learn, and remember to be compassionate with yourself. The point of this schedule is to give you a direction to move toward.

Don't let it be a source of frustration or shame.

Week	Goals
1	• Start journal; make entries no less often than every Wednesday night before bed. (1.1) This activity will continue for all weeks forever. • Identify distorted "I'm worthless" beliefs and automatic thoughts, do columns, and begin consistently talking back to thoughts. (2.5, 2.6, 2.7) • Begin practicing positive affirmations every day in front of the mirror. (5.4)
2	• Continue talking back to thoughts and continue positive affirmations. Monitor progress in journal. • Practice five-minute meditation every day as soon as I get to work. (4.2, 5.2) This activity will continue for all weeks forever.
3	• Continue talking back to thoughts and continue positive affirmations. Monitor progress in journal.
4	• Continue talking back to thoughts and continue positive affirmations. Monitor progress in journal.
5	• Continue talking back to thoughts only as needed. This activity will continue for all weeks forever. Positive affirmations can end this week. • Start facing exposures ranked 4 or lower when they come up. (3.6) This activity will continue for all weeks forever.
6	• Start taking salsa-dancing classes. (3.4, 15.4) First exposure—just show up. • Begin exposure success monitoring chart. This activity will continue for all weeks forever.
7	• Second salsa exposure—show up early and talk to one man, then take class.
8	• Third salsa exposure—show up early and start two separate conversations with different men, then take class.
9	• Fourth salsa exposure—show up early, start two separate conversations with different men, stay after class for no less than a half hour to socialize and dance.
10	• Fifth salsa exposure—show up early, start three separate conversations with different people, one of whom must be a woman. Stay after class to dance and socialize.

11	• Sixth salsa exposure—show up early, start three separate conversations with different people, one of which must involve a woman. After class, invite at least one woman to dance. • First willpower workout—I will open all doors with my left hand. (4.6)
12	• Repeat last week's salsa exposure. • Continue door-opening willpower workout. • Go fashion people–watching (19.3). Also, shop for new wardrobe, with emphasis on shoes and stylish clothes for salsa class. (19.4)
13	• Eighth salsa exposure—show up early, start three separate conversations with different people, one of which must involve a woman. Stay after, invite at least three women to dance, talk to at least three more people. • Continue door-opening willpower workout.
14	• Ninth salsa exposure—repeat early-arrival routine, dance with as many women as possible after class, ask at least one woman on a date and for her phone number. • New willpower workout—Start flossing every day when I brush my teeth. (4.6) This activity will continue for all weeks forever.
15	• Repeat salsa routine.
16	• Repeat salsa routine. • Get first new haircut. • Go shopping for more new clothing.
17	• Get gym membership. Hire trainer to teach me the basics of weightlifting. Set workout schedule, 6 a.m. on the following days: Monday, Tuesday, Thursday, Friday. (16.3) This activity will continue for all weeks forever. • Sign up for improv comedy classes; attend once per week (14.5). Quit salsa (unless I really like it).
18	• Continue improv comedy classes. • Exposure—Go to a popular bar in town. Stay for thirty minutes. People-watch (9.2, 10.3, 24.3).
19	• Continue improv comedy classes. • Exposure—Go to a popular bar in town. Walk up to one group and ask to hang out (8.11).

20	• Continue improv comedy classes. • **Begin posture training. Purchase watch to remind me to correct posture every thirty minutes. Plan implementation intentions. (11.2, 11.5)** • Exposure—Repeat last week's exposure.
21	• **Plan first social gathering. Invite friends from salsa, bars, and improv (15.7).** • Continue posture training. • Continue improv comedy classes. • Exposure—Repeat last week's bar exposure.
22	• Continue posture training. • Continue improv comedy classes. • **Go shopping for more new clothes.** • **Get second new haircut.** • **Exposure—Go to a popular bar in town. Walk up to one woman and flirt with her (21.3).**
23	• Continue posture training. • Continue improv comedy classes. • Exposure—Repeat last week's exposure. • **Begin looking for improv or other comedy performance opportunities. Schedule one for within the next three weeks (14.6).**
24	• Continue improv comedy classes. Otherwise, take a week off.
25	• **Sign up for jazz dance classes.** • Continue improv comedy classes. Perform ASAP. • **Begin voice training. Practice exercises from chapter 12 every day I do not have a class, immediately after dinner (12.3).**
26	• Continue jazz dance classes. • Continue improv comedy classes. If I haven't performed, I must perform this week (14.6). • Continue voice training. • **Plan second social gathering. Invite people from salsa, improv, bars, jazz dance.**
27	• Continue jazz dance classes. • Continue improv comedy classes. • Continue voice training.

28	• Assertiveness training begins. For two weeks, I will not say "sorry" (13.8). • Continue jazz dance classes. • Last week of improv comedy classes (unless I really like them). • Continue voice training. • **Get third new haircut.** • **If I need any new clothes, buy them. This activity will continue for all weeks forever.**
29	• Moratorium on "sorry" continues and ends this week. • Continue jazz dance classes. • Voice training continues and ends this week.
30	• **Make an online dating profile (23.1). Begin messaging five new women per day (23.2).** • Continue jazz dance classes. • **Sign up for adult gymnastics classes.** • **Request a table at a fancy restaurant, then cancel. Buy merchandise, then return it (13.11).** • **Begin making arrangements for trip in week 42.**
31	• Continue jazz dance classes. • Continue messaging five new women per day through online dating. • Continue gymnastics classes. • **Ask one person who regularly upsets me to stop doing the thing that upsets me.** • **Plan third social gathering. Invite people from salsa, improv, jazz dance, bars, and gymnastics.**
32	• Continue jazz dance classes. • Reduce online dating messaging to "as needed." • Continue gymnastics classes. • **Ask two more people who regularly upset me to stop doing what they do that upsets me.** • **Ask one person to help me with something (13.12).**
33	• Continue jazz dance classes. • Continue gymnastics classes. • **Remove the most toxic person I know from my life.**

34	• Continue jazz dance classes. • Continue gymnastics classes. • **Get fourth new haircut.**
35	• Continue jazz dance classes. • Continue gymnastics classes. • **Exposure—Go to a popular dance club in town. Stay for at least one hour.**
36	• Last week of jazz dance classes (unless I really like them). • Continue gymnastics classes. • **Sign up for social sports league.** • **Sign up for cooking classes.** • **Exposure—Go to a popular dance club in town. Dance during no fewer than ten songs.**
37	• Continue gymnastics classes. • Continue social sports league. • Continue cooking classes. • **Exposure—Go to a popular dance club in town. Dance with at least one woman, grinding if possible.** • **Plan fourth social gathering. Invite people from salsa, improv, jazz dance, gymnastics, social sports, cooking class, bars, and club.**
38	• Continue gymnastics classes. • Continue social sports league. • Continue cooking classes. • Exposure—repeat last week's exposure.
39	• Continue gymnastics classes. • (Probable) last week of social sports league. • Continue cooking classes.
40	• Continue gymnastics classes. • Continue cooking classes. • **Decide which haircut of the four I liked best. Ask barber to cut it that way from now on. This activity will continue as needed forever.**
41	• Last week of gymnastics classes (unless I really like them). • Last week of cooking classes (unless I really like them).
42–44	• **Take an extended vacation in an exotic and adventurous location (5.6).**

| 45 | • Continue developing new ways to become more awesome. |

Exercise 28.1 – Immediate – Write Out Your Self-Improvement Plan for the Next Twenty Weeks

Using Chuck's schedule as a model, write out your own self-improvement plan based on your own unique goals and weaknesses. Your plan should project out at least twenty weeks.

Conclusion

Thanks for taking the time to read *The Hot Guyde*. I hope it helps you change your life. Feel free to join the community at ***thehotguyde.com***, where you can get in touch with me and other guys working through the program. If you liked the book, please help me and other curious guys out by rating it on Amazon or wherever you may have purchased it. If you want to get in touch with me, I can be reached at **howie@thehotguyde.com**. I can't guarantee I'll be able to reply, but I read all my emails, and I'll appreciate receiving any feedback or stories you have to share. If, while reading *The Hot Guyde*, you encountered something you think is factually incorrect, please let me know. The science included in this book is still developing, and I'm not perfect, so I'm glad to have errors pointed out to me. I wish you luck on your journey.

General References and Recommended Reading

Alexander Technique
• *How You Stand, How You Move, How You Live: Learning the Alexander Technique to Explore Your Mind-Body Connection and Achieve Self-Mastery,* by Missy Vineyard (New York: Marlowe, 2007).

Assertiveness
• *No More Mr. Nice Guy!: A Proven Plan for Getting What You Want in Love, Sex, and Life,* by Robert A. Glover (Philadelphia: Running Press, 2003).

• *When I Say No, I Feel Guilty: How to Cope—Using the Skills of Systematic Assertive Therapy,* by Manuel J. Smith (New York: Dial Press, 1975).

• *The Assertiveness Workbook: How to Express Your Ideas and Stand Up for Yourself at Work and in Relationships,* by Randy J. Paterson (Oakland, CA: New Harbinger, 2000).

Body Language
• *The Definitive Book of Body Language,* by Allan Pease and Barbara Pease (New York: Bantam Books, 2006).

Cognitive Behavioral Therapy
• *Feeling Good: The New Mood Therapy,* by David D. Burns (New York: Morrow, 1980).

• *Cognitive Behavior Therapy: Basics and Beyond,* by Judith S. Beck, 2nd ed. (New York: Guilford Press, 2011).

Couples Therapy
• *The Seven Principles for Making Marriage Work,* by John M. Gottman and Nan Silver (New York: Crown, 1999).

• *Hold Me Tight: Seven Conversations for a Lifetime of Love,* by Sue Johnson (New York: Little, Brown, 2008).

Exercise and Nutrition

- *Bigger Leaner Stronger: The Simple Science of Building the Ultimate Male Body,* by Michael Matthews (Clearwater, FL: Oculus, 2014).
- *Starting Strength: Basic Barbell Training,* by Mark Rippetoe and Lon Kilgore, 2nd ed. (Wichita, TX: Aasgaard, 2007).

Exposure Therapy

- *Face Your Fears: A Proven Plan to Beat Anxiety, Panic, Phobias, and Obsessions,* by David F. Tolin (Hoboken, NJ: Wiley, 2012).

Fashion

- *Dress Like a Man: A Style Guide for Practical Men Wanting to Improve Their Professional Personal Appearance,* by Antonio Centeno and Geoffrey Cubbage (Real Men Real Style, 2013).
- *Kinowear Fashion Bible,* by Benoit Wojtenka and Geoffrey Bruyère (**www.kinowear.com**, 2016).

Habits

- *The Power of Habit: Why We Do What We Do in Life and Business,* by Charles Duhigg (New York: Random House, 2012).
- *Making Habits, Breaking Habits: Why We Do Things, Why We Don't, and How to Make Any Change Stick,* by Jeremy Dean (Boston: Da Capo Press, 2013).

Humor

- *The Comic Toolbox: How to Be Funny Even If You're Not,* by John Vorhaus (Los Angeles: Silman-James Press, 1994).
- *Ha! The Science of When We Laugh and Why,* by Scott Weems (New York: Basic Books, 2014).

Polyamory

- *Opening Up: A Guide to Creating and Sustaining Open Relationships,* by Tristan Taormino (Berkeley, CA: Cleis Press, 2018).
- *More Than Two: A Practical Guide to Ethical Polyamory,* by Franklin Veaux and Eve Rickert (Portland, OR: Thorntree Press, 2014).

Sex

• *Come As You Are: The Surprising New Science That Will Transform Your Sex Life,* by Emily Nagoski (New York: Simon and Schuster, 2015).

• *She Comes First: The Thinking Man's Guide to Pleasuring a Woman,* by Ian Kerner (New York: HarperCollins, 2010).

Shaving

• *The Art of Shaving; or, Shaving Made Easy—What the Man Who Shaves Ought to Know* (New York: Twentieth Century Correspondence School, 2012).

Social Skills

• *The Lost Art of Listening: How Learning to Listen Can Improve Relationships,* by Michael P. Nichols (New York: Guilford Press, 2009).

• *How to Win Friends and Influence People,* by Dale Carnegie, rev. ed. (New York: Simon and Schuster, 1981).

• *The Charisma Myth: How Anyone Can Master the Art and Science of Personal Magnetism,* by Olivia Fox Cabane (New York: Portfolio/Penguin, 2012).

Social Status

• *The Psychology of Social Status,* by Joey T. Cheng, Jessica L. Tracy, and Cameron Anderson (Editors) (New York: Springer, 2014).

Willpower

• *The Willpower Instinct: How Self-Control Works, Why It Matters, and What You Can Do to Get More of It,* by Kelly McGonigal (New York: Avery/Penguin, 2012).

Notes

1 Robert A. Glover, *No More Mr. Nice Guy!: A Proven Plan for Getting What You Want in Love, Sex, and Life* (Philadelphia: Running Press, 2003).

2 V. A. Benassi, P. D. Sweeney, and C. L. Dufour, "Is There a Relation between Locus of Control Orientation and Depression?" *Journal of Abnormal Psychology* 97, no. 3 (1988): 357–67.

3 J. D. Baron and D. A. Cobb-Clark, "Are Young People's Educational Outcomes Linked to Their Sense of Control?" *SSRN Electronic Journal*, retrieved from http://ftp.iza.org/dp4907.pdf.

4 L. Vijayashree and M. Jagdischchandra, "Locus of Control and Job Satisfaction: PSU Employees," *Serbian Journal of Management* 6, no. 2 (2011): 193–203.

5 C. R. Anderson, "Locus of Control, Coping Behaviors, and Performance in a Stress Setting: A Longitudinal Study," *Journal of Applied Psychology* 62, no. 4 (1977): 446–51.

6 A. C. Butler, J. E. Chapman, E. M. Forman, and A. T. Beck, "The Empirical Status of Cognitive-Behavioral Therapy: A Review of Meta-Analysis," *Clinical Psychology Review* 26, no. 1 (2006): 17–31; D. L. Chambless and T. H. Ollendick, "Empirically Supported Psychological Interventions: Controversies and Evidence," *Annual Review of Psychology* 52 (2001): 685–716.

7 Judith S. Beck, *Cognitive Behavior Therapy: Basics and Beyond,* 2nd ed. (New York: Guilford Press, 2011).

8 David D. Burns, *Feeling Good: The New Mood Therapy* (New York: Morrow, 1980).

9 J. M. G. Evans, S. D. Hollon, R. J. DeRubeis, J. M. Piasecki, W. M. Grove, M. J.

Garvey et al., "Differential Relapse Following Cognitive Therapy and Pharmacology for Depression," *Archives of General Psychiatry* 49 (1992): 802–8; S. D. Hollon, R. J. DeRubeis, and M. E. P. Seligman, "Cognitive Therapy and the Prevention of Depression," *Applied and Preventive Psychiatry* 1 (1992): 89–95.

[10] How the brain processes forbidden content: R. J. Giuliano and N. Y. Wicha, "Why the White Bear Is Still There: Electrophysiological Evidence for Ironic Semantic Activation during Thought Suppression," *Brain Research* 1316 (2010): 62–74.

[11] D. M. Wegner, *White Bears and Other Unwanted Thoughts: Suppression, Obsession, and the Psychology of Mental Control* (New York: Guilford Press, 1994).

[12] D. M. Wegner, *White Bears and Other Unwanted Thoughts: Suppression, Obsession, and the Psychology of Mental Control* (New York: Guilford Press, 1994). Examples of ironic rebound: D. M. Wegner, "How to Think, Say, or Do Precisely the Worst Thing for Any Occasion," *Science* 325 (2009): 48–50.

[13] A. Tversky and D. Kahneman, "Availability: A Heuristic for Judging Frequency and Probability," *Cognitive Psychology* 5 (1973): 207–32.

[14] J. L. S. Borton, L. J. Markowitz, and J. Dieterich, "Effects of Suppressing Negative Self-Referent Thoughts on Mood and Self–Esteem," *Journal of Social and Clinical Psychology* 24 (2005): 172–90.

[15] Giuliano and Wicha, "Why the White Bear Is Still There."

[16] S. Hoffman and J. Smits, "Cognitive-Behavioral Therapy for Adult Anxiety Disorders," *Journal of Clinical Psychiatry* 69, no. 4 (2008): 621–32.

[17] I. Marks, "Exposure Therapy for Phobias and Obsessive-Compulsive Disorders," *Hospital Practice* 14, no. 2 (1979): 101–8

[18] D. Ougrin, "Efficacy of Exposure versus Cognitive Therapy in Anxiety Disorders: Systematic Review and Meta-Analysis," *BMC Psychiatry* 200, no. 11 (2011): 200.

[19] L. G. Ost, T. Alm, M. Brandberg, and E. Breitholtz, "One vs. Five Sessions of

Exposure and Five Sessions of Cognitive Therapy in the Treatment of Claustrophobia," *Behaviour Research and Therapy* 39 (2001): 167–83; M. L. Moulds and R. D. Nixon, "In Vivo Flooding for Anxiety Disorders: Proposing Its Utility in the Treatment of Post-Traumatic Stress Disorder," *Journal of Anxiety Disorders* 20 (2006): 498–509.

[20] David F. Tolin, *Face your Fears: A Proven Plan to Beat Anxiety, Panic, Phobias, and Obsessions* (Hoboken, NJ: Wiley, 2012).

[21] X. T. Wang and R. D. Dvorak, "Sweet Future: Fluctuating Blood Glucose Levels Affect Future Discounting." Psychological Science 21 (2010): 183–88; M. Symmonds, J. J. Emmanuel, M. E. Drew, R. L. Batterham, and R. J. Dolan, "Metabolic State Alters Economic Decision Making under Risk in Humans." PLoS ONE 5 (2010): e11090; C. N. DeWall, T. Deckman, M. T. Gailliot, and B. J. Bushman, "Sweetened Blood Cools Hot Tempers: Physiological Self-Control and Aggression." Aggressive Behavior 37 (2011): 73–80; M. T. Gailliot, R. F. Baumeister, C. N. DeWall, J. K. Maner, E. A. Plant, D. M. Tice, L. E. Brewer, and B. J. Schmeichel, "Self-Control Relies on Glucose as a Limited Energy Source: Willpower Is More Than a Metaphor." Journal of Personality and Social Psychology 92 (2007): 325–36.

[22] R. Kurzban, "Does the Brain Consume Additional Glucose During Self-Control Tasks?" *Evolutionary Psychology* 8 (2010): 244–59.

[23] Y. Suchy, Y. "Executive Functioning: Overview, Assessment, and Research Issues for Non-Neuropsychologists," *Annals of Behavioral Medicine* 37 (2009): 106–16.

[24] S. C. Segerstrom, J. K. Hardy, D. R. Evans, and N. F. Winters, "Pause and Plan: Self-Regulation and the Heart," in *How motivation affects cardiovascular response: Mechanisms and applications,* ed. G. Gendolla and R. Wright (Washington, DC: American Psychological Association).

[25] S. C. Segerstrom and L. S. Nes, "Heart Rate Variability Reflects Self-Regulatory Strength, Effort, and Fatigue," *Psychological Science* 18 (2007): 275–81; J. T.

Ingjaldsson, J. C. Laberg, and J. F. Thayer, "Reduced Heart Rate Variability in Chronic Alcohol Abuse: Relationship with Negative Mood, Chronic Thought Suppression, and Compulsive Drinking," *Biological Psychiatry* 54 (2003): 1427–36; J. F. Thayer, A. L. Hansen, E. Saus-Rose, and B. H. Johnsen, "Heart Rate Variability, Prefrontal Neural Function, and Cognitive Performance: The Neurovisceral Integration Perspective on Self-Regulation, Adaptation, and Health," *Annals of Behavioral Medicine* 37 (2009): 141–53; see also F. C. M. Geisler and T. Kubiak, "Heart Rate Variability Predicts Self-Control in Goal Pursuit," *European Journal of Personality* 23 (2009): 623–33.

[26] Sung Kyun Park et al., "Air Pollution and Heart Rate Variability," *Epidemiology* 19, no. 1 (2008): 111–20.

[27] C. B. Taylor, "Depression, Heart Rate–Related Variables and Cardiovascular Disease," *International Journal of Psychophysiology* 78 (2010): 80–88.

[28] L. Solberg Nes, C. R. Carlson, L. J. Crofford, R. de Leeuw, and S. C. Segerstrom, "Self-Regulatory Deficits in Fibromyalgia and Temporomandibular Disorders," *Pain* 151 (2010): 37–44.

[29] R. F. Baumeister, T. F. Heatherton, and D. M. Tice, *Losing Control: How and Why People Fail at Self-Regulation* (San Diego: Academic Press, 1994); M. I. Inzlicht and J. N. Gutsell, "Running on Empty: Neural Signals for Self-Control Failure," *Psychological Science* 18 (2007): 933–37.

[30] M. Muraven and D. Shmueli, "The Self-Control Costs of Fighting the Temptation to Drink," *Psychology of Addictive Behaviors* 20 (2006): 154–60.

[31] J. Duffy and S. M. Hall, "Smoking Abstinence, Eating Style, and Food Intake," *Journal of Consulting and Clinical Psychology* 56 (1988): 417–21.

[32] R. Sinha, C. Lacadie, P. Skudlarski, R. Fulbright, B. Rounsaville, T. Kosten, and B. Wexler, "Neural Activity Associated with Stress-Induced Cocaine Craving: A Functional Magnetic Resonance Imaging Study," *Psychopharmacology* 183 (2005): 171–80.

[33] H. Chun, V. M. Patrick, and D. J. MacInnis, "Making Prudent vs. Impulsive Choices: The Role of Anticipated Shame and Guilt on Consumer Self-Control," *Advances in Consumer Research* 34 (2007): 715–19.

[34] T. McFarlane, J. Polivy, and C. P. Herman, "Effects of False Weight Feedback on Mood, Self-Evaluation, and Food Intake in Restrained and Unrestrained Eaters," *Journal of Abnormal Psychology* 107 (1998): 312–18.

[35] J. Polivy and C. P. Herman, "Dieting and Binging: A Causal Analysis," *American Psychologist* 40 (1985): 193–201.

[36] C. E. Adams and M. R. Leary, "Promoting Self-Compassionate Attitudes toward Eating among Restrictive and Guilty Eaters," *Journal of Social and Clinical Psychology* 26 (2007): 1120–44.

[37] M. J. A. Wohl, T. A. Pychyl, and S. H. Bennett, "I Forgive Myself, Now I Can Study: How Self-Forgiveness for Procrastinating Can Reduce Future Procrastination," *Personality and Individual Differences* 48 (2010): 803–8.

[38] M. R. Leary, E. B. Tate, C. E. Adams, A. B. Allen, and J. Hancock, "Self-Compassion and Reactions to Unpleasant Self-Relevant Events: The Implications of Treating Oneself Kindly," *Journal of Personality and Social Psychology* 92 (2007): 887–904.

[39] N. Trumpeter, P. J. Watson, and B. J. O'Leary, "Factors within Multidimensional Perfectionism Scales: Complexity of Relationships with Self-Esteem, Narcissism, Self-Control, and Self-Criticism," *Personality and Individual Differences* 41 (2006): 849–60

[40] "New Year's Resolution Statistics" (n.d.), retrieved August 5, 2015, from http://www.statisticbrain.com/new-years-resolution-statistics/.

[41] J. Polivy and C. P. Herman, "If at First You Don't Succeed: False Hopes of Self-Change," *American Psychologist* 57 (2002): 677–89.

[42] A. Fishbach and R. Dhar, "Goals as Excuses or Guides: The Liberating Effect of Perceived Goal Progress on Choice," *Journal of Consumer Research* 32 (2005): 370–

–77; A. Mukhopadhyay and G. V. Johar, "Indulgence as Self-Reward for Prior Shopping Restraint: A Justification-Based Mechanism," *Journal of Consumer Psychology* 19 (2009): 334–45; D. G. Mick and M. Demoss, "Self-Gifts: Phenomenological Insights from Four Contexts," *Journal of Consumer Research* 17 (1990): 322–32; U. Khan and R. Dhar, "Licensing Effect in Consumer Choice," *Journal of Marketing Research* 43 (2006): 259–66.

[43] B. Monin and D. T. Miller, "Moral Credentials and the Expression of Prejudice," *Journal of Personality and Social Psychology* 81 (2001): 33–43.

[44] S. Sachdeva, R. Iliev, and D. L. Medin, "Sinning Saints and Saintly Sinners," *Psychological Science* 20 (2009): 523–28.

[45] A. Fishbach and R. Dhar, "Goals as Excuses or Guides: The Liberating Effect of Perceived Goal Progress on Choice," *Journal of Consumer Research* 32 (2005): 370–77.

[46] R. J. Tanner and K. A. Carlson, "Unrealistically Optimistic Consumers: A Selective Hypothesis Testing Account for Optimism in Predictions of Future Behavior," *Journal of Consumer Research* 35 (2009): 810–22.

[47] E. Pronin, C. Y. Olivola, and K. A. Kennedy, "Doing unto Future Selves as You Would Do unto Others: Psychological Distance and Decision Making," *Personality and Social Psychology Bulletin* 34 (2008): 224–36.

[48] J. P. Mitchell, J. Schirmer, D. L. Ames, and D. T. Gilbert, "Medial Prefrontal Cortex Predicts Intertemporal Choice," *Journal of Cognitive Neuroscience* 23 (2011): 857–66.

[49] H. Ersner-Hershfield, D. G. Goldstein, W. F. Sharpe, J. Fox, L. Yeykelvis, L. L. Carstensen, and J. Bailenson, "Increasing Saving Behavior through Age-Progressed Renderings of the Future Self," *Journal of Marketing Research,* 48 (2011): S23-S37; J. Peters and C. Buchel. "Episodic Future Thinking Reduces Reward Delay Discounting through an Enhancement of Prefrontal-Mediotemporal Interactions," *Neuron* 66 (2010): 138–48; E. C. Murru and K. A.

Martin Ginis, "Imagining the Possibilities: The Effects of a Possible Selves Intervention on Self-Regulatory Efficacy and Exercise Behavior," *Journal of Sport and Exercise Psychology* 32 (2010): 537–54.

[50] H. Rachlin, *The Science of Self-Control* (Cambridge, MA: Harvard University Press, 2000), 126–27.

[51] J. A. Brefczynski-Lewis, A. Lutz, H. S. Schaefer, D. B. Levinson, and R. J. Davidson, "Neural Correlates of Attentional Expertise in Long-Term Meditation Practitioners," *Proceedings of the National Academy of Sciences* 104 (2007): 11483–88; E. Baron Short, S. Kose, Q. Mu, J. Borckardt, A. Newberg, M. S. George, and F. A. Kozel, "Regional Brain Activation during Meditation Shows Time and Practice Effects: An Exploratory fMRI Study," *Evidence-Based Complementary and Alternative Medicine* 7 (2007): 121–27; E. Luders, A. W. Toga, N. Lepore, and C. Gaser, "The Underlying Anatomical Correlates of Long-Term Meditation: Larger Hippocampal and Frontal Volumes of Gray Matter," *Neuroimage* 45 (2009): 672–78

[52] C. Peressutti, J. M. Martin-Gonzalez, J. M. García-Manso, and D. Mesa, "Heart Rate Dynamics in Different Levels of Zen Meditation," *International Journal of Cardiology* 145 (2010): 142–46

[53] R. F. Baumeister, M. Gailliot, C. N. DeWall, and M. Oaten, "Self-Regulation and Personality: How Interventions Increase Regulatory Success, and How Depletion Moderates the Effects of Traits on Behavior," *Journal of Personality* 74 (2006): 1773–801; M. Muraven, R. F. Baumeister, and D. M. Tice, "Longitudinal Improvement of Self-Regulation through Practice: Building Self-Control Strength through Repeated Exercise," *Journal of Social Psychology* 139 (1999): 446–57; M. Muraven, "Building Self-Control Strength: Practicing Self-Control Leads to Improved Self-Control Performance," *Journal of Experimental Social Psychology* 46 (2010): 465–68; M. Oaten and K. Cheng, "Improvements in Self-Control from Financial Monitoring," *Journal of Economic Psychology* 28 (2007): 487–501.

54 S. E. Carrell, M. Hoekstra, and J. E. West, "Is Poor Fitness Contagious? Evidence from Randomly Assigned Friends," Working Paper 16518, National Bureau of Economic Research (2010).

55 N. A. Christakis and J. H. Fowler, "The Spread of Obesity in a Large Social Network over 32 Years," *New England Journal of Medicine* 357 (2007): 370–79.

56 J. N. Rosenquist, J. Murabito, J. H. Fowler, and N. A. Christakis, "The Spread of Alcohol Consumption Behavior in a Large Social Network," *Annals of Internal Medicine* 152 (2010): 426–33; N. A. Christakis and J. H. Fowler, "The Collective Dynamics of Smoking in a Large Social Network," *New England Journal of Medicine* 358 (2008): 2249–58; S. C. Mednick, N. A. Christakis, and J. H. Fowler, "The Spread of Sleep Loss Influences Drug Use in Adolescent Social Networks," *PLoS ONE* 5 (2010): e9775.

57 A. Fishbach and Y. Trope, "Implicit and Explicit Mechanisms of Counteractive Self-Control," in *Handbook of Motivation Science*, ed. James Y. Shah and W. Gardner (New York: Guilford Press, 2007).

58 Sarah Bowen and Alan Marlatt, "Surfing the Urge: Brief Mindfulness-Based Intervention for College Student Smokers," *Psychology of Addictive Behaviors* 23, no. 4 (2009): 666–71.

59 Andrea Stocco, Christian Lebiere, and John R. Anderson, "Conditional Routing of Information to the Cortex: A Model of the Basal Ganglia's Role in Cognitive Coordination," *Psychological Review* 117, no. 2 (2010): 541–74.

60 F. Gregory Ashby and John M. Ennis, "The Role of the Basal Ganglia in Category Learning," PSYCHOLOGY OF LEARNING AND MOTIVATION 46 (2006): 1–36; F. G. Ashby, B. O. Turner, and J. C. Horvitz, "Cortical and Basal Ganglia Contributions to Habit Learning and Automaticity," TRENDS IN COGNITIVE SCIENCES 14 (2010): 208–15; C. Da Cunha et al., "Learning Processing in the Basal Ganglia: A Mosaic of Broken Mirrors," BEHAVIOURAL BRAIN RESEARCH 199 (2009): 157–70.

61 Ann M. Graybiel, "The Basal Ganglia and Chunking of Action Repertoires,"

NEUROBIOLOGY OF LEARNING AND MEMORY 70 (1998): 119–36.

[62] A. DelParigi et al., "Successful Dieters Have Increased Neural Activity in Cortical Areas Involved in the Control of Behavior," INTERNATIONAL JOURNAL OF OBESITY 31 (2007): 440–48; A. DelParigi et al., "Persistence of Abnormal Neural Responses to a Meal in Postobese Individuals," INTERNATIONAL JOURNAL OF OBESITY 28 (2004): 370–77; A. C. Janes et al., "Brain fMRI Reactivity to Smoking-Related Images before and during Extended Smoking Abstinence," EXPERIMENTAL AND CLINICAL PSYCHOPHARMACOLOGY 17 (December 2009): 365–73; D. Mcbride et al., "Effects of Expectancy and Abstinence on the Neural Response to Smoking Cues in Cigarette Smokers: An fMRI Study," NEUROPSYCHOPHARMACOLOGY 31 (December 2006): 2728–38; R. Sinha and C. S. Li, "Imaging Stress-and Cue-Induced Drug and Alcohol Craving: Association with Relapse and Clinical Implications," DRUG AND ALCOHOL REVIEW 26, no. 1 (January 2007): 25–31; E. Tricomi, B. W. Balleine, and J. P. O'Doherty, "A Specific Role for Posterior Dorsolateral Striatum in Human Habit Learning," EUROPEAN JOURNAL OF NEUROSCIENCE 29, no. 11 (June 2009): 2225–32.

[63] M. Maltz, *Psycho-Cybernetics: A New Way to Get More Living out of Life* (Englewood Cliffs, NJ: Prentice-Hall, 1960).

[64] P. Lally, C. H. M. van Jaarsveld, H. W. W. Potts, and J. Wardle, "How Are Habits Formed?: Modelling Habit Formation in the Real World," *European Journal of Social Psychology* 40 (6): 998–1009.

[65] K. C. Berridge and M. L. Kringelbach, "Affective Neuroscience of Pleasure: Reward in Humans and Animals," PSYCHOPHARMACOLOGY 199 (2008): 457–80; Wolfram Schultz, "Behavioral Theories and the Neurophysiology of Reward," ANNUAL REVIEW OF PSYCHOLOGY 57 (2006): 87–115.

[66] P. M. Gollwitzer and P. Sheeran, "Implementation Intentions and Goal Achievement: A Meta-Analysis of Effects and Processes," *Advances in Experimental Social Psychology* 38 (2006): 69–119.

[67] M. A. McDaniel and G. O Einstein. "Strategic and Automatic Processes in

Prospective Memory Retrieval: A Multiprocess Framework," *Applied Cognitive Psychology* 14, no. 7 (2000): S127–S144.

[68] P. Lally, J. Wardle, and B. Gardner, "Experiences of Habit Formation: A Qualitative Study," *Psychology, Health, and Medicine* 16, no. 4 (2011): 484–89.

[69] E. L. Deci and R. M. Ryan, *Intrinsic Motivation and Self-Determination in Human Behavior* (New York: Plenum, 1985).

[70] K. Bate, J. Malouff, E. Thorsteinsson, and N. Bhullar, "The Efficacy of Habit Reversal Therapy for Tics, Habit Disorders, and Stuttering: A Meta-Analytic Review," *Clinical Psychology Review* 31 no. 5 (2011): 865–71.

[71] M. A. Adriaanse, J. M.F van Oosten, D. T. D. de Ridder, J. B. F. de Wit, and C. Evers, "Planning What Not to Eat: Ironic Effects of Implementation Intentions Negating Unhealthy Habits," *Personality and Social Psychology Bulletin* 37, no. 1 (2011): 69.

[72] W. Wood, L. Tam, and M. G. Witt, "Changing Circumstances, Disrupting Habits," *Journal of Personality and Social Psychology* 88, no. 6 (2005): 918.

[73] L. Festinger, *A Theory of Cognitive Dissonance* (Stanford: Stanford University Press, 1957); L. Festinger, "Some Attitudinal Consequences of Forced Decisions," *Acta Psychologica* 15 (1959): 389–90.

[74] C. B. Becker, S. Bull, K. Schaumberg, A. Cauble, and A. Franco, "Effectiveness of Peer-Led Eating Disorders Prevention: A Replication Trial," *Journal of Consulting and Clinical Psychology* 76, no. 2 (2008): 347–54; T. A. Brown and P. K. Keel, "A Randomized Controlled Trial of a Peer Co-Led Dissonance-Based Eating Disorder Prevention Program for Gay Men," *Behaviour Research and Therapy* 74 (2015): 1–10.

[75] W. Chiou and C. Wan, "Using Cognitive Dissonance to Induce Adolescents' Escaping from the Claw of Online Gaming: The Roles of Personal Responsibility and Justification of Cost," *CyberPsychology and Behavior* 10, no. 5 (2007): 663–70.

[76] S. Takaku, "Reducing Road Rage: An Application of the Dissonance-Attribution Model of Interpersonal Forgiveness," *Journal of Applied Social Psychology* 36, no. 10 (2006): 2362–78.

[77] T. J. Kaptchuk, E. Friedlander, J. M. Kelley et al., "Placebos without Deception: A Randomized Controlled Trial in Irritable Bowel Syndrome," *PLoS ONE* 5, no. 12 (2010) doi: 10.1371/journal.pone.0015591

[78] William Bosl, quoted in Olivia Fox Cabane, *The Charisma Myth: How Anyone Can Master the Art and Science of Personal Magnetism* (New York: Portfolio/Penguin, 2012), 24; see also S. Harris, S. A. Sheth, and M. S. Cohen, "Functional Neuroimaging of Belief, Disbelief, and Uncertainty," *Annals of Neurology* 63 (2008): 14.

[79] D. R. Carney, A. J. C. Cuddy, and A. J. Yap, "Power Posing: Brief Nonverbal Displays Affect Neuroendocrine Levels and Risk Tolerance," *Psychological Science* 21 (2010): 1363–68.

[80] Amy J. C. Cuddy, Caroline A. Wilmuth, Andy J. Yap, and Dana R. Carney, "Preparatory Power Posing Affects Nonverbal Presence and Job Interview Performance," *Journal of Applied Psychology* 100, no. 4 (2015): 1286–95.

[81] H. S. Song and P. M. Lehrer, "The Effects of Specific Respiratory Rates on Heart Rate and Heart Rate Variability," *Applied Psychophysiology and Biofeedback* 28 (2003): 13–23.

[82] A. Maratos, M. Crawford, and S. Procter, "Music Therapy for Depression: It Seems to Work, But How?" *British Journal of Psychiatry* 199, no. 2 (2011): 92–93.

[83] BBC, "The Songs That Saved Your Life," Poll for BBC 6 Music, BBC (2004), http://news.bbc.co.uk/2/hi/entertainment/3547347.stm.

[84] J. S. Jenkins, "The Mozart Effect," *Journal of the Royal Society of Medicine* 94, no. 4 (2001): 170–72.

[85] Dale Carnegie, *How to Win Friends and Influence People,* rev. ed. (New York: Simon and Schuster, 1981), 100.

[86] Ibid, 111.

[87] H. Roediger and J. Karpicke, "Repeated Retrieval during Learning is the Key to Enhancing Long-Term Retention," *Journal of Memory and Language* 57 (2006): 151–62.

[88] This advice comes from Trey Parker and Matt Stone, creators of the TV show *South Park.* "Stand In: Trey Parker and Matt Stone" (2016), retrieved February 23, 2016, from http://www.mtvu.com/video/?vid=689002.

[89] Albert Mehrabian, *Nonverbal Communication* (New Brunswick, NJ: Aldine Transaction, 1972).

[90] H. S. Friedman, "The Relative Strength of Verbal vs. Nonverbal Cues," *Personality and Social Psychology Bulletin* 4 (1978): 147–50.

[91] R. S. Feldman, P. Philippot, and R. J. Custrini, "Social Competence and Noverbal Behavior," in *Fundamentals of Nonverbal Behavior,* ed. R. S. Feldman and B. Rime (Cambridge: Cambridge University Press, 1991), 329–50; J. A. Hubbard and J. D. Coie, "Emotional Correlates of Social Competence in Children's Peer Relationships," *Merrill Palmer Quarterly* 40 (1994): 1–20.

[92] M. Robin DiMatteo, Ron D. Hays, and Louise M. Prince, "Relationship of Physicians' Nonverbal Communication Skill to Patient Satisfaction, Appointment Noncompliance, and Physician Workload," *Health Psychology* 5, no. 6 (1986): 581–94.

[93] B. M. Depaulo, J. J. Lindsay, B. E. Malone, L. Muhlenbruck, K. Charlton, and H. Cooper, "Cues to Deception," *Psychological Bulletin* 129, no. 1 (2003): 74–112; M. Hartwig and C. F. Bond, "Why Do Lie-Catchers Fail? A Lens Model Meta-Analysis of Human Lie Judgments," *Psychological Bulletin* 137, no. 4 (2003): 643–59.

[94] P. Ekman, W. V. Friesen, and M. O'Sullivan, "Smiles When Lying," *Journal of Personality and Social Psychology* 54 (1988): 414–20.

[95] University of Granada, "'Pinocchio Effect' Confirmed: When You Lie, Your Nose Temperature Rises," *ScienceDaily* (3 December 2012),

www.sciencedaily.com/releases/2012/12/121203081834.htm.

[96] Desmond Morris, *Bodytalk: A World Guide to Gestures* (London: Jonathan Cape, 1994).

[97] P. Ekman and W. Friesen, "Nonverbal Leakage and Clues to Deception," *Psychiatry Journal for the Study of Interpersonal Processes* 32, no. 1 (1969): 88–106.

[98] T. L. Chartrand and J. A. Bargh, "The Chameleon Effect: The Perception-Behavior Link and Social Interaction," *Journal of Personality and Social Psychology* 76, no. 6 (1999): 893–910.

[99] J. C. Magee and A. D. Galinsky, "Social Hierarchy: The Self-Reinforcing Nature of Power and Status," *Academy of Management Annals* 2 (2008): 351–98; A. Mazur, "A Cross-Species Comparison of Status in Small Established Groups," *American Sociological Review* 38 (1973): 513–30.

[100] I. D. Chase, C. Tovey, D. Spangler-Martin, and M. Manfredonia, "Individual Differences versus Social Dynamics in the Formation of Animal Dominance Hierarchies," *Proceedings of the National Academy of Sciences* 99 (2002): 5744–49.

[101] J. T. Cheng, J. L. Tracy, and J. Henrich, "Pride, Personality, and the Evolutionary Foundations of Human Social Status," *Evolution and Human Behavior* 31 (2010): 334–47.

[102] Cheng, Tracy, and Henrich, "Pride, Personality."

[103] R. Boyd and P. J. Richerson, *Culture and the Evolutionary Process* (Chicago: University of Chicago Press, 1985); K. N. Laland and B. G. Galef, *The Question of Animal Culture* (Cambridge, MA: Harvard University Press, 2009).

[104] J. K. Maner and N. Mead, "The Essential Tension between Leadership and Power: When Leaders Sacrifice Group Goals for the Sake of Self-Interest," *Journal of Personality and Social Psychology* 99 (2010): 482–97.

[105] D. M. Buss, M. Gomes, D. S. Higgins, and K. Lauterbach, "Tactics of

Manipulation," *Journal of Personality and Social Psychology* 52 (1987): 1219–29; J. A. Howard, P. Blumstein, and P. Schwartz, "Sex, Power, and Influence Tactics in Intimate Relationships," *Journal of Personality and Social Psychology* 51 (1986): 102–9; L. M. Kyl-Heku and D. M. Buss, "Tactics as Units of Analysis in Personality Psychology: An Illustration Using Tactics of Hierarchy Negotiation," *Personality and Individual Differences* 21 (1996): 497–517.

[106] G. A. Van Kleef, A. C. Homan, C. Finkenauer, S. Gündemir, and E. Stamkou, "Breaking the Rules to Rise to Power: How Norm Violators Gain Power in the Eyes of Others," *Social Psychological and Personality Science* 2 (2011): 500–507; D. Keltner, R. C. Young, E. A. Heerey, C. Oemig, and N. D. Monarch, "Teasing in Hierarchical and Intimate Relations," *Journal of Personality and Social Psychology* 75 (1998): 1231–47; D. Kipnis, J. Castell, M. Gergen, and D. Mauch, "Metamorphic Effects of Power," *Journal of Applied Psychology* 61 (1976): 127–35.

[107] T. A. Judge, J. E. Bono, R. Ilies, and M. W. Gerhardt, "Personality and Leadership: A Qualitative and Quantitative Review," *Journal of Applied Psychology* 87 (2002): 765–80; R. G. Lord, C. L. De Vader, and G. M. Alliger, "A Meta-Analysis of the Relation between Personality Traits and Leadership Perceptions: An Application of Validity Generalization Procedures," *Journal of Applied Psychology* 71 (1986): 402–10.

[108] R. J. Foti and N. M. Hauenstein, "Pattern and Variable Approaches in Leadership Emergence and Effectiveness," *Journal of Applied Psychology* 92 (2007): 347–55.

[109] C. Anderson and G. J. Kilduff, "Why Do Dominant Personalities Attain Influence in Face-to-Face Groups? The Competence-Signaling Effects of Trait Dominance," *Journal of Personality and Social Psychology* 96 (2009): 491–503.

[110] P. D. Harms, B. W. Roberts, and D. Wood, "Who Shall Lead? An Integrative Personality Approach to the Study of the Antecedents of Status in Informal Social Organizations," *Journal of Research in Personality* 41 (2007): 689–99.

[111] D. R. Ames and F. J. Flynn, "What Breaks a Leader: The Curvilinear Relation between Assertiveness and Leadership," *Journal of Personality and Social Psychology* 92 (2007): 307–24.

[112] Anderson and Kilduff, "Why Do Dominant Personalities Attain Influence."

[113] T. A. Judge and D. M. Cable, "The Effect of Physical Height on Workplace Success and Income: Preliminary Test of a Theoretical Model," *Journal of Applied Psychology* 89 (2004): 428–41; D. M. Fessler, C. Holbrook, and J. K. Snyder, "Weapons Make the Man (Larger): Formidability Is Represented as Size and Strength in Humans," *PLoS ONE* 7 (2012): e32751; A. A. Marsh, H. Y. Henry, J. C. Schechter, and R. J. R. Blair, "Larger Than Life: Humans' Nonverbal Status Cues Alter Perceived Size," *PLoS ONE* 4 (2009): e5707; T. W. Schubert, S. Waldzus, and S. R. Giessner, "Control over the Association of Power and Size," *Social Cognition* 27 (2009): 1–19; W. D. Dannenmaier and F. J. Thumin, "Authority Status as a Factor in Perceptual Distortion of Sizes," *Journal of Social Psychology* 63 (1964): 361–65; P. R. Wilson, "Perceptual Distortion of Height as a Function of Ascribed Academic Status," *Journal of Social Psychology* 74 (1968): 97–102.

[114] *Ibid*

[115] S. Alrajih and J. Ward, "Increased Facial Width-to-Height Ratio and Perceived Dominance in the Faces of the UK's Leading Business Leaders," *British Journal of Psychology* 105: 153–161; K. A. Valentine, N. P. Li, L. Penke, and D. I. Perrett, "Judging a Man by the Width of His Face: The Role of Facial Ratios and Dominance in Mate Choice at Speed-Dating Events," *Psychological Science* 25: 806–11; M. P. Haselhuhn and E. M. Wong, "Bad to the Bone: Facial Structure Predicts Unethical Behaviour," *Proceedings of the Royal Society B: Biological Sciences* 279 (2012): 571–76; E. M. Wong, M. E. Ormiston, and M. P. Haselhuhn, "A Face Only an Investor Could Love: CEOs' Facial Structure Predicts Their Firms' Financial Performance," *Psychological Science* 22 (2011): 1478–83.

[116] D. R. Feinberg, B. C. Jones, A. C. Little, D. M. Burt, and D. I. Perrett,

"Manipulations of Fundamental and Formant Frequencies Influence the Attractiveness of Human Male Voices," *Animal Behaviour* 69 (2005): 561–68; D. A. Puts, S. J. Gaulin, and K. Verdolini, "Dominance and the Evolution of Sexual Dimorphism in Human Voice Pitch," *Evolution and Human Behavior* 27 (2006): 283-96; D. A. Puts, C. R. Hodges, R. A. Cárdenas, and S. J. Gaulin, "Men's Voices as Dominance Signals: Vocal Fundamental and Formant Frequencies Influence Dominance Attributions among Men," *Evolution and Human Behavior* 28 (2007): 340–44; R. C. Anderson and C. A. Klofstad, "Preference for Leaders with Masculine Voices Holds in the Case of Feminine Leadership Roles," *PLoS ONE* 7 (2012): e51216; C. A. Klofstad, R. C. Anderson, and S. Peters, "Sounds Like a Winner: Voice Pitch Influences Perception of Leadership Capacity in Both Men and Women," *Proceedings of the Royal Society B: Biological Sciences* 279 (2012): 2698–704; C. C. Tigue, D. J. Borak, J. J. O'Connor, C. Schandl, and D. R. Feinberg, "Voice Pitch Influences Voting Behavior," *Evolution and Human Behavior* 33 (2012): 210–16; W. J. Mayew, C. A. Parsons, and M. Venkatachalam, "Voice Pitch and the Labor Market Success of Male Chief Executive Officers," *Evolution and Human Behavior* 34 (2013): 243–48; M. Stel, E. van Dijk, P. K. Smith, W. W. van Dijk, and F. M. Djalal, "Lowering the Pitch of Your Voice Makes You Feel More Powerful and Think More Abstractly," *Social Psychological and Personality Science* 3 (2012): 497–502; J. T. Cheng, J. L. Tracy, S. Ho, and J. Henrich, "Listen, Follow Me: Changes in Vocal Pitch Predict Social Rank" *Journal of Experimental Psychology: General* 145, no. 5, (2013): 536-47.

[117] D. R. Carney, J. A. Hall, and L. S. LeBeau, "Beliefs about the Nonverbal Expression of Social Power," *Journal of Nonverbal Behavior* 29 (2005): 105–23; A. A. Marsh, H. Y. Henry, J. C. Schechter, and R. J. R. Blair, "Larger Than Life: Humans' Nonverbal Status Cues Alter Perceived Size," *PLoS ONE* 4 (2009): e5707; A. F. Shariff and J. L. Tracy, "Knowing Who's Boss: Implicit Perceptions of Status from the Nonverbal Expression of Pride," *Emotion* (Washington, DC) 9 (2009):

631–39; J. L. Tracy and D. Matsumoto, "The Spontaneous Expression of Pride and Shame: Evidence for Biologically Innate Nonverbal Displays," *Proceedings of the National Academy of Sciences* 105 (2008): 11655–60; L. Huang, A. D. Galinsky, D. H. Gruenfeld, and L. E. Guillory, "Powerful Postures versus Powerful Roles: Which Is the Proximate Correlate of Thought and Behavior?" *Psychological Science* 22 (2011): 95–102; J. H. Riskind and C. C. Gotay, "Physical Posture: Could It Have Regulatory or Feedback Effects on Motivation and Emotion?" *Motivation and Emotion* 6 (1982): 273–98; L. Z. Tiedens and A. R. Fragale, "Power Moves: Complementarity in Dominant and Submissive Nonverbal Behavior," *Journal of Personality and Social Psychology* 84 (2003): 558–68; Carney, Cuddy, and Yap, "Power Posing".

[118] Chase, Tovey, Spangler-Martin, and Manfredonia, "Individual Differences versus Social Dynamics."

[119] E. K. Sadalla, D. T. Kenrick, and B. Vershure, "Dominance and Heterosexual Attraction," *Journal of Personality and Social Psychology* 52 (1987): 730–38.

[120] J. R. Burger and M. Cosby, "Do Women Prefer Dominant Men? The Case of the Missing Control Condition," *Journal of Research in Personality* 33 (1999): 358–68.

[121] L. Jensen-Campbell, W. Graziano, and S. West, "Dominance, Prosocial Orientation, and Female Preferences: Do Nice Guys Really Finish Last?" *Journal of Personality and Social Psychology* 68, no. 3 (1995): 421–40; J. K. Snyder, L. A. Kirkpatrick, and H. C. Barrett, "The Dominance Dilemma: Do Women Really Prefer Dominant Mates?" *Personal Relationships* 15 (2008): 425–44.

[122] C. Anderson, S. E. Spataro, and F. J. Flynn, "Personality and Organizational Culture as Determinants of Influence," *Journal of Applied Psychology* 93 (2008): 702–10.

[123] J. E. Driskell and B. Mullen, "Status, Expectations, and Behavior: A Meta-Analytic Review and Test of the Theory," *Personality and Social Psychology Bulletin* 16 (1990): 541–53; C. L. Ridgeway, "Status in Groups: The Importance of

Motivation," *American Sociological Review* 47 (1982): 76–88; R. Willer, "Groups Reward Individual Sacrifice: The Status Solution to the Collective Action Problem," *American Sociological Review* 74 (2009): 23–43; C. L. Ridgeway, "Nonverbal Behavior, Dominance, and the Basis of Status in Task Groups," *American Sociological Review* 52 (1987): 683–94; V. Griskevicius, J. M. Tybur, and B. Van den Bergh, "Going Green to Be Seen: Status, Reputation, and Conspicuous Conservation," *Journal of Personality and Social Psychology* 98 (2010): 392–404; C. L. Hardy and M. Van Vugt, "Nice Guys Finish First: The Competitive Altruism Hypothesis," *Personality and Social Psychology Bulletin* 32 (2006): 1402–13.

[124] Ridgeway, "Status in Groups"; Willer, "Groups Reward Individual Sacrifice"; Griskevicius, Tybur, and Van den Bergh, "Going Green to Be Seen"; Hardy and Van Vugt, Nice Guys Finish First."

[125] J. Berger, S. J. Rosenholtz, and M. Zelditch, "Status-Organizing Processes," *Annual Review of Sociology* 6 (1980): 479–508.

[126] C. Anderson, S. Brion, D. A. Moore, and J. A. Kennedy, "A Status-Enhancement Account of Overconfidence," *Journal of Personality and Social Psychology* 103 (2012): 718–35.

[127] Anderson and Kilduff, "Why Do Dominant Personalities Attain Influence"; G. E. Littlepage, G. W. Schmidt, E. W. Whisler, and A. G. Frost, "An Input-Process-Output Analysis of Influence and Performance in Problem-Solving Groups," *Journal of Personality and Social Psychology* 69 (1995): 877–89.

[128] C. M. Steckler and J. L. Tracy, "The Emotional Underpinnings of Social Status," in J. T. Cheng, J. L. Tracy, and C. Anderson (eds), *The Psychology of Social Status*, (New York: Springer, 2014), 201–24.

[129] M. Chudek, S. Heller, S. Birch, and J. Henrich, "Prestige-Biased Cultural Learning: Bystander's Differential Attention to Potential Models Influences Children's Learning," *Evolution and Human Behavior* 33 (2012): 46–56.

[130] J. Henrich and F. J. Gil-White, "The Evolution of Prestige: Freely Conferred

Deference as a Mechanism for Enhancing the Benefits of Cultural Transmission," *Evolution and Human Behavior* 22 (2001): 165–96; J. T. Cheng and J. L. Tracy, "The Impact of Wealth on Prestige and Dominance Rank Relationships," *Psychological Inquiry* 24 (2013): 102–8.

[131] P. F. Grundy and C. J. Roberts, "Does Unequal Leg Length Cause Back Pain? A Case-Control Study," *Lancet* 2, no. 8397 (August 4, 1984): 256–58; D. Grob, H. Frauenfelder, and A. F. Mannion, "The Association between Cervical Spine Curvature and Neck Pain," *European Spine Journal* 16, no. 5 (2007): 669–78; P. B. O'Sullivan, A. J. Smith, D. J. Beales, and L. M. Straker, "Association of Biopsychosocial Factors with Degree of Slump in Sitting Posture and Self-Report of Back Pain in Adolescents: A Cross-Sectional Study," *Physical Therapy* 91, no. 4 (2011), 470-83.

[132] J. Vernikos, *Sitting Kills, Moving Heals: How Everyday Movement Will Prevent Pain, Illness, and Early Death—and Exercise Alone Won't* (Fresno, CA: Linden Publishing, 2011).

[133] J. M. Muyor, P. A. López-Miñarro, and A. J. Casimiro, "Effect of Stretching Program in an Industrial Workplace on Hamstring Flexibility and Sagittal Spinal Posture of Adult Women Workers: A Randomized Controlled Trial," *Journal of Back and Musculoskeletal Rehabilitation* 25, no. 3 (2012): 161–69.

[134] Woolhouse, Jeremy. "Semi+Supine." Digital image. Guide to Semi-supine Practice - Poise Alexander Technique. July 1, 2012. http://www.poisealexandertechnique.com.au/articles/2014/10/9/guide-to-semi-supine-practice.

[135] G. L. Stewart, S. L. Dustin, M. R. Barrick, and T. C. Darnold, "Exploring the Handshake in Employment Interviews," *Journal of Applied Psychology* 93, no. 5 (September 2008): 1139–46.

[136] Cheng et al., "Listen, Follow Me."

[137] Feinberg, Jones, Little, Burt, and Perrett, "Manipulations of Fundamental and

Formant Frequencies"; Puts, Gaulin, and Verdolini, "Dominance and the Evolution of Sexual Dimorphism"; Puts, Hodges, Cárdenas, and Gaulin, "Men's Voices as Dominance Signals."

[138] D. A. Puts, "Mating Context and Menstrual Phase Affect Women's Preferences for Male Voice Pitch," *Evolution and Human Behavior* 26 (2005): 388–97; D. R. Feinberg, B. C. Jones, M. J. Law-Smith, F. R. Moore, L. M. DeBruine, R. E. Cornwell, S. G. Hillier, and D. I. Perrett, "Menstrual Cycle, Trait Estrogen Level, and Masculinity Preferences in the Human Voice," *Hormones and Behavior* 49 (2006): 215–22.

[139] H. Davis, "The Uptalk Epidemic: Can You Say Something without Turning It into a Question?" *Psychology Today* (October 6, 2010), available at https://www.psychologytoday.com/blog/caveman-logic/201010/the-uptalk-epidemic; M. Ching, "The Question Intonation in Assertions," *American Speech* 57 (1982): 95–107.

[140] Robin Lakoff, "Language and Woman's Place," *Language in Society* 2, no. 1 (1973): 45–80.

[141] M. J. Smith, *When I Say No, I Feel Guilty: How to Cope—Using the Skills of Systematic Assertive Therapy* (New York: Dial Press, 1985).

[142] Sharon Anthony Bower and Gordon H. Bower, *Asserting Yourself: A Practical Guide for Positive Change,* 2nd ed. (Reading, MA.: Addison-Wesley, 1991).

[143] Thomas Gordon and W. Sterling Edwards, *Making the Patient Your Partner: Communication Skills for Doctors and Other Caregivers* (Westport, CT: Auburn House, 1997).

[144] Jensen-Campbell, Graziano, and West, "Dominance, Prosocial Orientation, and Female Preferences."

[145] Sascha Topolinski, Katja Likowski, Peter Weyers, and Fritz Strack, "The Face of Fluency: Semantic Coherence Automatically Elicits a Specific Pattern of Facial Muscle Reactions," *Cognition and Emotion* 23, no. 2 (2009): 260–71.

[146] Alison Gopnik, "Explanation as Orgasm," *Minds and Machines* 8 (1998): 101–18, 103.

[147] Karli Watson, Benjamin Matthews, and John Allman, "Brain Activation During Sight Gags and Language-Dependent Humor," *Cerebral Cortex* 17 (2007): 314–24.

[148] Robert R. Provine, "Laughter," *American Scientist* (January-February 1996): 38-47

[149] O. Aragon, J. A. Bargh, M. S. Clark, and R. L. Dyer, "Dimorphous Expressions of Positive Emotion: Displays of Both Care and Aggression in Response to Cute Stimuli," *Psychological Science* 26, no. 3 (2015): 259-273.

[150] M. Cowan and A. Little, "The Effects of Relationship Context and Modality on Ratings of Funniness," *Personality and Individual Differences* 54, no. 4 (2013): 496–500.

[151] R. R. Provine and K. R. Fischer, "Laughing, Smiling, and Talking: Relation to Sleeping and Social Context in Humans," *Ethology* 83, no. 4 (1989): 295–305.

[152] A. M. Rankin and P. J. Philip, "An Epidemic of Laughing in the Bukoba District of Tanganyika," *Central African Journal of Medicine* 9 (1963): 167–70.

[153] Göran Nerhardt, "Humor and Inclination to Laugh: Emotional Reactions to Stimuli of Different Divergence from a Range of Expectancy," *Scandinavian Journal of Psychology* 11 (1970): 185–95.

[154] Scott Weems, *Ha! The Science of When We Laugh and Why* (New York: Basic Books, 2014).

[155] Joke #6, 100 *Funniest Jokes of All Time* (n.d.), retrieved November 11, 2015, from http://www.bluedonut.com/jokes.htm.

[156] F. P. Piercy and S. K. Piercy, "Interpersonal Attraction as a Function of Propinquity in Two Sensitivity Groups," *Psychology: A Journal of Human Behavior* 9, no. 1 (1972): 27–30; James H. S. Bossard, "Residential Propinquity as a Factor in Marriage Selection," *American Journal of Sociology* 38, no. 2 (1932): 219–24.

[157] L. Craft and F. Perna, "The Benefits of Exercise for the Clinically Depressed,"

Primary Care Companion to the Journal of Clinical Psychiatry 6, no. 3 (2004): 104–11; C. Anderson-Hanley, J. P. Nimon, and S. C. Westen, "Cognitive Health Benefits of Strengthening Exercise for Community-Dwelling Older Adults," *Journal of Clinical and Experimental Neuropsychology* 32, no. 9 (2010): 996–1001; P. O'Connor, M. Herring, and A. Caravalho, "Mental Health Benefits of Strength Training in Adults," *American Journal of Lifestyle Medicine* 4, no. 5 (2010): 377–96.

[158] C. Wrann, J. White, J. Salogiannnis, D. Laznik-Bogoslavski, J. Wu, D. Ma, J. D. Lin, M. E. Greenberg, and B. M. Spiegelman, "Exercise Induces Hippocampal BDNF through a PGC-1α/FNDC5 Pathway," *Cell Metabolism* 18, no. 5 (2013): 649–59.

[159] Brad J. Schoenfeld, "The Mechanisms of Muscle Hypertrophy and Their Application to Resistance Training," *Journal of Strength and Conditioning Research* 24, no. 10 (2010): 2857–72.

[160] Shane Schwanbeck, Philip D. Chilibeck, and Gordon Binsted, "A Comparison of Free Weight Squat to Smith Machine Squat Using Electromyography," *Journal of Strength and Conditioning Research* 23, no. 9 (2009): 2588–91; Evan E. Schick, Jared W. Coburn, Lee E. Brown, Daniel A. Judelson, Andy V. Khamoui, Tai T. Tran, and Brandon P. Uribe, "A Comparison of Muscle Activation between a Smith Machine and Free Weight Bench Press," *Journal of Strength and Conditioning Research* 24, no. 3 (2010): 779–84.

[161] P. Gentil, S. R. Soares, M. C. Pereira, R. R. Cunha, S. S. Martorelli, A. S. Martorelli, and M. Bottaro, "Effect of adding single-joint exercises to a multi-joint exercise resistance-training program on strength and hypertrophy in untrained subjects," *Applied Physiology, Nutrition, and Metabolism* 38, no. 3 (2013), 341-344.

[162] William J. Kraemer, Kent Adams, Enzo Cafarelli, Gary A. Dudley, Cathryn Dooly, Matthew S. Feigenbaum, Steven J. Fleck, Barry Franklin, Andrew C. Fry, Jay R. Hoffman, Robert U. Newton, Jeffrey Potteiger, Michael H. Stone, Nicholas A.

Ratamess, and Travis Triplett-Mcbride, "American College of Sports Medicine Position Stand: Progression Models in Resistance Training for Healthy Adults," *Medicine and Science in Sports and Exercise* 41, no. 3 (2009): 687–708. doi: 10.1249/MSS.0b013e3181915670.

[163] Kraemer et al., "American College of Sports Medicine Position Stand"; G. T. Mangine, J. R. Hoffman, A. M. Gonzalez, J. R. Townsend, A. J. Wells, A. R. Jajtner et al., "The Effect of Training Volume and Intensity on Improvements in Muscular Strength and Size in Resistance-Trained Men," *Physiological Reports* 3, no. 8 (2015): e12472; Rhea et al., "Meta-Analysis".

[164] Ioannis G. Fatouros, Athanasios Chatzinikolaou, Symeon Tournis, Michalis G. Nikolaidis, Athanasios Z. Jamurtas, Ioannis I. Douroudos, Ioannis Papassotiriou, Petros M. Thomakos, Kyriakos Taxildaris, George Mastorakos, and Asimina Mitrakou, "Intensity of Resistance Exercise Determines Adipokine and Resting Energy Expenditure Responses in Overweight Elderly Individuals," *Diabetes Care* 32, no. 12 (2009): 2161–67.

[165] Belmiro Freitas de Salles, Roberto Simão, Fabrício Miranda, Jefferson da Silva Novaes, Adriana Lemos, and Jeffrey M. Willardson, "Rest Interval between Sets in Strength Training," *Sports Medicine* 39, no. 9 (2009): 765–77; Jeffrey M. Willardson and Lee N. Burkett, "The Effect of Different Rest Intervals between Sets on Volume Components and Strength Gains," *Journal of Strength and Conditioning Research* 22, no. 1 (2008): 146–52, doi: 10.1519/JSC.0b013e31815f912d; Jeffrey M. Willardson and Lee N. Burkett, "The Effect of Rest Interval Length on Bench Press Performance with Heavy vs. Light Loads," *Journal of Strength and Conditioning Research* 20, no. 2 (2006): 396–99.

[166] M. Wernborn, J. Augustsson, and R. Thomeé, "The Influence of Frequency, Intensity, Volume and Mode of Strength Training on Whole Muscle Cross-Sectional Area in Humans," *Sports Medicine* 37, no. 3 (2007): 225-64.

[167] Kraemer et al., "American College of Sports Medicine Position Stand"

[168] J. Mclester, P. Bishop, J. Smith, L. Wyers, B. Dale, J. Kozusko, M. Richardson, M. E. Nevett, and R. Lomax, "A Series of Studies—A Practical Protocol for Testing Muscular Endurance Recovery," *Journal of Strength and Conditioning Research* 17, no. 2 (2003): 259–73.

[169] P. Bishop, E. Jones, and A. Woods, "Recovery from Training: A Brief Review," *Journal of Strength and Conditioning Research* 22, no. 3 (2008): 1015–24.

[170] Gary A. Sforzo, Beth G. McManis, Dennis Black, D. Luniewski, and Kent Scriber, "Resilience to Exercise Detraining in Healthy Older Adults," *Journal of the American Geriatrics Society* 43, no. 3 (1995): 209–15.

[171] Schoenfeld, "Mechanisms of Muscle Hypertrophy"; Rhea et al., "Meta-Analysis."

[172] Disa L. Hatfield, William J. Kraemer, Barry A. Spiering, Keijo Häkkinen, Jeff S. Volek, Tomoko Shimano, Luuk P. Spreuwenberg, Ricardo Silvestre, Jakob L. Vingren, Maren S. Fragala, Ana L. Gómez, Steven J. Fleck, Robert U. Newton, and Carl M. Maresh, "The Impact of Velocity of Movement on Performance Factors in Resistance Exercise," *Journal of Strength and Conditioning Research* 20, no. 4 (2006): 760–66; Joanne Munn, Robert D. Herbert, Mark J. Hancock, and Simon C. Gandevia, "Resistance Training for Strength: Effect of Number of Sets and Contraction Speed," *Medicine and Science of Sports and Exercise* 37, no. 9 (2005): 1622–26.

[173] Munn et al., "Resistance Training for Strength"; Hatfield et al., "Impact of Velocity of Movement"; Christopher M. Neils, Brian E. Udermann, Glenn A. Brice, Jason B. Winchester, and Michael R. McGuigan, "Influence of Contraction Velocity in Untrained Individuals over the Initial Early Phase of Resistance Training," *Journal of Strength and Conditioning Research* 19, no. 4 (2005): 883–87; Eonho Kim, Alexis Dear, Steven L. Ferguson, Dongil Seo, and Michael G. Bemben, "Effects of Four Weeks of Traditional Resistance Training vs. Superslow Strength Training on Early Phase Adaptations in Strength, Flexibility, and Aerobic Capacity

in College-Aged Women," *Journal of Strength and Conditioning Research* 25, no. 11 (2011): 3006–13, doi: 10.1519/JSC.0b013e318212e3a2.

[174] Jason B. Winchester, Arnold G. Nelson, Dennis Landin, Michael A. Young, and Irving C. Schexnayder, "Static Stretching Impairs Sprint Performance in Collegiate Track and Field Athletes," *Journal of Strength and Conditioning Research* 22, no. 1 (2008): 13–19, doi: 10.1519/JSC.0b013e31815ef202; Antonio La Torre, Carlo Castagna, Elisa Gervasoni, Emiliano Cè, Susanna Rampichini, Maurizio Ferrarin, and Giampiero Merati, "Acute Effects of Static Stretching on Squat Jump Performance at Different Knee Starting Angles," *Journal of Strength and Conditioning Research* 24, no. 3 (2010): 687–94.

[175] Lawrence Hart, "Effect of Stretching on Sport Injury Risk: A Review," *Clinical Journal of Sport Medicine* 15, no. 2 (2005): 113.

[176] Peter C. D. Macpherson, M. Anthony Schork, and James A. Faulkner, "Contraction-Induced Injury to Single Fiber Segments from Fast and Slow Muscles of Rats by Single Stretches," *American Journal of Physiology—Cell Physiology* 271, no. 5 (1996): C1438–46.

[177] Danny J. McMillian, Josef H. Moore, Brian S. Hatler, and Dean C. Taylor, "Dynamic vs. Static-Stretching Warm Up: The Effect on Power and Agility Performance," *Journal of Strength and Conditioning Research* 20, no. 3 (2006): 492–99; Katherine Herman, Christian Barton, Peter Malliaras, and Dylan Morrissey, "The Effectiveness of Neuromuscular Warm-Up Strategies That Require No Additional Equipment for Preventing Lower Limb Injuries during Sports Participation: A Systematic Review," *BMC Medicine* 10 (July 19, 2012): 75.

[178] W. Schanke, "Electromyographical Analysis of the Pectoralis Major During Various Chest Exercises," Master's Thesis. University of Wisconsin (2012), https://minds.wisconsin.edu/handle/1793/62857; Valdinar de Araújo Rocha Júnior, Paulo Gentil, Elke Oliveira, and Jake do Carmo, "Comparison among the EMG activity of the pectoralis major, anterior deltoidis and triceps brachii during

the bench press and peck deck exercises," *Revista Brasileira de Medicina do Esporte* 13, No. 1 (2007): 51-54.

[179] Chris Barnett, Vaughan Kippers, and Peter Turner, "Effects of Variations of the Bench Press Exercise on the EMG Activity of Five Shoulder Muscles," *Journal of Strength and Conditioning Research* 9, no. 4 (1995): 222–27.

[180] Barnett, Kippers, Turner, "Effects of Variations."

[181] Juan C. Colado, Carlos Pablos, Ivan Chulvi-Medrano, Xavier Garcia-Masso, Jorgez Flandez, and David G. Behm, "The Progression of Paraspinal Muscle Recruitment Intensity in Localized and Global Strength Training Exercises Is Not Based on Instability Alone," *Archives of Physical Medicine and Rehabilitation* 92, no. 11 (2011): 1875–83.

[182] Martuscello, et al., "Systematic Review of Core Muscle"; Nuzzo, et al., "Trunk Muscle Activity."

[183] Nicolle Hamlyn, David G. Behm, and Warren B. Young, "Trunk Muscle Activation during Dynamic Weight- Training Exercises and Isometric Instability Activities," *Journal of Strength and Conditioning Research* 21, no. 4 (2007): 1108–12.

[184] M. Anders, "New Study Puts the Crunch on Ineffective Ab Exercises," Ace Fitness, http://www.acefitness.org/getfit/studies/BestWorstAbExercises.pdf (accessed August 2, 2016).

[185] John A. Hawley, "Molecular Responses to Strength and Endurance Training: Are They Incompatible?" *Applied Physiology, Nutrition, and Metabolism* 34, no. 3 (2009): 355–61; Gustavo A. Nader, "Concurrent Strength and Endurance Training: From Molecules to Man," *Medicine and Science of Sports and Exercise* 38, no. 11 (2006): 1965–70; Michael Leveritt, Peter J. Abernethy, Benjamin K. Barry, and Peter A. Logan, "Concurrent Strength and Endurance Training: A Review," *Sports Medicine* 28, no. 6 (1999): 413–27; Keijo Häkkinen, Markku Alen, William J. Kraemer, Esteban Gorostiaga, Mikel Izquierdo, Heikki Rusko, Jussi Mikkola, Arja

Häkkinen, Heli Valkeinen, E. Kaarakainen, Saara Romu, V. Erola, Juha Ahtiainen, and Leena Paavolainen, "Neuromuscular Adaptations during Concurrent Strength and Endurance Training versus Strength Training," *European Journal of Applied Physiology* 89, no. 1 (2003): 42–52.

[186] J. M. Wilson, P. J. Marin, M. R. Rhea, S. M. Wilson, J. P. Loenneke, and J. C. Anderson, "Concurrent Training: a meta-analysis examining interference of aerobic and resistance exercises," *Journal of Strength and Conditioning Research* 26, No. 8 (2012): 814-18.

[187] Angelo Tremblay, Jean-Aimé Simoneau, and Claude Bouchard, "Impact of Exercise Intensity on Body Fatness and Skeletal Muscle Metabolism," *Metabolism* 43, no. 7 (1994): 814–18; Jeffrey W. King, "A Comparison of the Effects of Interval Training vs. Continuous Training on Weight Loss and Body Composition in Obese Pre-Menopausal Women" (Thesis, East Tennessee State University, 2001), http://static.ow.ly/docs/Interval Training v Continuous Training_5gS.pdf; E. Gail Trapp, Donald J. Chisholm, Judith Freund, and Stephen H. Boutcher, "The Effects of High-Intensity Intermittent Exercise Training on Fat Loss and Fasting Insulin Levels of Young Women," *International Journal of Obesity* 32, no. 4 (2008): 684–91.

[188] Amy M. Knab, R. Andrew Shanely, Karen D. Corbin, Fuxia Jin, Wei Sha, and David C. Nieman, "A Forty-Five-Minute Vigorous Exercise Bout Increases Metabolic Rate for Fourteen Hours," *Medicine and Science in Sports and Exercise* 43, no. 9 (2011): 1643–48.

[189] Stephen H. Boutcher, "High-Intensity Intermittent Exercise and Fat Loss," *Journal of Obesity* 2011 (2011): 1-10.

[190] J. C. Gergley, "Comparison of Two Lower-Body Modes of Endurance Training on Lower-Body Strength Development While Concurrently Training," *Journal of Strength Conditioning Research* 23, No. 3 (2009): 979-87.

[191] Institute of Medicine, *Dietary Reference Intakes for Energy, Carbohydrate,*

Fiber, Fat, Fatty Acids, Cholesterol, Protein, and Amino Acids (Washington, DC: National Academies Press, 2005).

[192] Stuart M. Phillips and Luc J. C. Van Loon, "Dietary Protein for Athletes: From Requirements to Optimum Adaptation," *Journal of Sports Sciences* 29, no. S1 (2011): S29–S38; Peter W. Lemon, "Beyond the Zone: Protein Needs of Active Individuals," *Journal of the American College of Nutrition* 19, no. S5 (2000): 513S–21S.

[193] Eric R. Helms, Caryn Zinn, David S. Rowlands, and Scott R. Brown, "A Systematic Review of Dietary Protein during Caloric Restriction in Resistance Trained Lean Athletes: A Case for Higher Intakes," *International Journal of Sport Nutrition and Exercise Metabolism* 24, no. 2 (2014): 127–38.

[194] Shane Bilsborough and Neil Mann, "A Review of Issues of Dietary Protein Intake in Humans," *International Journal of Sport Nutrition and Exercise Metabolism* 16, no. 2 (2006): 129-52.

[195] Jason E. Tang, Daniel R. Moore, Gregory W. Kujbida, Mark A. Tarnopolsky, and Stuart M. Phillips, "Ingestion of Whey Hydrolysate, Casein, or Soy Protein Isolate: Effects on Mixed Muscle Protein Synthesis at Rest and Following Resistance Exercise in Young Men," *Journal of Applied Physiology* 107, no. 3 (2009): 987–92; D. W. West, N. A. Burd, V. G. Coffey, S. K. Baker, L. M. Burke, J. A. Hawley, et al., "Rapid aminoacidemia enhances myofibrillar protein synthesis and anabolic intramuscular signaling responses after resistance exercise," *American Journal of Clinical Nutrition* 94, no. 3 (2011): 795-803.

[196] Martial Dangin, Yves Boirie, Clara Garcia-Rodenas, Pierre Gachon, Jacques Fauquant, Philippe Callier, Olivier Ballèvre, and Bernard Beaufrère, "The Digestion Rate of Protein Is an Independent Regulating Factor of Postprandial Protein Retention," *Endocrinology and Metabolism* 280, no. 2 (2001): E340–E348.

[197] L. E. Norton, G. J. Wilson, D. K. Layman, C. J. Moulton, and P. J. Garlick, "Leucine content of dietary proteins is a determinant of postprandial skeletal

muscle protein synthesis in adult rats," *Nutrition and Metabolism* 9, no. 1 (2012): 67; Satoshi Fujita, Hans C. Dreyer, Micah J. Drummond, Erin L. Glynn, Jerson G. Cadenas, Fumiaki Yoshizawa, Elena Volpi, and Blake B. Rasmussen, "Nutrient Signalling in the Regulation of Human Muscle Protein Synthesis," *Journal of Physiology* 582, pt. 2 (2007): 813–23.

[198] Kevin D. Tipton, Tabatha A. Elliott, Melanie G. Cree, Steven E. Wolf, Arthur P. Sanford, and Robert R. Wolfe, "Ingestion of Casein and Whey Proteins Result in Muscle Anabolism after Resistance Exercise," *Medicine and Science in Sports and Exercise* 36, no. 12 (2004): 2073–81, doi: 10.1249/01.MSS.0000147582.99810.C5; Boirie et al., "Slow and Fast Dietary Proteins Differently Modulate Postprandial Protein Accretion," *Proceedings of the National Academy of Sciences USA* 94, no 26 (1997): 14930-35.

[199] Jorge E. Chavarro, Thomas L. Toth, Sonita M. Sadio, and Russ Hauser, "Soy Food and Isoflavone Intake in Relation to Semen Quality Parameters among Men from an Infertility Clinic," *Human Reproduction* 23, no. 11: 2584–90.

[200] Laura K. Beaton, Brianne L. McVeigh, Barbara L. Dillingham, Johanna W. Lampe, and Alison M. Duncan, "Soy Protein Isolates of Varying Isoflavone Content Do Not Adversely Affect Semen Quality in Healthy Young Men," *Fertility and Sterility* 94, no. 5 (2010): 1717-22; Mark Messina, "Soybean Isoflavone Exposure Does Not Have Feminizing Effects on Men: A Critical Examination of the Clinical Evidence," *Fertility and Sterility* 93, no. 7 (2010): 2095–104; Jill M. Hamilton-Reeves, Gabriela Vazquez, Sue J. Duval, William R. Phipps, Mindy S. Kurzer, and Mark J. Messina, "Clinical Studies Show No Effects of Soy Protein or Isoflavones on Reproductive Hormones in Men: Results of a Meta-Analysis," *Fertility and Sterility* 94, no. 3 (2010): 997–1007.

[201] Cara L. Frankenfeld, Charlotte Atkinson, Wendy K. Thomas, Alex Gonzalez, Tuija Jokela, Kristiina Wähälä, Stephen M. Schwartz, Shuying S. Lia, and Johanna W. Lampe, "High Concordance of Daidzein-Metabolizing Phenotypes in

Individuals Measured One to Three Years Apart," *British Journal of Nutrition* 94, no. 6 (2005): 873–76.

[202] James D. House, Jason Neufeld, and Gero Leson, "Evaluating the Quality of Protein from Hemp Seed (Cannabis sativa L.) Products through the Use of the Protein Digestibility-Corrected Amino Acid Score Method," *Journal of Agricultural and Food Chemistry* 58, no. 22 (2010): 11801–7.

[203] François Mariotti, Maria E. Pueyo, Daniel Tomé, Serge Bérot, Robert Benamouzig, and Sylvain Mahé, "The Influence of the Albumin Fraction on the Bioavailability and Postprandial Utilization of Pea Protein Given Selectively to Humans," *Journal of Nutrition* 131, no. 6 (2001): 1706–13.

[204] Carol S. Johnston, Sherrie L. Tjonn, Pamela D. Swan, Andrea White, Heather Hutchins, and Barry Sears, "Ketogenic Low-Carbohydrate Diets Have No Metabolic Advantage over Nonketogenic Low-Carbohydrate Diets," *American Journal of Clinical Nutrition* 83, no. 5 (2006): 1055–61; Shane A. Phillips, Jason W. Jurva, Amjad Q. Syed, Amina Q. Syed, Jacquelyn P. Kulinski, Joan Pleuss, Raymond G. Hoffmann, and David D. Gutterman, "Benefit of Low-Fat over Low-Carbohydrate Diet on Endothelial Health in Obesity," *Hypertension* 51, no. 2 (2008): 376–82; Frank M. Sacks, George A. Bray, Vincent J. Carey, Steven M. Smith, Donna H. Ryan, Stephen D. Anton, Katherine McManus, Catherine M. Champagne, Louise M. Bishop, Nancy Laranjo, Meryl S. Leboff, Jennifer C. Rood, Lilian de Jonge, Frank L. Greenway, Catherine M. Loria, Eva Obarzanek, and Donald A. Williamson, "Comparison of Weight- Loss Diets with Different Compositions of Fat, Protein, and Carbohydrates," *New England Journal of Medicine* 360 (February 26, 2009): 859–73, doi: 10.1056/NEJMoa0804748; Cynthia A. Thomson, Alison T. Stopeck, Jennifer W. Bea, Ellen Cussler, Emily Nardi, Georgette Frey, and Patricia A. Thompson, "Changes in Body Weight and Metabolic Indexes in Overweight Breast Cancer Survivors Enrolled in a Randomized Trial of Low-Fat vs. Reduced Carbohydrate Diets," *Nutrition and*

Cancer 62, no. 8 (2010): 1142–52, doi:10.1080/01635581.2010.513803.

[205] Andrew Creer, Philip Gallagher, Dustin Slivka, Bozena Jemiolo, William Fink, and Scott Trappe, "Influence of Muscle Glycogen Availability on ERK1/2 and Akt Signaling after Resistance Exercise in Human Skeletal Muscle," *Journal of Applied Physiology* 99, no. 3 (2005): 950–56.

[206] Robert A. Robergs, David R. Pearson, David L. Costill, William J. Fink, David D. Pascoe, Michael A. Benedict, Charles P. Lambert, and Jeffrey J. Zachweija, "Muscle Glycogenolysis during Differing Intensities of Weight- Resistance Exercise," *Journal of Applied Physiology* 70, no. 4 (1991): 1700–1706; P. Knuiman, M. T. Hopman, and M. Mensink, "Glycogen availability and skeletal muscle adaptations with endurance and resistance exercise," *Nutritions and Metabolism* 12, no. 1 (2015): 59.

[207] Lyonel Benjamin, Peter Blanpied, and Linda Lamont, "Dietary Carbohydrate and Protein Manipulation and Exercise Recovery in Novice Weight-Lifters," *Journal of Exercise Physiology* 12, no. 6 (2009): 33; Krista R. Howarth, Stuart M. Phillips, Maureen J. MacDonald, Douglas Richards, Natalie A. Moreau, and Martin J. Gibala, "Effect of Glycogen Availability on Human Skeletal Muscle Protein Turnover during Exercise and Recovery," *Journal of Applied Physiology* 109, no. 2 (2010): 431–8.

[208] Sharon L. Miller and Robert R. Wolfe, "Physical Exercise as a Modulator of Adaptation to Low and High Carbohydrate and Low and High Fat Intakes," *European Journal of Clinical Nutrition* 53, no. S1 (1999): S112–19; Howarth et al., "Effect of Glycogen Availability."

[209] Amy R. Lane, Joseph W. Duke, and Anthony C. Hackney, "Influence of Dietary Carbohydrate Intake on the Free Testosterone: Cortisol Ratio Responses to Short-Term Intensive Exercise Training," *European Journal of Applied Physiology* 108, no. 6 (2010): 1125–31.

[210] Miller and Wolfe, "Physical Exercise as a Modulator."

[211] C, Wang, D. H. Catlin, B. Starcevic, D. heber, C. Ambler, N. Berman, G. Lucas, A. Leung, K. Schramm, P. W. Lee, L. Hull, and R. S. Swerdloff, "Low-fat high-fiber diet decreased serum and urine androgens in men," *Journal of Clinical Endocrinology and Metabolism* 90, no. 6 (2005), 3550-9; E. K. Hämäläinen, H. Adlercreutz, P. Puska, P. Pietinen, "Decrease of serum total and free testosterone during a low-fat high-fibre diet," *Journal of Steroid Biochemistry* 18, no. 3 (1983): 369-70.

[212] D. M. Muoio, J. J. Leddy, P. J. Horvath, A. B. Awad, D. R. Pendergast, "Effect of dietary fat on metabolic adjustments to maximal VO2 and endurance in runners," *Medicine and Science in Sports and Exercise* 26, no. 1 (1994): 81-8; P. J. Horvath, C. K. Eagen, N. M. Fisher, J. J. Leddy, D. R. Pendergast, "The effects of varying dietary fat on performance and metabolism in trained male and female runners," *Journal of the American College of Nutrition* 19, no. 1 (2000): 52-60.

[213] Rajiv Chowdhury, Samantha Warnakula, Setor Kunutsor, Francesca Crowe, Heather A. Ward, Laura Johnson, Oscar H. Franco, Adam S. Butterworth, Nita G. Forouhi, Simon G. Thompson, Kay-Tee Khaw, Dariush Mozaffarian, John Danesh, and Emanuele Di Angelantonio, "Association of Dietary, Circulating, and Supplement Fatty Acids with Coronary Risk: A Systematic Review and Meta-Analysis," *Annals of Internal Medicine* 160, no. 6 (2014): 398–406.

[214] "Saturated Fats" (2015), retrieved December 2, 2015, from http://www.heart.org/HEARTORG/GettingHealthy/NutritionCenter/HealthyEatin g/Saturated-Fats_UCM_301110_Article.jsp#.Vl8rntKrSUk.

[215] Nathalie T. Bendsen, Ryan Christensen, Else M. Bartels, and Arne Astrup, "Consumption of Industrial and Ruminant Trans Fatty Acids and Risk of Coronary Heart Disease: A Systematic Review and Meta-Analysis of Cohort Studies," *European Journal of Clinical Nutrition* 65, no. 7 (2011): 773–83, doi:10.1038/ejcn.2011.34; Michael Lefevre, Jennifer C. Lovejoy, Steven R. Smith, James P. DeLany, Catherine Champagne, Marlene M. Most, Yvonne Denkins, Lilian de Jonge, Jennifer Rood, and George A. Bray, "Comparison of the Acute

Response to Meals Enriched with Cis- or Trans-Fatty Acids on Glucose and Lipids in Overweight Individuals with Differing FABP2 Genotypes," *Metabolism—Clinical and Experimental* 54, no. 12 (2005): 1652–58, doi: 10.1016/j.metabol.2005.06.015; Dariush Mozaffarian, Tobias Pischon, Susan E. Hankinson, Nader Rifai, Kaumudi Joshipura, Walter C. Willett, and Eric B. Rimm, "Dietary Intake of Trans Fatty Acids and Systemic Inflammation in Women," *American Journal of Clinical Nutrition* 79, no. 4 (2004): 606–12; Jorge Salmerón, Frank B. Hu, JoAnn E. Manson, Meir J. Stampfer, Graham A. Colditz, Eric B. Rimm, and Walter C. Willett, "Dietary Fat Intake and Risk of Type 2 Diabetes in Women," *American Journal of Clinical Nutrition* 73, no. 6 (2001): 1019–26.

[216] Institute of Medicine, *Dietary Reference Intakes for Energy.*

[217] Fabio Levi, Cristina Pasche, Franca Lucchini, Liliane Chatenoud, David R. Jacobs Jr., and Carlo La Vecchia, "Refined and Whole Grain Cereals and the Risk of Oral, Oesophageal, and Laryngeal Cancer," *European Journal of Clinical Nutrition* 54, no. 6 (2000): 487–89; Dagfinn Aune, Doris S. M. Chan, Darren C. Greenwood, Ana Rita Vieira, Deborah A. Navarro Rosenblatt, Rui Vieira, and Teresa Norat, "Dietary Fiber and Breast Cancer Risk: A Systematic Review and Meta-Analysis of Prospective Studies," *Annals of Oncology* 23, no. 6 (2012): 1394–402.

[218] Mark A. Pereira, Eilis O'Reilly, Katarina Augustsson, Gary E. Fraser, Uri Goldbourt, Berit L. Heitmann, Goran Hallmans, Paul Knekt, Simin Liu, Pirjo Pietinen, Donna Spiegelman, June Stevens, Jarmo Virtamo, Walter C. Willett, and Alberto Ascherio, "Dietary Fiber and Risk of Coronary Heart Disease," *Archives of Internal Medicine: A Pooled Analysis of Cohort Studies* 164, no. 4 (2004): 370–76; Eric B. Rimm, Alberto Ascherio, Edward Giovannucci, Donna Spiegelman, Meir J. Stampfer, and Walter C. Willett, "Vegetable, Fruit, and Cereal Fiber Intake and Risk of Coronary Heart Disease among Men," *Journal of the American Medical Association* 275, no. 6 (1996): 447–51; Lisa Brown, Bernard Rosner, Walter W. Willett, and Frank M. Sacks, "Cholesterol-Lowering Effects of Dietary Fiber: A

Meta-Analysis," *American Journal of Clinical Nutrition* 69, no. 1 (1999): 30–42.

[219] Manisha Chandalia, Abhimanyu Garg, Dieter Lutjohann, Klaus von Bergmann, Scott M. Grundy, and Linda J. Brinkley, "Beneficial Effects of High Dietary Fiber Intake in Patients with Type 2 Diabetes Mellitus," *New England Journal of Medicine* 342 (May 11, 2000): 1392–98, doi: 10.1056/NEJM200005113421903; Cynthia M. Ripsin, Joseph M. Keenan, David R. Jacobs Jr., Patricia J. Elmer, Robert R. Welch, Linda Van Horn, Kiang Liu, Wilfred H. Turnbull, Forrest W. Thye, Mark Kestin, Maren Hegsted, Dennis M. Davidson, Michael H. Davidson, Lynn D. Dugan, Wendy Demark-Wahnefried, and Stephanie Beling, "Oat Products and Lipid Lowering: A Meta-Analysis," *Journal of the American Medical Association* 267, no. 24 (1992): 3317–25, doi: 10.1001/jama.1992.03480240079039; June Stevens, "Does Dietary Fiber Affect Food Intake and Body Weight?" *Journal of the American Dietetic Association* 88, no. 8 (1988): 939–42, 945; Supriya Krishnan, Lynn Rosenberg, Martha Singer, Frank B. Hu, Luc Djoussé, L. Adrienne Cupples, and Julie R. Palmer, "Glycemic Index, Glycemic Load, and Cereal Fiber Intake and Risk of Type 2 Diabetes in U.S. Black Women," *Archives of Internal Medicine* 167, no. 21 (2007): 2304–9; Teresa T. Fung, Frank B. Hu, Mark A. Pereira, Simin Liu, Meir J. Stampfer, Graham A. Colditz, and Walter C. Willett, "Whole-Grain Intake and the Risk of Type 2 Diabetes: A Prospective Study in Men," *American Journal of Clinical Nutrition* 76, no. 3 (2002): 535–40.

[220] Yikyung Park, Amy F. Subar, Albert Hollenbeck, and Arthur Schatzkin, "Dietary Fiber Intake and Mortality in the NIH-AARP Diet and Health Study," *Archives of Internal Medicine* 171, no. 12 (2011): 1061–68.

[221] Institute of Medicine, *Dietary Reference Intakes for Energy*.

[222] Institute of Medicine, *Dietary Reference Intakes: Water, Potassium, Sodium, Chloride, and Sulfate* (Washington, DC: National Academies Press, 2005).

[223] E. Guallar, S. Stranges, C. Mulrow, L. J. Appel, and E. R. Miller, "Enough Is Enough: Stop Wasting Money on Vitamin and Mineral Supplements," *Annals of*

Internal Medicine 159, no. 12 (2013): 850-1; S. Fortmann, B. Burda, C. Senger, J. Lin, and E. Whitlock, "Vitamin and Mineral Supplements in the Primary Prevention of Cardiovascular Disease and Cancer: An Updated Systematic Evidence Review for the U.S. Preventive Services Task Force," *Annals of Internal Medicine* (2013): 824–34; F. Grodstein, J. O'Brien, J. Kang, R. Dushkes, N. Cook, O. Okereke, J. Manson, R. Glynn, J. Buring, J. Gaziano, and H. Sesso, "Long-Term Multivitamin Supplementation and Cognitive Function in Men," *Annals of Internal Medicine* 159, no. 12 (2013): 806–14; G. Lamas, R. Boineau, C. Goertz, D. Mark, Y. Rosenberg, M. Stylianou, T. Rozema, R. Nahin, L. Lindblad, E. Lewis, J. Drisko, and K. Lee, "Oral High-Dose Multivitamins and Minerals after Myocardial Infarction," *Annals of Internal Medicine* 159, no. 12 (2013): 797–805.

[224] N. Shute, "The Case against Multivitamins Grows Stronger" (December 13, 2013), retrieved December 2, 2015, from http://www.npr.org/sections/health-shots/2013/12/17/251955878/the-case-against-multivitamins-grows-stronger.

[225] "Learn More about Toothbrushes" (2016); retrieved January 27, 2016, from http://www.ada.org/en/science-research/ada-seal-of-acceptance/product-category-information/toothbrushes.

[226] D. W. Bartlett, B. G. Smith, and R. F. Wilson, "Comparison of the Effect of Fluoride and Non-Fluoride Toothpaste on Tooth Wear in Vitro and the Influence of Enamel Fluoride Concentration and Hardness of Enamel," *British Dental Journal* 176, no. 9 (1994): 346–48; M. Lagerweij, W. Buchalla, S. Kohnke, K. Becker, A. M. Lennon, and T. Attin, "Prevention of Erosion and Abrasion by a High Fluoride Concentration Gel Applied at High Frequencies," *Caries Research* 40, no. 2 (2006): 148–53; A. Hara, S. Kelly, C. González-Cabezas, G. Eckert, A. Barlow, S. Mason, and D. Zero, "Influence of Fluoride Availability of Dentifrices on Eroded Enamel Remineralization in Situ," *Caries Research* 43, no. 1 (2009): 57–63; C. Ganss, N. Schlueter, M. Hardt, P. Schattenberg, and J. Klimek, "Effect of Fluoride Compounds on Enamel Erosion in Vitro: A Comparison of Amine, Sodium, and

Stannous Fluoride," *Caries Research* 42, no. 1 (2008): 2–7; A. Magalhães, L. Comar, D. Rios, A. Delbem, and M. Buzalaf, "Effect of a 4 Percent Titanium Tetrafluoride (TiF4) Varnish on Demineralisation and Remineralisation of Bovine Enamel in Vitro," *Journal of Dentistry* 36, no. 2 (2008): 158–62.

[227] P. I. Eke, B. A. Dye, L. Wei, G. O. Thornton-Evans, and R. J. Genco, "Prevalence of Periodontitis in Adults in the United States: 2009 and 2010," *Journal of Dental Research* 91, no. 10 (2012): 914–20.

[228] "Learn More about Toothbrushes."

[229] R. Gerlach, "Tooth-Whitening Clinical Trials: A Global Perspective," *American Journal of Dentistry* 20 (2007): 3A–6A.

[230] A. M. Grunewald, M. Gloor, W. Gehring, and P. Kleesz, "Damage to the Skin by Repetitive Washing," *Contact Dermatitis* 32 (1995): 225–32.

[231] E. Larson, C. Friedman, J. Cohran, J. Treston-Aurand, and S. Green, "Prevalence and Correlates of Skin Damage on Hands of Nurses," *Heart and Lung* 26 (1997): 404–12; E. Larson, J. Leyden, K. McGinley, G. Grove, and G. Talbot, "Physiologic and microbiologic Changes in Skin Related to Frequent Handwashing," *Infection Control* 7, no. 2 (1986): 59-63.

[232] B. Burke, E. A. Eady, and W. J. Cunliffe, "Benzoyl Peroxide versus Topical Erythromycin in the Treatment of Acne Vulgaris," *British Journal of Dermatology* 108 (1983): 199–204.

[233] M. Ozolins, E. A. Eady, A. J. Avery et al., "Comparison of Five Antimicrobial Regimens for Treatment of Mild to Moderate Inflammatory Facial Acne Vulgaris in the Community: Randomised Controlled Trial," *Lancet* 364 (2004): 2188–95.

[234] M. Damhorst, "In Search of a Common Thread: Classification of Information Communicated through Dress," *Clothing and Textiles Research Journal* 8, no. 2 (1990): 1–12.

[235] "Seventeen On-Screen Couples Who Have ZERO Chemistry" (2015), retrieved December 17, 2015, from http://www.refinery29.com/2013/07/50844/worst-

movie-couples#slide.

[236] C. Ober, L. R. Weitkamp, N. Cox, H. Dytch, D. Kostyu, and S. Elias, "HLA and Mate Choice in Humans," *American Journal of Human Genetics* 61 (1997): 497–504.

[237] Puts, "Mating Context"; Feinberg et al., "Menstrual Cycle."

[238] A. Pease and B. Pease, *The Definitive Book of Body Language* (New York: Bantam Books, 2006).

[239] D. Walker and E. Vul, "Hierarchical Encoding Makes Individuals in a Group Seem More Attractive," *Psychological Science* 25, no. 1 (2014): 230–35.

[240] K. Light, K. Grewen, and J. Amico, "More-Frequent Partner Hugs and Higher Oxytocin Levels Are Linked to Lower Blood Pressure and Heart Rate in Premenopausal Women," *Biological Psychology* 69, no. 1 (2005): 5–21; K. Grewen, B. Anderson, S. Girdler, and K. Light, "Warm Partner Contact Is Related to Lower Cardiovascular Reactivity," *Behavioral Medicine* 29, no. 3 (2003): 123–30.

[241] M. Olff, J. L. Frijling, L. D. Kubzansky, B. Bradley, M. A. Ellenbogen, C. Cardoso, et al., "The role of oxytocin in social bonding, stress regulation and mental health: An update on the moderating effects of context and interindividual differences," *Psychoneuroendocrinology* 38, no. 9 (2013): 1883-94.

[242] Meredith L. chivers, Michael C. Seto, Martin L. Lalumière, Ellen Laan, and Teresa Grimbos, "Agreement of Self-Reported and Genital Measures of Sexual Arousal in Men and Women: A Meta-Analysis," *Archives of Sexual Behavior* 39, no. 1 (2010): 5-56.

[243] Erick Janssen and John Bancroft, "The Dual Control Model: The Role of Sexual Inhibition and Excitation in Sexual Arousal and Behavior," in *The Psychophysiology of Sex,* ed. Erick Janssen (Bloomington: Indiana University Press, 2007), 197.

[244] Katie McCall and Cindy Meston, "Cues Resulting in Desire for Sexual Activity in

Women," *Journal of Sexual Medicine* 3 (2006): 838–52.

[245] Cynthia A. Graham, Stephanie A. Sanders, Robin R. Milhausen, and Kimberly R. Mcbride, "Turning On and Turning Off: A Focus Group Study of the Factors That Affect Women's Sexual Arousal," *Archives of Sexual Behavior* 33, no. 6 (2004): 527–38.

[246] Ibid.

[247] Openstax College. "Figure 28 02 02." Digital image. File:Figure 28 02 02.jpg. May 2, 2013. Accessed November 7, 2016. https://commons.wikimedia.org/wiki/File:Figure_28_02_02.jpg.

[248] Barry R. Komisaruk, Nan Wise, Eleni Frangos, Wen-Ching Liu, Kachina Allen, and Stuart Brody, "Women's Clitoris, Vagina, and Cervix Mapped on the Sensory Cortex: fMRI Evidence," *Journal of Sexual Medicine* 8, no. 10 (2011): 2822–30.

[249] Chua Chee Ann, "A Proposal for a Radical New Sex Therapy Technique for the Management of Vasocongestive and Orgasmic Dysfunction in Women: The AFE Zone Stimulation Technique," *Journal of the British Association for Sexual and Marital Therapy* 12, no.4 (1997): 357-70; Komisaruk et al., "Women's Clitoris."

[250] C. Hazan and P. Shaver, "Attachment as an Organizational Framework for Research on Close Relationships," *Psychological Inquiry* 5, no. 1 (1994): 1–22.

[251] Mario Mikulincer, Victor Florian, and Aron Weller, "Attachment Styles, Coping Strategies, and Post-Traumatic Psychological Distress: The Impact of the Gulf War in Israel," *Journal of Personality and Social Psychology* 64 (1993): 817–26.

[252] James Coan, Hillary Schaefer, and Richard Davidson, "Lending a Hand," *Psychological Science* 17 (2006): 1–8.

[253] Jeffry Simpson, William Rholes, and Julia Nelligan, "Support Seeking and Support Giving within Couples in an Anxiety-Provoking Situation: The Role of Attachment Styles," *Journal of Personality and Social Psychology* 62 (1992): 434–46.

[254] J. Tucker, H. Friedman, D. Wingard, and J. Schwartz, "Marital History at Midlife

as a Predictor of Longevity: Alternative Explanations to the Protective Effect of Marriage," *Health Psychology* 15, no. 2 (1996): 94–101.

[255] Mario Mikulincer, "Adult Attachment Style and Information Processing: Individual Differences in Curiosity and Cognitive Closure," *Journal of Personality and Social Psychology* 72 (1997): 1217–30.

[256] Mario Mikulincer, "Attachment Style and the Mental Representation of the Self," *Journal of Personality and Social Psychology* 69 (1995): 1203–15.

[257] Mario Mikulincer, "Adult Attachment Style and Individual Differences in Functional versus Dysfunctional Experiences of Anger," *Journal of Personality and Social Psychology* 74 (1998): 513–24.

[258] Tucker et al., "Marital History at Midlife."

[259] James Coyne, Michael J. Rohrbaugh, Varda Shoham, John Sonnega, John M. Nicklas, and James Cranford, "Prognostic Importance of Marital Quality for Survival of Congestive Heart Failure," *American Journal of Cardiology* 88 (2001): 526–29; Jack H. Medalie and Uri Goldbourt, "Angina Pectoris among 10,000 Men," *American Journal of Medicine* 60 (1976): 910–21; Kristina Ortho-Gomer, Sarah Wamala, Myriam Horsten, Karen Schenck-Gustafsson, Neil Schneiderman, and Murray Mittleman, "Marital Stress Worsens Prognosis in Women with Coronary Heart Disease," *Journal of the American Medical Association* 284 (2000): 3008–14.

[260] Janice K. Kiecolt-Glaser, Timothy J. Loving, J. K. Stowell, William B. Malarkey, Stanley Lemeshow, Stephanie Dickinson, and Ronald Glaser, "Hostile Marital Interactions, Pro-Inflammatory Cytokine Production, and Wound Healing," *Archives of General Psychiatry* 62 (2005): 1377–84.

[261] Janice K. Kiecolt-Glaser, William B. Malarkey, Marie-Anne Chee, Tamara Newton, John T. Cacioppo, Hsiao-Yin Mao, and Ronald Glaser, "Negative Behavior during Marital Conflict Is Associated with Immunological Down-Regulation," *Psychosomatic Medicine* 55 (1993): 395–409.

[262] K. D. O'Leary, J. L. Christian, and N. R. Mendell, "A Closer Look at the Link between Marital Discord and Depressive Symptomatology," *Journal of Social and Clinical Psychology* 13 (1994): 33–41.

[263] L. Gigy and J. Kelly, "Reasons for Divorce: Perspectives of Divorcing Men and Women," *Journal of Divorce and Remarriage* 18, no. 1 (1993), 169-188.

[264] Ted Huston, John Caughlin, Renate Houts, Shanna Smith, and Laura George, "The Connubial Crucible: Newlywed Years as Predictors of Marital Delight, Distress, and Divorce," *Journal of Personality and Social Psychology* 80 (2001): 237–52.

[265] J. M. Gottman and N. Silver, *The Seven Principles for Making Marriage Work* (New York: Crown, 1999).

[266] J. M. Gottman and R. W. Levenson, "What predicts change in marital interaction over time? A study of alternative models," *Family Process* 38, no. 2 (1999): 143-158.

[267] Gottman and Silver, *The Seven Principles*.

[268] Gottman and Silver, *The Seven Principles*.

Made in the USA
San Bernardino, CA
22 July 2017